The Lost Abbey of Eynsham

Steve Parrinder

ARCHAEOPRESS PUBLISHING LTD
Summertown Pavilion
18-24 Middle Way
Summertown
Oxford OX2 7LG

www.archaeopress.com

ISBN 978-1-78969-250-1
ISBN 978-1-78969-251-8 (e-Pdf)

Cover illustrations:
Medieval Eynsham Abbey, a view from the fishponds, from a print by Peter Lorimer © Eynsham Parish Council.
Dog's head gargoyle formerly in the Vicarage Garden. Now at the MRC, OCMS.

Printed in England by Severn, Gloucester

This book is available direct from Archaeopress or from our website www.archaeopress.com

For

Posy, Kate and Anna

Contents

List of Figures and Tables

Preface and Acknowledgements

On 4 December 1538, Eynsham Abbey was surrendered to the Crown. For over half a millennium the huge structure had dominated the village and the surrounding countryside, towering over the farms and cottages of Eynsham's inhabitants. Following the Dissolution in the 16th century, it was gradually demolished and pillaged for its building materials over the next 130 years or so. Now, nothing remains *in situ* above ground.[1] Attempts to discover the layout of the lost abbey buildings and what they may have looked like have been hampered by the fact that much of what may remain of the abbey church now lies beneath the graveyard of St Leonard's parish church. Until the late 20th century extension to the churchyard, most graves had been cut through construction and demolition layers and in at least one instance came across massive stone foundations.[2]

This study is, in part, a summary of the history of the Benedictine abbey from its foundation in about 1005 to its re-establishment in the 12th century; from its growth in the medieval period to its fall in the 16th century; from its disappearance to its rediscovery in more recent times. However, it is also an attempt to reconstruct what the abbey, or at least parts of it, may have looked like at various points in that history. This will necessarily require comparisons to be made with abbeys and cathedrals whose remains are more complete, and with other churches in Britain and Europe. It will also involve a degree of speculation, not to say guesswork. Although it might be argued that all conclusions should be based solely on the traces of the abbey that have so far emerged, it is worth repeating the old archaeological adage that 'absence of evidence is not necessarily evidence of absence.' It therefore seems reasonable at times to make particular assertions about Eynsham which apply to the generality of abbeys from the same period.

Numerous stones and artefacts from the abbey have been discovered and recorded over the last two hundred years. Most of the old houses, barns and walls in the central part of the village were built, at least partially, from material from Eynsham Abbey which was such a convenient quarry. Finely cut and chiselled ashlar blocks can be found in many places and even the rougher, uncut 'rubble' stone may have come from the infilling of an abbey wall or pier. In addition, there are many fragments of carved stones which formed arches, doors, windows and monuments of the abbey church and its associated monastic buildings. There are certainly many more in the village as when they were re-cycled by villagers in the past, the sculpted surface would more likely than not be placed on the inside of a wall, leaving the flat surface on the outside.

Larger abbey stones, as one might expect, were generally used in the foundation or bottom layers of walls and only in exceptional circumstances are ever likely to be recoverable. Smaller pieces, such as column fragments and mouldings, were used in the upper levels.

---

[1] It has been tentatively suggested by R.A. Chambers in Eynsham Abbey Excavations, ER 7, 1990, that part of the north gate to the abbey precinct may have been assimilated in the west end of St Leonard's parish church although this is 'not yet proven'. However, see the author's article on Thomas Hearne's Eynsham, ER 33, 2016 and Chapter 14.
[2] Gray M. and Clayton N., Excavations on the site of Eynsham Abbey 1971, *Oxoniensia*, Vol. XLIII, 1978.

Such was the case with worked stones recently recorded from collapsed walls in Conduit Lane, Lombard Street, Newland street, Abbey Farm and Holewelle field. The display of moulded stones in walls and gateposts is very much a 20th/21st century fashion and some of the above have been re-set and are now visible for the first time since the abbey's destruction.

The picture we have of the Eynsham Abbey is clearer than it was even 50 years ago thanks to the efforts of local historians and archaeologists, particularly the excavations of part of the abbey site between 1989 and 1992. It is still incomplete but enough has been uncovered to enable some tentative conclusions to be drawn. New discoveries are being made year on year and the evidence will need to be re-assessed in the future. It is known too that there are other collections of stones which have yet to be fully recorded and which may change our perceptions. Of course, there is a danger of assuming that all the ancient stones found in the village and its vicinity came from Eynsham Abbey. They may have come from other buildings or indeed from elsewhere, in the same way that some abbey stones have turned up in villages around or even further afield. Nevertheless, despite these caveats, it is important to make a start, to record what has been done and hopefully to provoke further research to rescue this lost abbey from oblivion.

This study would not have been possible but for the publications of others, many of them living in Eynsham, whose contributions I hope I have fully acknowledged. In addition, I am grateful to all the local residents, over 100, whose willingness to allow me to record stones and artefacts, and to use some of them for this book, has been indispensable. To respect their right to privacy, I have for the most part not included specific names and addresses but future researchers can contact the author for available details. However, an honourable mention should be made here of David Rivalin who has unearthed many stones in Holewelle Field and alerted me to others in the village. Likewise, Dr Bryan Hyde who entrusted me with his collection of abbey stones and Sonny Schneider who drained the race at Hardwick Mill to enable me to photograph an abbot's tombstone (Figure 259). I am grateful too to Peter Glare for his help with some of the medieval Latin of the *Eynsham Cartulary*.

David Moon at the Museum Resources Centre (MRC) at Standlake gave unprecedented access to the Eynsham material there, rescuing from deep storage some of the larger items and providing photographic facilities. Andy Libby, Ian Looker and the contractors E.S.S. were especially helpful in rescuing abbey stones from the collapsed Co-op wall in 2014.[3] Similarly, Gary Smith from Savvy construction who enabled me to photograph stones from the demolished stables of Beech Court House in Newland Street.

Thanks are also due to the following who have granted permission to use copyright material: Arts Council of England for Figure 129; Bodleian Library, University of Oxford for Figures 26, 27, 32, 37, 49, 51, 71, 98, 262, 264, 266, 268, 270; British Library Board for Figures 244 and 284; Sue Chapman for Figure 141; Corpus Christi College, Oxford for Figure 247; Paul Davies for Figure 12; English Heritage Archive for Figure 269; Eynsham History Group for

---

[3] Parrinder S., The Co-op Wall, *ER* 31, 2014.

articles by the author in the *Eynsham Record* and the use of the Bainbridge slide collection[4]; Eynsham Parish Council for the front cover print by Peter Lorimer; Alan Hardy for Figure 292; Paul Hughes for Figures 4, 42, 139 and 187; Kunstmuseum, Basel, for Figure 246; Oxford Archaeology for Figures 140, 159 and 216 ; Oxfordshire Architectural and Historical Society for Figure 277; Oxfordshire County Museums Service (Carol Anderson) for photos taken by the author at the Oxfordshire Museum Resources Centre, at Woodstock Museum and at the Vale and Downland Museum, Wantage; Oxfordshire History Centre for Figure 258; V&A Images for Figure 256. Every effort has been made to identify and secure permission from all those who hold copyright and the author accepts liability for any that have not been recognised. Full details of copyright are given in the 'List of Figures'. Unless otherwise stated, all photos are copyright of the author whose extensive archive will ultimately be available to others for future research.

The archaeologist Alan Hardy who was the principal supervisor of the excavation of 1989-92, read the first draft of the main text of this book, gave professional advice and provided an important corrective to some of my assumptions. His support, encouragement and friendship have been invaluable.

Special gratitude is due to the late Brian Atkins who, as editor of the *Eynsham Record* for 30 years, and President of the Eynsham History Group from 2002 to 2013, did so much to rescue the village's history and give the local community a sense of its roots. Shortly before he died, Brian charged me with the safekeeping of his significant collection of Eynsham Abbey stones but it would be more appropriate if they, and others found around the village or stored at the Museum Resources Centre at Standlake, could be displayed in a purpose-built museum. Any profits from this publication will be put towards a fund to realise this ideal.

Whereas I am indebted to all the above for their assistance, errors of fact or interpretation are entirely my responsibility. In particular, it will be apparent to specialist architectural historians that I lack expertise in some areas and I beg their forbearance. A glossary of some of the architectural terms used is provided in Appendix 4.

Lastly, historians are oft reminded that all history is contemporary history, that we view the past with the spectacles of the present and in the light of our current attitudes and prejudices. In this I am no exception, and however much one might acknowledge that the past is a different country, particularly as regards the belief systems of the medieval era, it is difficult to disguise the more secular and sceptical approaches of the early 21st century.

---

[4]   See Appendix 3

Chapter 1

Beginnings

The intelligible forms of ancient poets,
The fair humanities of old religion,
The power, the beauty and the majesty
That had their haunts in dale or piny mountain
Or forest, by slow stream or pebbly spring
Or chasms and watery depths: all these have vanish'd[1]

Long before the establishment of an abbey, Eynsham may have been an area of special significance. Its position, on a gravel terrace adjoining a fording point on the upper Thames, near the crossing of north-south and east-west land routes and containing many natural springs and exploitable resources, made it an attractive place for settlement from the earliest times. West Oxfordshire is rich in prehistoric remains and archaeological investigations on the Eynsham Abbey site in 1989-92 revealed the existence of a ditched enclosure dating to the Bronze Age or possibly even earlier.[2] Within the ditch was found a large, very weathered

Figure 1. The reconstructed henge monument at Stanton Harcourt (Oxon), known as 'The Devil's Quoits'.

---

[1] Extract from Samuel Taylor Coleridge, *Piccolomini*. All chapters start with the conceit of a quotation. Some are clearly appropriate; others may seem a contrivance.
[2] Hardy A. and Dodd A. and Keevill G.D. et al., *Aelfric's Abbey – Excavations at Eynsham Abbey, Oxfordshire, 1989-92*, English Heritage. Published by Oxford University School of Archaeology, 2003. Eynsham hit the national headlines in the very dry summer of 2018 when extensive crop marks from the same period were revealed in a field north of Foxley's Farm.

Figure 2.   Eynsham's 'Bronze Age' standing stone, re-erected in the Tolkein Memorial garden of St Peter's Roman Catholic church, Eynsham.

fragment of limestone, like those which make up the circular monument at nearby Great Rollright and the so-called 'Devil's Quoits' at Stanton Harcourt, one of the most important ritual complexes in Britain, which has been recently reconstructed (Figure 1).

The Eynsham stone has been re-erected in the Tolkein Memorial garden of St Peter's Roman Catholic Church (Figure 2). It is not unusual for ancient sites with religious connotations to be reused as such by later generations, thereby appropriating their spiritual ethos.

However, although an attractive proposition, it is important to be aware that there is as yet no archaeological evidence to suggest any religious or ritualistic significance of the Bronze Age enclosure, nor for the idea that it was associated with the 'standing stone'. Indeed, a report of 2001 concluded that it was most probable that the stone was brought to the site from elsewhere during the medieval period as foundation material for one of the abbey buildings.[3] Why the monks would have taken so much trouble when there was an abundant supply of stone locally is open to question but at present, the hypothesis that there was some sort of 'sacred' continuity to the site, is very much unproven.

The earliest documentary evidence for Eynsham occurs in the *Anglo-Saxon Chronicle*, 26 years before Saint Augustine came to England to start the conversion of southern Britain to Christianity. The entry for AD 571 reads: *In this year Cutha fought against the Britons at Biedcanford and captured four villages, Limbury, Aylesbury, Benson and Eynsham.*[4] Cutha (or Cuthwulf) was a King of the West Saxons and the *Chronicle* was recounting the triumph of these peoples over the natives of Britain. However, these early parts of the *Anglo-Saxon Chronicle* were actually written some 300 years later, during the reign of King Alfred the Great, and clearly have to be treated with caution. Although it might have been based on a strong oral tradition, the precise dating of events is misleading.

[3] Barclay A. and Boyle A. and Keevill G.D., A Prehistoric Enclosure at Eynsham Abbey, Oxfordshire, *Oxoniensia*, Vol. LXVI: pp. 105-162, 2001.
[4] Garmonsway G.N. (Trans.), *The Anglo-Saxon Chronicle*, J.M. Dent and Sons Ltd, Everyman's Library 1967.

The most that can be said is that Eynsham's reputation as an important centre probably had ancient roots. It is supportive of the idea that it may have had a major ecclesiastical establishment, a Minster of a large district or *parochia* with its own community of loosely organised priests, even before the foundation of the Benedictine abbey. The Minster, originally a centre for missionary work, would have had a number of dependant churches in its locality which owed symbolic tribute to the mother church. The siting of a Minster in an area of previous settlement was not atypical as the positioning of the Minsters at Abingdon and Bampton demonstrate. Archaeological finds at the Eynsham Abbey site included an unusually large assemblage of early and middle Saxon pottery, and the animal and fish bone evidence are suggestive of a privileged diet and high-ranking occupation by the early eighth century. The late 20th century excavations also turned up some rare eighth century coins infrequently found on standard domestic sites. Directly below the early 11th century abbey, evidence emerged of high-status timber structures with wall plaster which would also be consistent with Eynsham's role within the Minster system.[5]

Other documents provide further evidence of the idea that Eynsham was a distinguished place and 'originally more important than Oxford.'[6] About the year AD 821, the Archbishop of Canterbury, Wulfred, surrendered a huge estate of 300 hides at Eynsham to King Coenwulf of Mercia.[7] A hide was a variable measurement of land in the early medieval period but 300 hides might approximate in Oxfordshire to a vast 30,000 acres or more. The suggestion therefore, is that Eynsham was a prestigious and very wealthy religious centre which had been liberally endowed in the era of monastic revival in the late 7th or early 8th century. It has been postulated that the endowment was made by a 'sub-king' based at Eynsham itself and that there was some 'common element' in the foundation of the communities of Eynsham and St Frideswide in Oxford.[8] It is thought that Eynsham's estate probably included Cassington, Yarnton, Cogges, Stanton Harcourt and Water Eaton. Interestingly, other Minsters (e.g. Chertsey, Gloucester and Pershore) were also endowed with 300 hides indicating that this was the normal practice for the financing of religious houses. The argument for such an early religious foundation at Eynsham is also supported by the fact that it fills a gap between other Minster controlled districts in the region, for example Bampton upstream and St Frideswide's, Oxford, downstream.

This large estate at Eynsham appears to have been progressively eroded by secular rulers thereafter and one example of this occurred in AD 864 when Burgred, King of Mercia granted five hides at Water Eaton to Alwin, Bishop of Worcester with the proviso that the bishop paid the large sum of *30 shillings to Eynsham to that church from the tribute*. Clearly a church at Eynsham existed by this date and the implication is that Water Eaton had belonged to Eynsham which was now being dispossessed of it. Such expropriations of church land were not uncommon in the late 9th century and by the early 11th century Eynsham's extensive holdings seem to have been largely lost. The process of alienation of church land, as well as

[5]   Blair J., *Anglo Saxon Oxfordshire*, Alan Sutton Publishing Limited, 1994. A modern reconstruction of a section of the wall is displayed in Woodstock Museum alongside other Anglo-Saxon artefacts from Eynsham.
[6]   Blair J., Saint Frideswide Reconsidered, *Oxoniensia*, Vol. LII: pp. 71-127, 1987.
[7]   Campbell J. and John E. and Wormald P., *The Anglo-Saxons*, p. 174. Phaidon Press Ltd, 1982. Published by the Folio Society, 2018.
[8]   Blair, Saint Frideswide Reconsidered, op. cit.

increasing Viking raids, probably contributed to the decline of religious houses and regular observance of monastic customs.[9]

However, from the mid-10th century, under the influence of Archbishops Dunstan and Oswald and Bishop, later Saint, Aethelwold, there had been another religious revival in England. New monasteries were established and existing ones reinvigorated and regularized as Benedictine houses, following the *Rule* of St Benedict written in the early 6th century. Eynsham's establishment, or re-establishment in AD 1005 was a late example of this reforming process and the only one in Oxfordshire.[10] The context for its foundation charter was the devastating attacks by the Danes and widespread famine, *the most severe in living memory* according to the *Anglo-Saxon Chronicle*. For some, these events were evidence of a wrathful deity and seemed to presage the ending of the world, an idea given extra credence by the recent onset of the millennium. The perceived Viking threat had resulted in the massacre of Danes living in Oxford in 1002, in the course of which St Frideswide's church, its ornaments and library were burnt to the ground. A few years later, in 1009, marauding Norsemen exacted their revenge on the whole town.

Eynsham's foundation charter, 'one of the most imposing...of its age'[11], was issued by King Aethelred II, so called Ethelred the Unready. He stated that because of the *perilous times* occasioned by *the most savage assault of the rampaging barbarous enemies...afflicting us almost to the point of extinction*, he had *determined to appease God with a never-ending display of good works...*[12] The original charter does not survive but a copy was made in the late 12th century and appears as the first item in the *Eynsham Cartulary*. Although forgeries of such charters are certainly not unknown, the authenticity of Eynsham's document has not been disputed. Nevertheless, its appearance in the 1190s was fortuitous to say the least, as will be seen in Chapter Five. In the charter, the monastery at Eynsham was granted special privileges at the behest of one of Aethelred's leading noblemen, Aethelmaer the Stout, and was *now duly dedicated, in honour of St Saviour and all his Saints, and established at an important place, hard by the river Thames, called Eynsham...* St Mary and St Benedict were added to the dedication although eventually the abbey was referred to simply as St Mary's Eynsham. Aethelmaer declared that his intention was to retire to Eynsham himself and live in the monastic community. His precise motives are unclear but it has been suggested that it was prompted by his falling out of favour at Court and that this move may not have been entirely voluntary.[13]

The reference to Eynsham as under the protection of the king and as *an important place* is a further indication of Eynsham's contemporary significance, particularly as the word 'place' often carried the connotation of 'holy place' at the time. The fact that Aethelmaer *therein is establishing monks who will order their lives by the Rule* and that *he has appointed the abbot* also suggests that this was more a reordering of a pre-existing house rather than a brand-new foundation. This seems confirmed by the statement that 'Aethelmaer had received

[9]   An Eynsham stone, purporting to show Viking Runes was photographed by William Bainbridge in 1976. Whereabouts unknown.

[10]   Blair, *Anglo Saxon Oxfordshire*, op. cit.

[11]   Keynes S., King Aethelred's charter for Eynsham Abbey (1005) in *Early Medieval Studies in Memory of Patrick Wormald*. N. Brooks (ed.), Ashgate Publishing Ltd, 2008.

[12]   Gordon E., *Eynsham Abbey 1005-1228. A Small Window into a Large Room*, p. 10. Phillimore and Co. Ltd., 1990.

[13]   Jones C.A., *Aelfric's Letter to the Monks of Eynsham*, p.12. Cambridge University Press, 2006.

the *monastery* from his son-in-law Aethelweard through an exchange, a transaction which might have occurred some years before.'[14] On the other hand, as Salter pointed out, the term *monasterium* was often used of a church in the eleventh century so it is far from conclusive.[15] The foundation charter concludes with an extensive list of 86 prominent contemporaries including the royal family, both archbishops, the majority of bishops, 16 abbots, three ealdormen and 44 thegns.

The new abbot, *he who is there now*,[16] was to be Aelfric 'the Grammarian', one of the leading intellectuals and teachers of his day. Aelfric was born *c*. 955 and had a significant intellectual and spiritual pedigree having received his training at Winchester and serving under Bishop Aethelwold. He had been transferred *c*. 987 to Cerne Abbas (Cernel) in Dorset and had already collaborated with Aethelmaer in reforming the monastery there. It was at Cerne that most of Aelfric's literary activity took place and his extensive works include sermons, homilies, *Lives of Saints* and a *Grammar*, the earliest such work in medieval Europe.[17] He is best known for the *Colloquy* which aimed to teach correct Latin to young monks by means of a largely, but not totally rehearsed dialogue with them. However, it is also a subtle and detailed commentary on the lives of ordinary people in the society of his day, those who tend to be overlooked in most Anglo-Saxon literature. He has been described as 'the father, the inventor, of the rich tradition of plainly stated, undecorated, but vigorous and powerful English prose.'[18] The novices he instructed would have been taught in the cloister and kept apart from the regular monks.

It would seem that Aelfric arrived at Eynsham sometime between 1002 and 1005 and that the latter date, and the foundation charter, represents the end of the process for establishing the Benedictine House that may have begun some time before.[19] Aelfric's standing as the 'greatest prose writer of the Anglo-Saxon period'[20] was already high and his appointment to the abbacy of Eynsham was another sign of its existing reputation. Aelfric wrote a *Customary*, better known as his *Letter to the Monks of Eynsham*, setting out the practical implications of the Benedictine Rule because he felt that they needed to know what 'customs' they were committed to. He implies that what he calls *your brotherhood* had *until now* been ignorant of monastic practices which he was familiar with. This may not have been because they were novices but because they had, before 1005, adopted a less strict approach to the religious life.[21] The *Letter* uses as its main source the *Regularis Concordia* compiled by St Aethelwold and his fellow reformers at Winchester in the early 970s. It tailors the *Concordia* to the conditions that prevailed at the more modest Oxfordshire House and is a rare record of the daily detailed offices or liturgy that the monks of Eynsham were expected to perform.

---

[14] Keynes, op. cit., p. 455.
[15] Salter H.E., *Medieval Oxford*, Clarendon Press for the Oxford Historical Society, 1936.
[16] Salter H.E., *Eynsham Cartulary*, Vol. 1: p. 27, Oxford Historical Society, Clarendon Press, 1907.
[17] Garmonsway G.N. (ed.), *Aelfric's Colloquy*, Methuen's Old English Library, 1965.
[18] Campbell et al., op.cit., p. 284.
[19] Jones, op. cit.
[20] Greenfield S.B. and Calder D.G. and Lapidge M., *A New Critical History of Old English Literature*, New York, 1986. Quoted in Jones. op.cit.
[21] Gordon, *Eynsham Abbey*, op.cit.

Aelfric's patron, Aethelmaer, endowed the abbey with the manor of Eynsham, with an initial grant of 30 hides, as well as the church of St Ebbe's in Oxford, his urban manor with its two mills and several properties in Oxford, to provide the monks with rental income.[22] In addition, the abbey received many properties both in the county (Shifford, Yarnton, Shipton-on-Cherwell) and further afield in Gloucestershire (Mickelton), Warwickshire (Marlcliff), Worcestershire (Bentley), Surrey (Esher and Ditton) and Sussex (Rye) making a total of nearly 120 hides. Another estate at 'Burton' has not been identified.

Eynsham's wealth and status as a 'locus celebris' or famous place, seems confirmed by Bishop White Kennett writing in 1695. Quoting the antiquary Henry Spelman, Kennett claimed that in 1009 a Council was held at Eynsham 'by the advice of the Archbishops of York and Canterbury (and) many decrees were enacted.' However, it is probably right to treat this statement circumspectly as Kennett had a reputation for being 'a bold guesser.'[23] Nevertheless, the claim was reiterated in a chronology in the *Gentleman's Magazine* in 1820 which stated that a Wittenagemot was held at Eynsham by Ethelred the Unready in 1009.[24] The Wittenagemot or witan was an assembly of the most important magnates, both spiritual and temporal, in Anglo-Saxon England, an advisory body to the king. Further, an analysis of food remains found in the excavation of 1989-92 confirmed that the abbey was very comfortably off at this time by comparison with other late Saxon sites which might support the idea that it was an important venue for leading dignitaries of the kingdom.

Aelfric probably died around AD 1010 which is when his literary output ceased and he was almost certainly buried within his abbey near the high altar. Aethelmaer vanishes from the records after 1014 although his role in the founding of Eynsham's abbey was still remembered by monks there over 100 years later.[25] The memory of Aelfric lasted much longer and a window in the chancel of St Leonard's church reminds parishioners even today of Eynsham's long spiritual heritage (Figure 3). A blue plaque to commemorate Eynsham's first abbot may also be shortly installed on the market hall.

The history of the abbey from 1010 to 1109 is not entirely clear and subject to some disputation. It would seem that during the reign of King Cnut (1016-35), Eynsham was dispossessed of several of its properties and went into decline. These included Marlcliff, Bentley, Esher and Ditton, Shipton-on-Cherwell, the unidentified Burton, and Rye with its harbour and salt pans.[26] However, it survived, as evidenced by the fact that around 1051 *the abbot and all the community of Eynsham* were witnesses to an agreement made at the shire moot concerning the lease of Great Tew by St Albans Abbey.[27]

---

[22] Salter, *Medieval Oxford*, op. cit. implies that one of these mills was later known as Blackfriars Mill, mentioned in an Eynsham charter of 1091 which referred to it as having been built some time ago.

[23] Salter, *Cartulary* op.cit., p. xiii. Kennett also claimed that Heamund Bishop of Sherborne, who was killed at the battle of Meretun in 871, was buried at Eynsham *a famous place fit for the sepulture of Bishops soon after honoured with a cell of religion.* Kennett's *Parochial Antiquities*, 1818.

[24] Gomme G.L. (ed.), *The Gentleman's Magazine Library 1731-1868*, Elliot Stock 1897.

[25] Keynes, op.cit., p. 473.

[26] A 'quatrefoil' silver penny from the reign of Cnut has been found on the site of Eynsham Abbey and donated by Mr Roland Oakeley to the Eynsham History Group. Atkins B., *Buried Treasure*, ER 2, 1985.

[27] Gordon, op. cit.

Figure 3.   *Stained glass window depicting Aelfric in the south wall of the chancel of St Leonard's parish church, Eynsham. In memory of William Nash Bricknell, vicar, who died in 1928.*

In the autumn of 1066, William 'The Bastard' invaded England. One chronicler subsequently claimed that *Eynsham Abbey had been laid waste at the Conquest and its brethren had fled away, frightened of the enemy.* The source for this apocalyptic assessment of the impact of the Conquest is the *Life* of St Hugh of Lincoln, written by Adam, one-time prior and later Abbot of Eynsham Abbey in the early 13th century, some 14 decades after the event. Although he may have had access to documents now lost, there are other reasons for doubting the authority of Adam's account, as will be discussed later. Additionally, when he wrote his *Life* Adam was almost certainly living in Lincoln where the folk memory of the Conqueror's 'Harrowing of the North' was still strong. Not unreasonably perhaps, he may have assumed that William's reign of terror there was but a continuation of what had happened in the home counties. In actual fact, the Conqueror's army had crossed the Thames further south, at Wallingford, before closing in on London. Oxford, just 14 miles north of Wallingford was left untouched and it would be surprising if nearby Eynsham was less fortunate.

A more reliable source is the Conqueror's 'Domesday' Survey of 1086 which stated that *The Bishop of Lincoln holds Eynsham himself and the monk Columban from him...Land for 18 ploughs; he found as many…The value is and was £20.*[28] In other words, Eynsham was worth the same amount in 1086 as had been the case in the reign of Edward the Confessor which doesn't seem supportive of the idea that it had suffered total depredation at the hands of the Normans. 'Domesday' does state that seven of the abbey's 13 properties in Oxford were derelict but this was the case with many of the houses in the town which seems to have been in decay. 'Domesday' has Eynsham itself with only 15½ hides (not the 30 which Aethelmaer had given) and it retained Shifford, Yarnton, Mickelton, the Oxford property and five hides in Little Rollright. Eynsham's annual income in 1086 has been calculated at a mere £40-9s-0d, about a tenth of that of Abingdon and one of the lowest in the country.[29]

But, although Eynsham's wealth had shrunk, its endowment was 'still perfectly viable.'[30] The archaeological investigation of part of the abbey site, 1989-92, found no evidence that the Saxon abbey had been *laid waste* and its inmates dispersed. Indeed, the remains of a large kitchen and annexe dating to the end of the 11th century were found, indicating the survival of a significant community. Once again, the evidence of the diet of the inmates, particularly the high levels of fish consumption, supports the idea of continued occupation by some fairly well-off monks at this time and certainly no great poverty.

It is possible that the later chronicler was confusing the events of 1066 with what is said to have happened in 1070 when, the *Anglo-Saxon Chronicle* recorded, *the king had all the monasteries in England plundered.* Certainly, the predatory approach of the Norman invaders is well documented by contemporaries like William of Poitiers and the spoils of conquest were distributed far and wide. From the nearby abbey at Abingdon for example, the chronicler detailed the seizure of *a wealth of gold and silver vestments, books and vessels of different kinds intended for the rites and honour of the church.* Even newly imported Norman monks participated in the process and confiscated gold and silver treasures given to Abingdon by St Athelwold and sent them across the channel to their mother house of Jumièges. Like many imperialists, the Normans implicitly justified their colonialism by contemptuously characterising the natives as barbaric, uncouth, effete and decadent. They therefore had no compunction about destroying the Anglo-Saxon religious and artistic heritage in the quest to enrich themselves.[31]

The Conqueror's first appointment to an English bishopric was Remigius of Fécamp who, in 1067 was given the see of Dorchester which stretched from the river Humber in the north to the Thames in the south (see Figure 4).

It is claimed by some that Remigius should be credited with the re-foundation of the abbey after the Conquest but the evidence does not seem supportive of this as discussed above. In 1072, Remigius, perhaps mindful of the threat posed to his northern properties by the ambitions of the Archbishopric of York, decided to move his bishop's seat from Dorchester to Lincoln and began to construct a new cathedral there. Then, towards the end of his life in 1091, Remigius, aware of his mortality and the imminence of divine judgement for his sins,

[28] Morris J., *Domesday Book, Oxfordshire*, p. 6. Phillimore, 1978.
[29] Gordon E., Eynsham Charters, *ER* 4, 1987.
[30] Hardy et al., op. cit. p. 10.
[31] Dodwell C.R., *Anglo-Saxon Art: A New Perspective*, Manchester University Press, 1982.

Figure 4.   Map of the 11th century diocese of Dorchester/ Lincoln. Design by Paul Hughes.

notably simony, developed plans to join Eynsham with the Minster at Stow in Lincolnshire creating a new Benedictine monastery. The latter, dedicated like Eynsham to St Mary, was to be directly under the bishop's patronage and Columban, presumably the same man referred to in Eynsham in 1086, was to be the new abbot of the merged institutions. Stow's foundation charter refers to the bequest of Eynsham as an *outstanding benefaction*[32] which would hardly have been the case if it was derelict or a dormant institution. However, some doubts have been expressed as to the charter's authenticity, suggesting that it might have been forged at Eynsham which would somewhat undermine the validity of the statement.[33]

In the event, the proposed union didn't survive as after Remigius died in 1092, his successor Robert Bloet, concerned that his predecessor had been overly generous in his grants of land to Stow, reversed the decision to merge the two institutions. The monks of Stow were therefore transferred to Eynsham and Abbot Columban. Bishop Blouet, at the insistence of the king, granted Eynsham additional properties in the south of the diocese to

---

[32] Gordon, *Eynsham Abbey*, op. cit.
[33] Carpenter D.X., *The Charters of William II and Henry I – Eynsham Abbey*, https://actswilliam2henry1.wordpress. com, 2016.

recompense them for the loss of Stow and the bequests that had been made to the Minster there previously. Amongst the gifts that Stow had received were lands in the north of England (Newark, Fledborough, Brampton and Marton), supposedly given to the Minster before the Conquest by Earl Leofric and his wife, the legendary Lady Godiva. The bishop's compensation included the valuable manors and churches of Charlbury, South Stoke and Woodcote in Oxfordshire and Histon in Cambridgeshire.[34] Small wonder therefore that the monks of Eynsham included Leofric and Godiva in their prayers for founders and benefactors thereafter.

Bishop Bloet, who was also chancellor of England, seems to have been closely associated with Eynsham which he also valued as an attractive and convenient base closer to the centre of royal power. Bloet died of a stroke in 1123, falling from his horse whilst out hunting with King Henry I at Woodstock. Although his body was taken back to Lincoln, his entrails were buried in Eynsham Abbey, probably at the east end of the new abbey church which would have been the first part of the Norman structure to be completed. Bequeathing the abbey your bowels and intestines may not seem like much of a compliment but it was believed they were symbolic of your inner soul.[35]

---

[34] Curthoys J., Christ Church, Eynsham Abbey and its Cartulary, *ER* 30, 2013.
[35] Some sources, for example the 14th century chronicler Henry Knyghton, have claimed that the bowels of Remigius were also buried at Eynsham. See Dugdale W., *Monasticon Anglicanum*, Vol. 3: Note l on page 1.

Chapter 2

Aelfric's Abbey

He adorned the church with Gospel-Books made from pure silver and gold as well as with the most precious gems, with censers and cruets, cast basins and silver repoussé candelabras, and many other fine objects appropriate both for the monk's rites about the altar and for the comeliness of the church.[1]

For the purposes of this chapter, the term 'Anglo-Saxon' refers to buildings and artefacts which seem to date to the period before the re-building of the abbey in the 12th century. For, despite the Norman Conquest, 1066 did not mark a complete break with the past. Saxon masons did not suddenly disappear but undoubtedly continued to build in the style to which they were accustomed for years thereafter, albeit under the supervision and/or patronage of their new masters. Equally, Norman methods and styles of building were known in England even before William's invasion but took time to be adopted throughout the land. Not surprisingly therefore, the half century after the Conquest has frequently been referred to by architectural historians as the 'Saxo-Norman Overlap.'

The evidence for the Anglo-Saxon abbey at Eynsham is scant but tantalising. In 1971, what may have been part of the Minster's cemetery was discovered in the north-west corner of Nursery Field and more human bones have been found in the same area in recent years.[2] However, it was the archaeological investigation of a small part of the abbey site between 1989 and 1992 which brought more significant results. It revealed 'substantial, regularly planned stone buildings' which had been rapidly constructed in the first years of the 11th century and aligned north-west to south-east.[3] Defined largely by robber trenches the buildings were difficult to interpret with certainty. However, it was inferred that one of the structures was the southern narrow passage of a cloister floored in 5cm thick mortar, which seems to have been the Saxon practice even in important churches such as St Augustine's Canterbury or Glastonbury.[4]

The open space, or garth, to its north may have been surrounded on all sides by building ranges, including the abbey church. If correct, this would make the Eynsham 'enclosed' cloister one of the first in this country, prefiguring the standard Norman practice for religious houses. In his *Letter to the Monks of Eynsham* Aelfric himself made several references to a cloister that the brothers should avail themselves of in mild winter weather. It was also used by the abbot to hear his monks' confessions and for processions on Palm Sunday.[5]

---

[1] Chronicon Abingdon, Quoted in Dodwell C.R., *Anglo-Saxon Art: A New Perspective*, Manchester University Press, 1982.
[2] Gray M. and Clayton N., Excavations on the site of Eynsham Abbey 1971, *Oxoniensia*, Vol. XLIII, 1978.
[3] Hardy A. and Dodd A. and Keevill G.D. et al., *Aelfric's Abbey - Excavations at Eynsham Abbey, Oxfordshire, 1989-92*, English Heritage. Published by Oxford University School of Archaeology, 2003.
[4] Taylor H.M., *Anglo-Saxon Architecture* Vol. 3, Cambridge University Press, 1978. Parts of the floor are stored at the MRC whilst others are held privately.
[5] Jones C.A., *Aelfric's Letter to the Monks of Eynsham*, Cambridge University Press, 2006.

The use of the cloister for public penitence and correction of faults may imply the lack of a separate chapter house where these were usually heard. On the other hand, Aelfric does refer to a *domus*, a distinct building where monks could read and chant together in cold weather and which possibly performed the same function as a chapter house in the winter months. He also mentions a *sacristy*, a room for storing vestments, sacred vessels and documents, and there was to be an *auditorium* where the monks could converse if there was *a pressing need.*

In addition, Aelfric mentions a *refectory* which was prohibited to all secular persons excepting the king and his heirs. This may have been the use put to the large rectangular hall that was found in the excavation, extending south-west from the cloister. Attached to the hall by a wall was a building with a cellar or undercroft which may have been used for storage. Part of another structure to the north-west of the hall was also uncovered, as well as a south range extending east from the south of the hall with an open yard or garden between it and the cloister. To the south of the whole complex was a boundary ditch turning north-east into Nursery field and presumably linking with the northern edge of the abbey precinct along the Oxford Road. From the dimensions of the cloister it was possible to speculate as to the size of the abbey church although it was suggested that the existing Minster church may have been retained as the basis for the claustral layout. Given the orientation of the later parish church it was also suggested that a Saxon gatehouse chapel, on the same alignment as the excavated buildings, probably existed on the site of St Leonard's but this is unlikely to be provable.

Among the small Saxon finds discovered by the archaeologists were some pieces of blue painted glass and an unfinished fragment of a Saint carved from walrus ivory, both of which accord with the idea that the abbey was a high status foundation. The excavation also unearthed a very weathered capital or base which could have come from a pre-Conquest context. More certainly Saxon was a tiny fragment of interlace (Figure 5) which may have come from a cross shaft and bears comparison with the 10th century example in Wantage museum (Figure 6). Two pieces of another possible cross shaft have also been found in a

Figure 5.   Fragment of a Saxon cross found in the excavation of 1989-92 and now in the Museum Resources Centre (MRC) at Standlake (Oxon) in the care of the Oxfordshire County Museums Service (OCMS).

Figure 6.   *Part of a 10th century cross shaft in the Vale and Downland Museum at Wantage (Berks).*

Figure 7.   *Two parts of a possible cross shaft found in Holewelle Field, Eynsham.*

field south of the Saxon abbey (Figure 7). Though badly damaged, the design shares some of the characteristics of a 9th century shaft fragment built into the church wall at Colerne (Wilts) and another in the museum at Glastonbury Abbey (Figure 8).

The most interesting find of the excavation was a block of small-scale blind arcading which, it has been suggested, may have been part of a unique late Anglo-Saxon liturgical furnishing, a stone screen around an altar perhaps (Figure 9). The use of blind arcading occurs on a number of important Saxon churches, notably on the early 11th century church of St Laurence in Bradford-on-Avon (Wilts). However, such small-scale arcading is very unusual although it can be detected

Figure 8.   Part of a Saxon cross shaft in Glastonbury Abbey Museum (Somerset).

Figure 9.   Piece of Saxon small-scale blind arcading found in the excavation of 1989-92 and now at the MRC, OCMS. At the time of writing this is now on display at the Anglo-Saxon gallery in Woodstock Museum along with other finds from the abbey site.

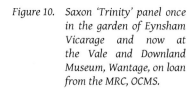

Figure 10.   Saxon 'Trinity' panel once in the garden of Eynsham Vicarage and now at the Vale and Downland Museum, Wantage, on loan from the MRC, OCMS.

on the door imposts of the tower entrance at Earls Barton in Northamptonshire, a famous Saxon survival. The sculpture from Eynsham adds to the evidence that Aelfric's Abbey was indeed a distinguished building, reflecting its importance in England's 11th century ecclesiastical administration.

Apart from the excavation finds there are a number of other pieces of stonework which might shed light on the Saxon abbey at Eynsham. One such is a stone currently on loan to the Vale and Downland Museum in Wantage from the Museum Resources Centre at Standlake (Figure 10).

Measuring roughly 43cm x 51cm on its longest edge it is certainly extraordinary. The triangular larger head with its lined forehead, heavy brows, drilled eyes, flaring nostrils and slit mouth looks quite primitive but the two smaller heads have a distinctly classical feel. The three-quarters relief is on a flat rectangular base, approximately four centimetres thick and may have been a panel attached to the abbey church, possibly to represent the Trinity like that which once adorned the late 10th century tower of the New Minster at Winchester. What appears to be the tip of a pointed arch may indicate that the Eynsham slab was set above a triangular headed window.

Such randomly placed sculpted panels are not unknown in Anglo-Saxon architecture. A much weathered slab, possibly showing Christ in Majesty, appears above a window on the west face of the Saxon tower of St Peter-at-Gowts, Lincoln. At Deerhurst (Gloucs) at the south corner of the ruined apse is a not dissimilar face to that on the Eynsham slab at Wantage (Figure

Figure 11.   Saxon sculpture of an angel built into the exterior east wall of St Mary, Deerhurst (Gloucs).

11). Dated to the 10th century it is said to be the head of an angel still *in situ* and Pevsner claims it shows Byzantine influence.[6] Closer to home, at Langford (Oxon) there is, on the south face of the tower, a sculpted panel with two kilted figures supporting a sundial which breaks into the pilaster strip in the centre of the wall. The pioneering art historian A.W. Clapham, writing in 1930, was quite dismissive of such 'rustic art which is represented by a number of rude, ill-formed, and worse executed figures scattered in certain remote churches of the midlands...' The Eynsham carvings are certainly crude but nevertheless interesting and the details have been obscured by weathering and the loss of any pigment that may have been applied.[7] Many Anglo-Saxon carvings appear to have been painted and Aelfric himself states in his *Colloquy* that the stone crosses of his day were coloured.

In addition, a number of stones have recently turned up which may relate to the late Saxon abbey although equally they could have come from an early Anglo-Norman building. Among these is a plain cone-shaped free-standing block capital fallen from a collapsed field wall in what

Figure 12.   Small, double-splayed window built into a garden wall in Mill Street, Eynsham. Photo by Paul Davies.

---

[6]   Pevsner N. (ed.), *The Buildings of England – Gloucestershire: The Vale and the Forest of Dean*, Penguin Books, 1970.
[7]   The stone was in much better condition when it was photographed by Henry Taunt in the garden of the Vicarage in the late nineteenth century.

Figure 13. Loose stone with a rebate and square hole. Now in a house in Mill Street.

was the monastic precinct. 38cm square at its head and roughly chamfered to 25cm square at its base, the stone could have topped a column possibly in a crypt, cloister arcade or belfry opening in a tower. Though much smaller it bears comparison with those in the crypt at Repton, the uncarved capitals in St George's chapel at Oxford castle or the capitals to the western baluster shafts at Brixworth.[8]

Then there are four single-stone slabs, two half fragments, with holes cut through to form small windows or ventilation holes such as are sometimes seen in Saxon buildings like the staircase tower at Brixworth and the original east end of the chancel at Daglingworth (Gloucs). In three instances the stones are rectangular, the heads of the windows are roughly rounded and the openings are splayed on both sides. One of these has been built into a garden wall of a house in Mill Street (Figure 12) and the other two fragments came from collapsed walls in the village. The fourth stone, in a house in Mill Street is roughly square with a slight taper. A hole with a chamfer has been cut, with a rebate which may have held a piece of glass, a frame holding a skin or a small shutter (Figure 13).

So what might Eynsham's Anglo-Saxon abbey have looked like? The most obvious problem in answering this question is the limited extent of the 1989-92 excavation which, if the interpretation is correct, just clipped part of the south range of the cloister and revealed a few of the buildings close to it. Although a later copy of the 1005 foundation charter survives, there are no written records which relate to the building of the abbey. Indeed, the date of the charter itself does not necessarily indicate the start or completion of the building process and the existing Minster buildings may well have been incorporated in the new abbey structures.

To try to build a picture of Eynsham's Saxon abbey it is necessary therefore to rely on the studies of other Anglo-Saxon churches but that also raises issues. Of the thousands of Anglo-Saxon churches which there may have been, less than 400 survive to any degree. In part this may be because many Saxon churches were built of wood, especially in areas where good building stone was at a premium, and were later replaced by larger buildings to

---

[8] It has recently been concluded that the tower of St George at Oxford Castle was part of the very late pre-Conquest town defenses rather than an early Norman construction. Blair J., *Building Anglo-Saxon England*, p. 399, Princeton University Press, 2018.

Figure 14.   Polygonal Saxon apse at All Saints, Wing (Bucks).

meet the needs of the growing population in the 12th and 13th centuries. Of Saxon stone buildings extant, the majority have been altered or extended by later generations and it is not always easy to discriminate with certainty between Saxon and Norman work or to discern the extent of the earliest structure buried under or even within the existing one. Nevertheless, if for no other reason than general interest it is worth speculating and perhaps proffering a number of alternatives for Eynsham's Saxon abbey. Some of the particular features of Saxon ecclesiastical architecture are discussed with reference to a number of churches in central and southern England.

Firstly, Eynsham's Saxon building was to serve a monastic community and not just the needs of a small parish, although references in Aelfric's *Letter* indicate that it was used for services and baptism by the latter. As Aelfric makes clear, it was also large enough to support the schooling of boys at the monastery before they became fully fledged monks. Additionally, it was renowned throughout England and its first abbot was among the most distinguished scholars in Western Christendom. Aelfric had been a monk at Winchester which by the late 10th century was one of the largest abbeys in southern England vying with Canterbury, Glastonbury, Sherborne and Cirencester. Eynsham was probably not on the same scale but given its status it would certainly be appropriate to draw inferences about its form and layout from larger surviving monastic churches such as Brixworth (Northants), Deerhurst (Gloucs) or Reculver (Kent). All of these had semi-circular apsidal east ends and relatively wide naves with 'aisles' divided into porticuses or chapels. In his *Letter to the Monks of Eynsham* Aelfric refers to the porticus of the south and north aisles in his description of the celebrations at the end of Holy Week. It would not be unreasonable to suppose that Eynsham's church also contained an apse like that which still survives at Wing (Bucks), with a crypt below it (Figure 14).

According to Alan Hardy, the existence of a semi-circular apse at Eynsham is 'not inconsistent' with the anomalies picked up by the geophysical investigation of part of the

Nursery Field to the east of the main excavation. On the other hand, the survey also revealed a rectangular structure situated to the east along the axis of the possible position of the late Saxon church. If the cloister was larger than supposed, then this might be an instance of a square-ended chancel which was more popular generally in Anglo Saxon churches. It might also be an example of an exterior eastern crypt such as was added to the apsidal east end at Winchester. Alternatively, it is known that some significant monastic settlements were characterised by a number of separate churches rather than a single abbey. St Augustine's Canterbury for example, had four churches built in a row. Glastonbury, Rochester and Monkwearmouth had three and Lindisfarne and Hexham two. Such a possibility should not be discounted for Eynsham too but more archaeological excavations would be needed to confirm it. Aelfric's *Customary* implies the existence of at least two churches although one of these may have been the possible gatehouse chapel referred to above.

Lest it be thought that the claims for a large Saxon ecclesiastical establishment at Eynsham are exaggerated, it is worth pointing out that the surviving Oxfordshire churches with significant Saxon remains, Langford, North Leigh and St Michael's, Oxford, demonstrate a certain ambitiousness in late 10th/early 11th century architecture. It is unlikely that Eynsham would be subordinate to any of these. Indeed, the reverse is true. Only the tower survives of St Michael's but at Langford and North Leigh there is clear evidence that the towers there were axial, standing between a chancel to the east and a nave to the west. Langford has some particularly elaborate features: unique belfry windows, pilaster strips and two stone roods, crucifixes, re-set in the walls of the later south porch (Figures 15 and 16). That which is built into the east wall of the porch has a monumental quality of dignified simplicity, a form that conveys majesty and power despite the fact that the head

of Christ is missing. Its date is controversial but as Taylor has pointed out, it bears comparison with the fragments of the undoubted late Saxon rood at Bitton (Gloucs).[9]

Figure 15.   Saxon stone Rood on the east wall of the south porch of St Matthew, Langford (Oxon).

---

[9]   Taylor H.M. and J., *Anglo-Saxon Architecture*, Vols.1 & 2, Cambridge University Press, 1965.

Figure 16.   Re-constructed Saxon stone Rood on the south wall of the porch at Langford.

The other rood at Langford, in the gable of the south porch, has been incorrectly reassembled so that the figures of his mother Mary and St John are facing the wrong way. However, the distorted figure of Jesus effectively conveys the agony of the Passion as in the much-mutilated Saxon roods at Breamore and Headbourne Worthy (Hants). Both the roods at Langford are not in their original position, usually above the chancel arch, and indeed at least one of them may have been brought from elsewhere.

The main fabric of the walls of Eynsham Abbey would most probably have been of coursed 'rubble', uncut stone, plastered inside and probably outside as well. The church at Brixworth (Northants) provides a good example of this rubble construction and shows the re-use of Roman tiles for the voussoirs of windows, doors and the nave arcade (Figure 17). Brixworth was one of the largest Anglo-Saxon churches in England and provides another illustration of why the remains of Eynsham's Saxon abbey are difficult to identify. Unworked rubble stone is impossible to date on its own and it is quite likely that the rubble stone first quarried by the Anglo-Saxons has been re-cycled in the construction of the village's houses, walls and even St Leonard's church, most of which is of rubble construction.

There are very few Anglo-Saxon churches with walls of ashlar and even then the exposed surfaces are often quite rough. In most Saxon churches however, the corner stones, quoins,

Figure 17.   All Saints, Brixworth (Northants).

were constructed of large and irregularly shaped stones. A number of these megaliths, coarsely dressed, can be found in the walls of houses in Eynsham and may conceivably have come from its Saxon abbey.

One method of constructing such quoins which is generally agreed to reliably denote Saxon structures is 'long and short' work, tall stones and short horizontal ones, laid alternately. Good examples of this technique occur on the tower of Earls Barton (Northants) (Figure 18), Odda's Chapel at Deerhurst (Gloucs) and the tower of St Michael's in Oxford. Another feature of some churches which is characteristic of the Anglo-Saxon style is the use of pilaster strips or lesenes, square sectioned 'columns' attached to a wall. These were in part to assist the masons in the construction of rubble walls but they were also partly decorative and reminiscent of timber framing. These were especially prevalent in central and southern England and good examples can be found at Wing (Figure 14), Earls Barton (Figure 18) and Langford (Figure 22).

Openings in walls, both windows and doorways, would generally be round-headed, although triangular and flat headed arches were also sometimes used. Unlike their Norman counterparts, Saxon masons tended to construct their arches from rubble, like Brixworth,

Figure 18.   *Saxon tower of All Saints, Earls Barton (Northants).*

Figure 19.   *Tower arch at St Peter, Wooton Wawen (Warks).*

or of large stones that ran through or half through the thickness of the walls as at Wootton Wawen in Warwickshire (Figure 19).

Double-splayed windows, i.e. splayed internally and externally with an opening in the middle of the wall, were common in late Anglo-Saxon churches, especially in the south of England (Breamore, Deerhurst, Odda's Chapel and Tichborne (Figure 20)).

Figure 20.   *Double splayed Saxon window in the chancel of St Andrew, Tichborne (Hants).*

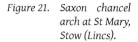

Figure 21. Saxon chancel arch at St Mary, Stow (Lincs).

Whereas Norman doorways were generally well proportioned and recessed in separate orders with angle shafts and capitals, Saxon ones were usually tall and narrow and cut straight through walls with imposts of square or rectangular through-stone slabs. Jambs were usually plain although at Britford (Wilts), sculpted panels were used. It has been suggested by Taylor that these tall doorways were to allow a cross or large candelabra to be carried in procession. Again, this idea is supported by reference to Aelfric who talks about a new fire being *struck from stone at the entrance of the church* to light a candle in the mouth of an image of a snake, fixed to a pole, and carried inside to kindle all the lights. Major openings such as chancel arches or belfry openings, sometimes used capitals as at Bibury (Gloucs) or Langford (Oxon) but these are rare and not used in an architecturally logical way. Chancel arches could be very wide and tall in larger Saxon churches, appropriate for buildings served by a number of clergy. That at Wing, for example, spans six metres and that at Brixworth is as high as seven metres. At St Mary's Stow, Eynsham's erstwhile partner, the arches of the crossing are truly monumental and of a scale in excess of any other surviving pre-conquest cruciform church (Figure 21).

Figure 22.   Saxon tower of Langford church (Oxon).

Aelfric's *Letter* contains a number of references to the ringing of bells, particularly on feast days and when children were baptised, which implies that Eynsham had a campanile. Substantial towers were a feature of the greater Saxon churches, most frequently placed at the west end of the church where they might also serve as porches, or axial where they sometimes formed a nave. These were tall and heftily built and in some cases consisted of three or four receding stages separated by string courses. Their strength and impressiveness meant that some important examples survived the post-Conquest rebuilding, notably at St Michael's Oxford; Earls Barton and Brixworth (Northants) and Langford (Figure 22) and North Leigh (Oxon). Belfry openings in Saxon towers were quite distinctive, often consisting of double round-headed openings supported by central mid-wall shafts or balusters supporting a rectangular stone or abacus which ran through the thickness of the wall.[10] Sometimes, as at St Michael's Oxford, the abaci project from the surface of the wall.

Based on the examples discussed, Eynsham's Saxon abbey church and some of its associated structures could have looked something like the visualisation below (Figure 23).

One aspect of Anglo-Saxon architecture which has largely been lost is the decoration of churches. According to literary sources, like the Abingdon Chronicle referred to at the head of the chapter, many churches were sumptuously painted, hung with embroideries and richly adorned with carvings and gold and silver objects. In fact, the internal beautification of Saxon churches was probably more important to the Saxons themselves than the structure that housed it.[11] The results of weathering, looting by the Vikings and later by the Conqueror and his followers, have left Saxon churches bare and sterile. Just a few fragments of wall paintings survive at Winchester and Nether Wallop in Hampshire (Figure 24) although the expertise of some Saxon book illuminators and metalworkers can still be appreciated in libraries and museums and may have provided an inspiration for larger scale murals.[12]

---

[10] Fisher E.A., *Anglo-Saxon Towers – An Architectural and Historical Study,* David & Charles Ltd, 1969.

[11] Dodwell, op. cit.

[12] The Nether Wallop painting depicts one of two angels which originally flanked Christ in Majesty within a mandorla, an almond shaped panel, as in *British Library Cotton MS Vespasian A viii, f. 2v,* a charter for the New Minster, Winchester, AD 966.

Figure 23. *Imaginative re-construction of Eynsham Abbey's Saxon church, cloister and some associated buildings. Posy Parrinder.*

Figure 24. *Saxon wall painting on the chancel arch at St Andrew, Nether Wallop (Hants).*

Figure 25.   Detail of the Bayeux Tapestry

English embroideries in particular, were much prized across Europe and one outstanding example of the skills of Anglo-Saxon textile workers in Canterbury survives as the 'Bayeux Tapestry' depicting the Norman invasion and the killing of the last English king (Figure 25).[13]

---

[13] Actually, the example shown is not the 'Bayeux Tapestry' but a copy of it made by some ladies from Leek in Staffordshire in the 1880s which is on display in Reading Museum. The copy is mostly accurate although the Victorians seem to have baulked at some details. They gelded the horses and embroidered a pair of shorts on a border figure who in the original was depicted proudly showing his genitals.

Chapter 3

Re-Foundation

Without the Normans, what would it have ever been.[1]

Eynsham Abbey was 're-established' by the Conqueror's youngest son, Henry 1, on Christmas Day 1109. In part at least, this may have been due to his desire to associate himself with a famous foundation, but it was also no doubt motivated by a sense that Norman architecture could demonstrate the superiority of the new culture over that of the natives. In addition, Eynsham was conveniently close to the Royal manor and hunting lodge of Woodstock and would serve as a useful annex to the limited accommodation there. A new and much grander Romanesque building at Eynsham was therefore to replace the Saxon structures which were then demolished. There are, as yet, no written records which might inform us of the process although it is possible that the incidence of gifts to the abbey may relate to stages of its construction. It is notable for example, that Eynsham received a large number of donations in the second half of the 12th century which may have been responses to appeals to enable the completion of the abbey church and the other monastic buildings. These bequests, mostly within Oxfordshire, included eight churches, a chapel, several portions of tithes, six mills, a manor, two meadows and land in excess of 1000 acres.

The new foundation charter aimed to *restore and confirm the abbey of Eynsham* which had *Right until now...lain deserted, with its affairs in disarray.* However, this was clearly an exaggeration, designed to suggest that the king's patronage was worthy of even greater acclaim, as another Royal writ issued *on behalf of the abbot of Eynsham* sometime between 1100 and 1107, had exempted the men of Eynsham from the duty of participating in the chase and beating the forest for game whilst the king's household was lodged at the abbey.[2] The foundation charter confirmed Eynsham's ownership of its Domesday properties, the gifts of Bishop Bloet and the grants made by individuals to the abbey previously. In addition, Henry gave the abbot the right of holding a manorial court, arbitrating in property disputes, taxing tenants and even hanging thieves caught within the manor although this latter franchise was modified by his daughter Matilda.[3] The abbot was still claiming the right to gallows in 1274/5.[4]

The date of foundation is not necessarily indicative of the start of rebuilding and it may be that the Saxon structures continued to be inhabited for quite a time as the new Norman church was planned and then built to the north of it. Temporary facilities would also need to be constructed before the demolition of the old abbey could begin and some

---

[1] The historian R.A. Brown's poetic rendering of Thomas Carlyle's belief that the Norman Conquest had benefited England.
[2] Gordon E., *Eynsham Abbey 1005-1228 A Small Window into a Large Room*, Phillimore and Co. Ltd., 1990.
[3] Chambers E., *Eynsham Under the Monks*, p. 7, Oxfordshire Record Society, Oxford, 1936.
[4] Crossley A., *Victoria History of the County of Oxford*, Vol. XII: p 142, Oxford University Press, 1990. University of London Institute of Historical Research.

evidence of these emerged in the course of the archaeological excavation in 1989-92. It may be significant that one of the early 12th century abbots of the new foundation was a certain Walter who had been prior of St Albans. As abbot, Walter and his prior would have played a part in the planning of the new building and it is possible that he would have employed masons that he was familiar with at St Albans, at least one of whom was also employed at Reading.[5] It is worth noting that Henry 1 was also the patron of Reading Abbey. That the abbey was intimately involved in such temporal affairs, even in lesser building projects, would seem amply demonstrated by the construction of a vicarage for a church it appropriated. Eynsham's abbot and chapter determined that it should be built of oak, specified dimensions of 26 feet by 20 feet and ordained that it should have a buttery at one end and a chamber and a privy at the other.[6]

Once the Eynsham site had been cleared and levelled the new abbey would start to take shape. Unlike its Saxon predecessor, the bulk of the Norman abbey church would have been built of ashlar, carefully dressed stones of more or less uniform size and rectangular to square shape, for ease of handling and laying in accurate courses. A large number of these stones can be seen in many buildings around the village. However, it is also probable that much of the Saxon rubble walling would have been incorporated into the new building as infill for walls and pillars which were more substantial after the Conquest. Most of the worked stones are of limestone, which ranges in colour from the palest yellow from the famous Taynton quarries near Burford, to a deep tawny brown from the Banbury area. Oxfordshire is rich in local stone quarries, some of the finest in England, making it likely that many of the masons were from the area too.

The usual practice was to start at the east end of the church followed by the cloister south of the nave, the sacristy, chapter house, scriptorium, dormitory, refectory, kitchen, latrines, domestic ranges, an infirmary complex and lodgings for visitors. It has been suggested that the new east-west alignment of the abbey was at least partially determined by the desire to preserve the grave of the revered Aelfric and incorporate it within the new chapter house.[7] On the other hand, the different orientation of the Saxon and Norman abbeys may be a reflection of the different times of the year that the buildings were laid out. In mid-summer the setting sun more nearly approximates to the position of Aelfric's church whereas the Norman structure is aligned closer to sunset in mid-winter. The west front of the abbey church would be the last part of the main buildings to be constructed but this would by no means end the construction process and the abbey would continue to be repaired, updated and altered throughout the medieval period. Most large abbeys and cathedrals could take many decades to complete. The cathedral church at Canterbury for example, begun by Archbishop Lanfranc in 1070 was not dedicated until 1130 and building operations could sometimes be interrupted by the vagaries of winter weather.[8]

---

[5] Parrinder S., Romanesque Sculpture from Reading Abbey, Unpublished MA dissertation, Birkbeck College, University of London, 1982.

[6] Gies F. and J., Life in a Medieval Village, p. 153, Folio Society, London, 2002.

[7] Hardy A. and Dodd A. and Keevill G.D. et al., Aelfric's Abbey - Excavations at Eynsham Abbey, Oxfordshire, 1989-92, English Heritage. Published by Oxford University School of Archaeology, 2003.

[8] Gervase's contemporary account of the construction of Canterbury reproduced in Willis R., The Architectural History of Canterbury Cathedral, 1845. Republished by Tiger of the Stripe, 2006.

Finances and political considerations – for example the uncertainties created by the civil war between King Stephen and Empress Matilda between 1135 and 1154 – may also have impacted on the pace of building and therefore the nature of its architectural decoration. Reading Abbey for example, had been founded in 1121 but although Henry I was buried before the high altar there in 1135 it does seem to have suffered some setbacks during 'The Anarchy'. The final consecration of Reading by Archbishop Thomas Becket did not occur until 1164. The Peterborough Chronicler detailed at length *the atrocities and cruelties wrought upon the unhappy people of this country* during Stephen's reign.[9] Nor were churches or monasteries immune from the general lawlessness which prevailed and it would not be in the least surprising if, like Reading, there was a lull in Eynsham's building activity at this time. Eynsham itself attempted to take advantage of the confusion of Stephen's reign by trying to claim possession of three Oxford churches, Holy Trinity, St. Clement's and St. Mildred's and their assets. However, when its weak claim was disputed and tried by the Bishop of Winchester about 1142, Eynsham's abbot failed to turn up to make his case.[10] Money, or rather the lack of it, could certainly have been an issue as Gervase's contemporary account of the reconstruction of the east end of Canterbury Cathedral makes clear. He noted that in the ninth year of building England's premier cathedral, *no work was done for want of funds.*

Another factor which could have influenced Eynsham's architecture was that the Bishop of Lincoln for much of the early part of the re-founded abbey's history was Bishop Alexander (1123-1148). Sometimes known as Alexander the Magnificent he was famous for his extravagant tastes and love of ostentatious decoration. He is thought to have lavishly restored Lincoln Cathedral after a disastrous fire in 1141, *making it more beautiful than it was before, and second to none in the kingdom.*[11] This view however, has recently been disputed by Rachel Moss who believes that the remodelling of Lincoln's west front was more feasibly carried out by one of Alexander's successors later in the century, possibly in the final years of Bishop Robert de Chesney who died in 1166.[12]

Interestingly, the art historian Nicholas Pevsner finds parallels between the west front of Lincoln and the sculptures of Malmesbury's south porch which undoubtedly date to the 1170s.[13] Moss's argument is perhaps lent further weight by the fact that Alexander had sided with Matilda and was arrested by Stephen in Oxford and imprisoned for a while. If she is correct, and if Eynsham followed the pattern of Lincoln, the west front of Eynsham's abbey may also not have been completed until the third quarter of the 12th century. Given the prominent part played by the De Chesney family in the endowment of Eynsham Abbey in the second half of the 12th century this would not seem unreasonable. This hypothesis would also seem to be supported by the archaeology and by much of the carved stone found in the village.

---

[9] Garmonsway G.N. (Trans.), *The Anglo-Saxon Chronicle*, p. 264, J.M. Dent and Sons Ltd, Everyman's Library, 1967.
[10] Salter H.E., *Medieval Oxford*, Oxford Historical Society, 1936.
[11] Henry of Huntingdon, quoted by Zarnecki G., Carved Stones from Newark Castle – Additional Notes, *Further Studies in Romanesque Sculpture*, Pindar Press, London 1992.
[12] Moss R., *Romanesque Chevron Ornament*, p. 39, British Archaeological Reports, International Series 1908, Archaeopress, 2009.
[13] Pevsner N. and Cherry B., *The Buildings of England - Wiltshire*, Penguin Books, 1975.

Figure 26. Eynsham's Market Cross drawn by J.C. Buckler in the early 19th century. The Bodleian Library, University of Oxford, MS Top Oxon a 66 f.258. According to Thomas Symonds, vicar of Eynsham at the time, the cross was 'Inclosed with an Iron Palisade in the year 1825 with the hope of protecting this beautiful Piece of Antiquity.'

The growth of the abbey would have been helped by special privileges given by the Bishop of Lincoln, most famously the gift by Bishop Alexander in 1138 of ancient offerings known as 'smoke-farthings' or Pentecostals. These were donations of a farthing, a quarter of a penny, from every house, due to Lincoln cathedral at Pentecost but henceforth, so far as Oxfordshire was concerned, payable to Eynsham. They were worth £7-5s-½d per annum by 1535. Great processions to deliver the sums would be made to the abbey yearly from every parish in the county and it was expected that some of those in attendance would make extra offerings. The *Cartulary* indeed, refers to gifts of gold, silver and silk.[14]

A weekly Sunday market was also established in Eynsham, granted in the early years of the reign of King Stephen (1135-1154). It is thought that the grant included the right to determine the weights, measures and prices of bread and ale. Apart from increasing Eynsham's status, the market, like the processionals, would bring more people to the town and the abbey would profit from fees, levies and offerings for prayers. The market cross in the Square, dated by some to *c.* 1300 and by others to the later medieval period, was supposedly put up by the monks of Eynsham Abbey and originally contained figures under canopies in its lower tier (Figure 26). There survives the lower part of a similar cross, erected by Eynsham Abbey in the churchyard at Yarnton which was part of its possessions.[15] It was also in King Stephen's reign that Eynsham was asked to take charge of a religious house called Pheleleie which belonged to the manor of Bloxham but was situated in Wychwood forest in Stonesfield. It was a hermitage or small community of Benedictines headed by a prior, and the monks and their endowments were transferred to Eynsham when one of the abbots called Walter was administering it. It is unclear what properties or benefits accrued to Eynsham as a result.

[14] Salter H.E., *Eynsham Cartulary*, Vol. 1: pp. 424 & 427, Oxford Historical Society, Clarendon Press, 1907.
[15] The Eynsham cross had deteriorated so badly by 1987 that it was replaced by a modern copy. Fragments of the original are stored in the Museum Resources Centre, Standlake.

Stephen's rival, Matilda, granted Eynsham the church and manor of Combe in 1141, and the patronage of North Leigh church was given to the abbey by John of St John, lord of the honour of St Valery, between 1140 and 1150.[16] Such gifts, which included the right to nominate the rector, the advowson, and receive a proportion of his income from offerings, mortuaries, the glebe and tithes, were believed to guarantee the donor significant spiritual benefits. Other patrons of Eynsham Abbey at this time included Robert D'Oyly, the founder of the nearby Augustinian abbey at Osney. He gave land to Eynsham and was buried there when he died about 1130. Roger D'Oyly, probably Robert's nephew, also gave land to the abbey when two of his sons became monks at Eynsham.[17] Robert's wife Edith, donated one of her villeins on her lands at Claydon *with his wife, children and all his cattle in free alms for ever*. This was not the only case of people being used as chattels as in about 1150, Geoffrey de Clinton of Cassington gave Eynsham Abbey a certain Hugh de Sumerford in restitution for a cope which he had borrowed and lost![18]

Major lay benefactors involved members of the extended De Chesney family, including Ralf Murdac and Henry de Oxonia, Sheriff of Oxford in 1153 and 1154 and father of John de Oxonia, Bishop of Norwich. Perhaps the most surprising of patrons was David, King of Scotland, the Empress Matilda's uncle, who gave Eynsham the living at Merton between 1123 and 1148. It paid the abbey 30 shillings annually. As has been said, gifts to the abbey had a particular purpose as is made clear, for example, by a grant by Richard de Submuro of Eynsham *for the welfare of my soul and of my ancestors and heirs.* Between 1197 and 1208 he gave the monastery a virgate (about 30 acres) of land in Eynsham *with all the crofts and meadow and one messuage (dwelling house) at Tilgaresle belonging to the same, with all its appurtenances and customs. Moreover I have given and granted to the said abbot and monks all the land which I had at Ludemere with its meadows and appurtenances.*[19]

King Stephen's successor, Henry II, added further privileges, including a fair twice a year and free passage throughout the land for all food and clothing for Eynsham's monks. One of the fairs coincided with the Pentecost processions and thereby attracted large crowds to the town and prosperity to the monastery although they could also result in riots such as that which occurred in 1296 when several students from Oxford were killed and wounded.[20] The other fair was held after the feast of St Mary's Assumption to Heaven on August 15th, a date that was of course particularly dear to the abbey.

By 1175, the main abbey buildings must have been complete, or at least nearly so, for on 26 November of that year King Henry II came to Eynsham to confer on John of Oxford the See of Norwich. He was consecrated Bishop of the East Angles just over two weeks later at Lambeth. Eleven years after, from 25 May to 2 June 1186, Henry held a council at Eynsham, possibly in the nave of the abbey church. Whereas the King resided at Woodstock and rode over daily, the abbey was used as a convenient hotel for other attendees. Baldwin, the Archbishop of Canterbury, was put up in the abbey and some of the other bishops, abbots,

---

[16] Crossley, op.cit., but thought to have been lost by 1200.
[17] Mason E., The D'Oyly Family and Eynsham Abbey, *ER* 22, 2005.
[18] Chambers, op. cit., p. 24.
[19] Chambers, op. cit., p. 11.
[20] Crossley, op. cit., p. 108.

barons and their retinues were probably housed there too. Eynsham lay just within the huge diocese of Lincoln and at that council Hugh of Avalon, Prior of the Charterhouse of Witham in Somerset, was elected Bishop of Lincoln in Eynsham Abbey.[21] At the same time bishops were elected for Worcester, Hereford and Exeter.[22]

By this date it might be assumed that the rest of the Abbey complex, including extensive guest accommodation, was largely realized and there were frequent visits by Royalty and leading ecclesiastics thereafter. Some of the archaeological finds on the abbey site tend only to be associated with structures patronised by medieval society's higher status individuals. One example would be the excavation of a very unusual pottery vessel known as an aquamanile, a jug holding water for washing hands during formal dining. The Eynsham aquamanile is particularly special in that it was in the form of a horse and rider. Such military connotations would seem inappropriate for an abbey but for the fact that it frequently welcomed prominent men with their knightly attendants. Such visits could be a mixed blessing. When Richard II and his court stayed at Gloucester Abbey for example, it was later said that the monastery was so over-crowded that it looked *more like a market than a house of religion* and the cloister garth was *so flattened by wrestling and ball games that it was hopeless to expect the grass to survive*.[23] Eynsham Abbey often complained of the considerable expense of providing such hospitality to the *concourse of magnates* but there were also benefits to the town and abbey from entertaining such wealthy personages. Sometimes too, the abbey was able to secure more property by way of recompense, thereby increasing its income.

What might Eynsham's new abbey have looked like? We are fortunate that an Oxford antiquarian, Anthony Wood, visited the abbey site in September 1657, just before the final demolition of the abbey church. His rough sketch (Figure 27) of what he saw actually tells us a great deal about the character of the new abbey's building.

Looking from the inside of the church facing west, it shows that the nave had largely disappeared although Wood gives an indication of the pier bases which appear to be circular. If Wood is to be trusted, the nave arcade was of six or seven bays. The crossing and monk's choir would have been further east and separated from the nave by a screen as the nave was reserved for the lay brothers who worked on the abbey's estate. The two substantially Romanesque towers were still standing but the large west window between them, its gable surmounted by a cross, was a later addition in the gothic style. The configuration of the tracery has been obscured by Wood's labelling, or else it had broken away, but it is likely to be in the Perpendicular style of the 15th century. The window had a small Norman doorway below and the suggestion of a galilee or porch between the two towers.

The northern tower was better preserved and more elaborate. It had buttresses at the angles and presumably at least one stair turret as Wood draws a little figure on the roof.

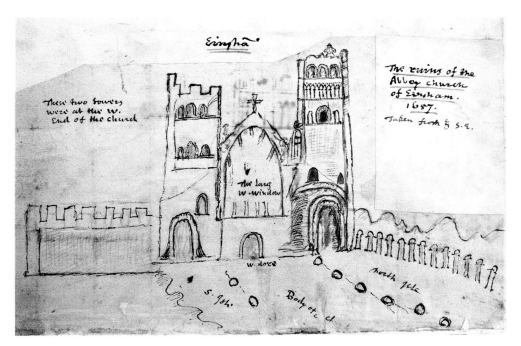

Figure 27. Anthony Wood's sketch of the inside of the Eynsham Abbey church looking west shortly before its final demolition after 1657. The Bodleian Library, University of Oxford, MS Wood E1 f. 45R.

There are three tiers of windows above the roof line, separated by string courses. At the top, three openings or blind arcade; in the middle a blind arcade of interlacing arches forming points; below, a large window flanked by two smaller blank arches. There also seems to have been a large window or doorway on the south side of the tower, presumably giving access to the south tower or nave roof. This latter would probably have been of timber originally like most abbey churches but may have been replaced by stone vaulting at a later date because of the risk of fire. The southern tower is simpler/more ruinous with two tiers of three windows and crowned with battlements. A good example of the form of ornamentation on the northern tower, albeit on a somewhat grander scale, can be found on the central tower of Tewkesbury Abbey which probably dates to the second quarter of the 12th century (Figure 28). The decoration covers all four sides as it probably did at Eynsham.

The Eynsham towers had lower openings facing into the church which probably provided access to the triforium, or gallery, which ran above the nave, choir and transepts. In accordance with normal practice, a clerestory or row of windows above the triforium would admit light to the central parts of the building. At the base of both towers and below the gothic window are the main interior doors into the church from the west front, leading into the nave and its aisles. As with the other openings, they consist of Norman arches of

Figure 28.   Tewkesbury Abbey (Gloucs). Central
crossing tower.

continuous orders without capitals and
columns. Whether this reflected reality,
like the south doors at Malmesbury and
Langford or the west door at Iffley, or
was just the consequence of the rough
drafting skills of Wood is difficult to say
although he does use small horizontal
lines to indicate capitals in the blind
arcade on the north tower and along
the wall of the north aisle. If the orders
of the arches were continuous, it might
support the idea of a later 12th century

Figure 29.   Castle Acre Priory (Norfolk). The inside of
the Priory church looking west.

date for the west front of the abbey.[24] On the other hand there does appear to be a tradition of continuous orders in central and western England from an earlier date. To the south of the southern tower, and seemingly separated from it, is a wall with crenellation, possibly the remains of the boundary to the inner precinct of the abbey. Alternatively, it might be what survived of the western range of the cloisters.

Wood doesn't provide any kind of scale to his drawing but what he was looking at may have been similar to the still standing ruins of Castle Acre Priory in Norfolk (Figure 29).

The inner core of the walls and columns at Castle Acre are of rubble, faced with ashlar, a standard form of construction which was almost certainly used at Eynsham too. The

Figure 30.   Southwell Minster (Notts).
West front.

closest surviving parallel to Eynsham's west front is probably the façade of Southwell Minster in Nottinghamshire which dates, mostly, to the early part of the 12th century and which also has blank arches and arcades in the two towers (Figure 30). Here too though, the original Romanesque facade at the centre of the west elevation was replaced by a large perpendicular gothic window in the 15th century. Such improvements were popular in most abbeys and large churches as they let more light into the body of the church.

There are few complete and unaltered examples of Norman abbey west fronts in England. Kirkstall Abbey, Yorkshire, has a moulded central portal crowned by a gable with two large windows above and Perpendicular additions. Castle Acre Priory, Norfolk, has three elaborate doorways with much blind arcading above but like Kirkstall is otherwise semi-derelict. Reculver in Kent is very austere with a single western portal. Worksop Priory (Notts) has a complete Norman façade but with the unusual feature of a single large window above the central portal. St Mary's Priory, Chepstow (Gwent) has 12th century work in its lower stages, a richly decorated central doorway flanked by narrow blind arches and a trio of windows with chevron above. St Germans in Cornwall has two western towers with a porch under a gable and three Norman windows above (Figure 31). The original western façade of Eynsham Abbey may therefore have contained similar features to these examples but exactly how they were disposed will never be possible to say.

---

[24] Zarnecki G., *Later English Romanesque Sculpture 1140-1210*, p. 42, London 1953.

Figure 31. St Germans Priory (Cornwall). West front.

It is assumed that, in common with usual practice, there was a large central tower at the junction of the nave, transepts and chancel although as yet there is no physical evidence of such. Nevertheless, there exists a reverse seal of the abbey dating to 1255 which depicts the Virgin and Child seated within what may be a representation of Eynsham Abbey (Figure 32). Salter concludes, from the *Customary* of John of Wood Eaton, that this seal was first produced about the year 1228 at the end of the rule of Abbot Adam.[25] It has been shown that such seals can, in general terms, depict the main features of buildings they are associated with, such as those of the early church of Christ Church Cathedral, Canterbury.[26] Likewise at Glastonbury, a seal of about 1175 is thought to have the only known representation of the Norman abbey church there before the disastrous fire of 1184.

In Eynsham's case, the conventual church is depicted as the throne or *sedes* of St Mary, to whom the abbey was dedicated. The seal seems

Figure 32. Eynsham Abbey Seal c. 1228. The Bodleian Library, University of Oxford, MS DD Queen's 288.

[25] Salter H.E., *Eynsham Cartulary*, Vol. 2: note on p. 174 and facing p. 176, Oxford Historical Society, Clarendon Press 1908.

[26] Zarnecki G. and Holt J. and Holland T. (eds), *English Romanesque Art 1066-1200*, p. 309 ff, Arts Council of Great Britain, 1984.

to show the abbey looking from the west. The two towers of the west front with their pyramidal roofs are clearly shown and between them the large central crossing tower with a short spire and pinnacles on its corners. The whole forms a canopy for the Virgin who is seated below a rounded arch supported by block capitals.

The north and south transepts would have adjoined the central tower to form the arms of the cross-shaped plan of the abbey church. They would probably have contained side chapels which were often used for the saying of masses for the deceased benefactors of the monastery. This generated a substantial amount of income for religious houses in the medieval era.

Although it only covered about 10% of the abbey precinct, the archaeological excavation of 1989-92 was able to infer the dimensions of the nave of the abbey church from the total length of the south walk of the cloister, roughly 33 metres. The width of the walk was estimated at roughly two and a half metres from wall to wall. The excavation of the west cloister walk uncovered a pavement of limestone flags and it is likely that the whole cloister was similarly floored. The archaeology also revealed that a circular lavatorium or lavabo was built in the south-west corner of the cloister garth to provide the monks with washing facilities before they ate. Although quite common in Europe, such free-standing lavabos

Figure 33.   Much Wenlock Priory (Shropshire). Lavabo in the cloister garth close to the west door of the refectory.

Figure 34.   Montreale Cathedral, Palermo, Sicily. Lavabo and cloister.

are unusual in England. A surviving example of such can be seen at Much Wenlock Priory in Shropshire (Figure 33) where just the base remains of a three-storied central structure once contained within an octagonal building outside the door to the refectory.

Secure dating evidence for Eynsham's lavabo was hard to come by but it was assigned to the second half of the 12th century. It seems to have been less elaborate than that at Much Wenlock and in general it may have functioned more like that still extant at Montreale in Sicily (Figure 34).

Unfortunately, there are no surviving Benedictine cloisters of this period *in situ* in England but Eynsham's cloister and lavabo with its associated buildings may have looked something like the imagined reconstruction below (Figure 35). The lavatorium was positioned close to one of the entrances to the refectory which was next to the whole length of the south walk of the cloister. The floor of the refectory seems to have been paved with flagstone and tile from the

Figure 35.   Imagined reconstruction of Eynsham's cloister and lavabo. Posy Parrinder.

Figure 36.   Wall-mounted pulpit in St Laurence, Combe Longa (Oxon).

beginning and the monks sat on benches and tables set on a step along just the south side of the building. This suggests that the standard refectory pulpit for readings from the Bible or other theological works, would have been placed on the north side. As no footings or foundations were found for such a structure the archaeologists concluded that the pulpit at Eynsham was built into the wall itself. A rare example of a medieval stone pulpit suspended from a wall in this way can be found in one of Eynsham's churches at nearby Combe Longa (Figure 36). The Combe example, built into its north wall, dates to the 14th century. It was probably part of the original fitments of the church but it is just possible that it may have been purloined from the abbey at the Dissolution.

Next to the west end of the refectory was the main kitchen, the original plan of which was unusual – a square with three-quarter 'apses' or turrets on its two southern corners. The original monk's kitchen at Glastonbury was of the same design. The Eynsham structure appears to have been almost immediately replaced by a larger rectangular building overlying it which was divided in two by an east-west oven range. The re-build was possibly necessitated by the need for a larger kitchen that was directly linked to the south west door of the refectory. Internally it measured approximately 10 x 15 metres, larger than the famous Great Kitchen of Stanton Harcourt Manor (Figure 37). Although the latter dates mostly to the 14th century, Eynsham's monks' kitchen may have functioned in the same way with the smoke from the central hearths and ovens escaping through louvres in the roof. The windows of the kitchen appear to have been unglazed and merely covered with canvas to keep out the rain. There is some evidence that the structure also contained two corner fireplaces such as can be found at the extant abbot's kitchen at Glastonbury (Figure 38).

It is thought that there was a separate bakehouse for making bread and a brewhouse for making the substantial quantities of beer consumed but as yet the location of these is unknown. South east of the kitchen was a large domestic range and latrine pit which replaced an earlier building in the second half of the 12th century. It has been suggested by Hardy that this building may have looked something like the hall of the castle at Christchurch, Hampshire, a remarkable late 12th century survival (Figure 39).

To its west was a small courtyard and on the other side of the courtyard, south of the kitchen, was a cellared building with a vault supported by a central column, possibly a food storage facility.

Figure 37.   The Great Kitchen of Stanton Harcourt Manor (Oxon). An 18th century print found in the papers of the Reverend Thomas Symonds, vicar of Eynsham 1826-45, The Bodleian Library, University of Oxford, MS Top Oxon b 275 f. 291a. Coincidentally, the building stands in the same relation to the two towers at Stanton Harcourt as did Eynsham's monastic kitchen to those of the Abbey's west front.

However, many of Eynsham's extensive abbey structures lay outside the excavated area and their exact location can only be second-guessed by comparison with other monastic complexes whose plans have been more completely revealed. It is assumed for example, that the chapter house, so called because a chapter of St Benedict's Rule was read at

Figure 38.   Glastonbury Abbey (Somerset). Fireplace in the abbot's kitchen.

Figure 39. Christchurch (Hants). The great hall of the castle.

daily business meetings here, lay just south of the abbey church off the east walk of the cloister. The chapter house probably followed the customary design of a central doorway from the cloister flanked by a window either side as can be seen for example at Buildwas Abbey (Salop) (Figure 40). Here the monks would have met every morning with the abbot

Figure 40. Buildwas Abbey (Shropshire). Entrance to the chapter house.

or prior to discuss the abbey's affairs and give out punishments for infringements of the *Rule*. The monk's dormitory may have lain to its south or possibly above it and an eastern range below. The monks would then have accessed the abbey church for early services via a night stair leading into the south transept.

After the Conquest, it was normal practice for a monastery's abbot to be provided for separately. At Eynsham, the abbot's lodging and kitchen is thought to have been off the west range of the cloister and may even have abutted the west front of the abbey as at Castle Acre Priory (Figure 41). Close by the western gate to the inner precinct, it would have enabled the abbot to welcome guests to the House and monitor the brethren's movements too. The abbot's kitchen would have provided a superior standard of food for him and the abbey's distinguished visitors as is made clear by accounts in the *Cartulary* although the main kitchen would also be used to prepare specialities if such visitors brought a large entourage with them.

The guest accommodation must have occupied a considerable area and it is thought that some of it, the almonry, for general visitors and/or pilgrims, may have been built to the north west of the precinct near where the 'Swan Inn' now is.[27] Interestingly, a Mr Malin, whose farmhouse and outbuildings were once located in Swan Street, claimed that when his farmyard was redeveloped for housing in the 1970s, the contractor putting in the groundworks broke into a stone vaulted cellar. Worried that the contract would be cancelled or delayed he told his men to fill it in and keep quiet about it.[28] In addition to the almonry and given the fact that the ground to the south of the precinct drops sharply to the flood plain, the main structures to house distinguished figures could also have been housed in the north of the precinct close to Oxford Road, or outside it altogether.[29]

Based on the geophysical survey of the Nursery Field which indicated a substantial group of buildings, the infirmary may have been sited to the east of the abbey church. It would have been a self-contained unit with its own kitchen, chapel, cemetery and accommodation for visitors. The discovery of encaustic tiles and a water system in the field in the 19th century adds weight to the idea (see chapter 14). Clearly, much more needs to be done before the precise location of all the constituent parts of the complex can be defined. Figure 42 shows what may have been the ground plan of the main Norman structures and their Saxon predecessors in relation to the modern village.[30]

[27] Chambers, op.cit., p. 77.

[28] As told in 2018 by Mr Malin to Heather Horner of the Oxfordshire Buildings Record and e-mailed by her to the author. The story was independently corroborated by Dave Russell, a long-term resident of the village. In 2006, in an interview with Eynsham's Junior History Group, Mr Malin also claimed to have found steps there under a large slab. The steps apparently went down to a huge tunnel going away towards Abbey Farm.

[29] It is sometimes claimed in the village that the house known as 'The Shrubbery' was part of, or contains parts of the abbey's guest accommodation. Secure evidence for the first assertion is not forthcoming although the house and garden does contain stone which clearly came from the abbey at the Dissolution.

[30] The illustration does not show the infirmary complex or the extensive guest accommodation and it is possible that the abbey church itself extended further to the east.

Figure 41. Castle Acre Priory (Norfolk). The abbot's house adjoining the west front of the Priory church.

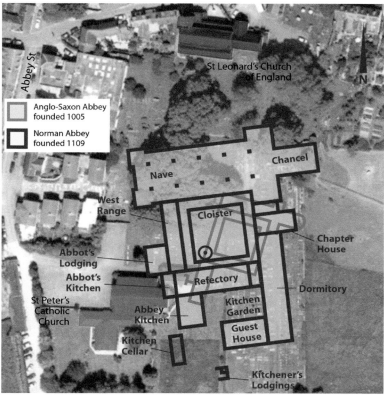

Figure 42. The ground plan of Eynsham's Norman abbey and its Saxon predecessor in relation to St Leonard's and St Peter's churches. Adapted by Paul Hughes from the leaflet *Eynsham Abbey, Archaeological Site Trail*, by Martin Flatman and Paul Hughes.

At the very end of the 12th century, Eynsham Abbey decided to build, or possibly rebuild, a small chapel for the parish to the north of the abbey precinct adjoining the market square. Until this time the parish could have used the nave or one of the aisles of the abbey church but this may have interfered with the monks' spiritual activities and had the potential for conflict between them and the villagers. When, for example, Bardney Abbey (Lincs) later petitioned the bishop to rebuild the parish church which had fallen down they complained that the villagers were *prone to wander and roam about in our conventual church in time of divine service, and to hinder, molest and disturb us in manifold ways...by their noise and uproar.*[31] The building of such parochial churches, adjoining the north gate of the monastic enclosure was a regular practice as demonstrated by two other local examples, St Lawrence's at Reading and St Nicholas' at Abingdon.

Eynsham's chapel, on the site of the bulk of the current south aisle of the parish church, was dedicated to St Leonard, a Saint popular with the Benedictines and patron of pregnant women and prisoners of war. Interestingly, the church follows more closely the orientation of the Saxon church rather than the Norman abbey. This may be an indication that in Saxon times, as previously mentioned, there was a small chapel on the St Leonard's site. The monastery would clearly have had an input as regards the chapel's architectural details which may shed light on the nature of changes made to the abbey itself. Moreover, the decision to build a separate church for the use of the village would have significant consequences for the abbey at the time of the Dissolution.

---

[31] Thompson A.H. (ed.), Visitations of Religious Houses in the Diocese of Lincoln Vol. 1 1420-1436: p.6, *Lincoln Record Society*, Vol. 7, 1913.

Chapter 4

Eynsham Abbey Stones

So many and so marvelous are the varieties of diverse shapes on every hand that we are more tempted to read in the stone than in our books and to spend the whole day in wondering at those things rather than in meditating the law of God. For God's sake, if men are not ashamed of these follies, why at least do they not shrink from the expense?[1]

Anthony Wood's drawing showed the ruins of the north wall of the abbey church along which are a regular series of small arches. This is probably blank arcading which was a popular form of Anglo-Norman decoration, particularly in large churches, cathedrals and abbeys. The example below (Figure 43) is an arcade dating to the first half of the 12th century in the north aisle of the Benedictine monastery in Ely, elevated to a Cathedral in 1109.

Figure 43.   Ely Cathedral (Cambs). North aisle.

---

[1]   Extract from St Bernard's 12th century complaint about the nature of some ecclesiastical sculpture. Quoted in Zarnecki G., *English Romanesque Sculpture 1066-1140*, p. 19, London, 1951.

Figure 44.   Column base with mason's laying out marks. Brian Atkins' collection.

Some of the stones found around the village would support the idea of such arcading at Eynsham too. Numerous column fragments, roughly 15cm in diameter, have been built into people's walls or litter their gardens. A fine column base (Figure 44) with the same moulding profile as those at Ely has been preserved, on which it is still possible to make out the mason's laying out marks.[2] The shaft which it supported would have been 15cm in diameter. Its excellent state of preservation would support the idea that it came from an internal feature in comparison to a similar base for a respond column which is very weathered (Figure 45).

Figure 45.   Column base found in Holewelle Field, Eynsham.

---

[2]   An identical stone has recently (2019) been discovered in a rockery at 'The Shrubbery.'

Figure 46. Cushion capital. Brian Atkins' collection. Once in Eynsham Vicarage garden.

The shaft in turn would have supported a capital such as the one here (Figure 46), a small (20cm x 23cm x 23cm) respond capital, carved on three sides with a familiar Anglo-Norman 'cushion' shape with vestigial leaves in two corners and a plain necking 15cm in diameter. The flat-blocked back indicates that it stood against a wall and again, given its largely unweathered state, from the interior of the abbey church. This capital would almost certainly have been painted originally, like the rest of the church. An interesting 12th century survival of such is in St Anselm's chapel in Canterbury Cathedral (Figure 47).

Another respond capital, of roughly the same dimensions, is carved on two sides with stylised foliage whose stems curl over at the ends (Figure 48). The angle between the two sides is filled with a flower bud and fans or flat leaves. This capital may have supported an arch above a door or may indeed have been part of the same blank arcading. This is difficult to date precisely but comparisons can be made with illuminated manuscripts to determine a general period. One of the 12th century manuscripts which is known to have

Figure 47. 12th century painting in St Anselm's chapel, Canterbury Cathedral (Kent).

been in Eynsham Abbey's library contains an elaborately decorated initial E (Figure 49). The distinctive flower form and the foliage stems that curl back on themselves, as well as the fan-shaped leaves, mirror those on the capital. Another fragment (Figure 50), possibly part of an abacus, has foliage with ball-like terminals similar to that in some of the simpler initials in the same manuscript (Figure 51). The manuscript dates to between 1130 and 1140

Figure 48.   Respond capital. Brian Atkins' collection. Once built into a gatepost of 'Newland House'.

and the initial is similar to those in the Winchcombe Psalter of the same date.[3] If one allows a generational gap between the production of the motifs in the MS and their use by the masons, then a date between the 1150s and 1160s would seem acceptable for this capital.

The form of decoration is similar to that found on some capitals now in the south transept of St Alban's abbey. These are clearly related to some of the work of master masons at Reading Abbey, of which more later.

Another capital can be found in the hallway between St Peter's church Eynsham and the adjoining Tolkein room (Figure 52). Although badly worn it is possible to make out some vestigial volutes. These are similar to those on the capitals of the tower arch on the interior of the tower of St Peter's church in Northampton (Figure 53) which is one of the most

Figure 49.   Initial E from a 12th century manuscript thought to have been in Eynsham Abbey's library. The Bodleian Library, University of Oxford, Bodl. 269, f. iiiv.

elaborately decorated Norman churches in the country and dates to the 1150s. Sculpture there is very distinctive and thought by some to be inspired by Italian models. Contacts

---

[3]   Kauffmann C.M., *Romanesque Manuscripts 1066-1190*, Harvey Miller, London 1975.

Figure 50.   Fragment of sculpted stone, possibly part of an abacus. Brian Atkins' collection.

Figure 51.   Initial M. The Bodleian Library, University of Oxford, Bodl. 269 f. 30v.

with Europe, both politically and culturally were closer than might be thought and the result of trade, dynastic marriages and pilgrimage led to a wide diffusion of artistic styles and motifs.[4]

---

[4] For example, one of Henry II's daughters, Joan, married King William II of Sicily. Another, Eleanor, married the King of Castile. 13th and 14th century references in Eynsham's *Cartulary* suggest that such links were on-going.

Figure 52.   Volute capital built into the wall of the vestibule between St Peter's R.C. church and the Tolkein Room, Eynsham. Originally in the Vicarage garden.

Figure 53.   St Peter's, Northampton. Capitals of the tower arch.

Figure 54.   Fragment built into the front wall of 7 Newland Street, Eynsham.

Figure 55.   St Peter's, Northampton. Capital of the nave.

Built into a house in Newland Street is a very unusual fragment, possibly part of a capital, which also has clear parallels with St Peter's Northampton (Figure 54). Although difficult to see and badly worn, it is possible to make out a multi-stranded stem with a band across one end and an unusual palmette leaf, again with a clasp at its base. This form of decoration compares well with that found on the distinctive capitals and abaci in Northampton (Figure 55). The design is rare but can also be found on a capital of the south door at Oxhill (Warks), on some of the capitals of the crossing arch at Lambourn (Berks) and on the top of the font of St Mary Bourne (Hants).

Figure 56.   Eynsham's 'Agnus Dei' capital. Photographed by W. Bainbridge ©Eynsham History Group (EHG). Current whereabouts unknown.

One very interesting capital found in Eynsham, but now apparently lost, was sculpted with a crude 'Agnus Dei' on one side (Figure 56). Though not unknown on tympana, corbels, voussoirs and fonts, this is an unusual theme for an English Romanesque capital.[5] The Lamb of God has a halo, a leg supporting a cross and a foliate tail. Another side (Figure 57) shows an animal, possibly a griffin, with an intertwined tail ending in a heart-shaped leaf such as can be found on the left of the early 12th century tympanum in the north wall of Ampney St Mary (Gloucs) (Figure 58). Flatly carved, the Eynsham piece has the feel of Viking influenced art and with some of the designs which were used by the so-called 'Herefordshire School' of Romanesque sculpture. The foliage terminals on one side and the triangular leaf form of the second side are similar to those on the Agnus Dei tympanum reset in

Figure 57.   Another side of the 'Agnus Dei' capital. W. Bainbridge ©EHG.

a barn at Coleshill (Berks) (Figure 59) which Pevsner dates to the 11th century although the beaded roundel in which the Lamb is set has parallels with 12th century work from Reading and elsewhere. Eynsham's 'Agnus Dei' capital may well have been used on one of the doorways of the west front of the abbey, to remind both monks and others that they were entering the House of God.

Another large Romanesque capital, with fleshy sinuous dragons, appears in a photograph by Henry Taunt in the late nineteenth century but has since been lost. The remaining

---

[5]   Another example can be found at Southwell Minster (Notts).

Figure 58.   Ampney St Mary (Gloucs). Tympanum in north wall of the nave.

Figure 59.   Coleshill (Berks). Tympanum re-set in a barn wall of Strattenborough Castle Farm.

Figure 60.   Respond capital found in Holewelle Field, Eynsham.

Figure 61. St Mary, Barnsley (Gloucs). Capitals of the chancel arch.

Anglo-Norman capitals and responds found in the village are simply fluted or scalloped blocks, more popular from the mid-12th century. One small respond capital, dug up in Holewelle field (Figure 60) compares well, for example, with the chancel arch capitals in Barnsley church (Gloucs) (Figure 61) and those at Elkstone in the same county. They would originally have been painted and a surviving example of such decoration and adjoining painted chevron, can be found in the parish church at Hailes (Gloucs) (Figure 62).

Of two other fluted respond capitals, one is built into a garden wall in Newland Street (Figure 63) whilst another is in the garden of a house in Acre End Street (Figure 64).

Two composite corner respond capitals (Figure 65) excavated in the 1970s are now built, upside-down, into the Abbey Street 'cairn' and the top of a larger scalloped capital is built into the wall of 'Twelve Acre' farmhouse (Figure 66). A fragment of another small scalloped capital was discovered in the 1989-92 archaeological investigation.

Figure 62. Hailes church (Gloucs). Scalloped capital of the chancel arch.

Figure 63.   Scalloped or fluted capital, Newland Street, Eynsham. W. Bainbridge ©EHG.

Figure 64.   Scalloped or fluted capital, Acre End Street, Eynsham. W. Bainbridge ©EHG.

Figure 65.   Scalloped corner capitals. W. Bainbridge ©EHG. Now built into the Abbey Street 'cairn', Eynsham.

Figure 66. Scalloped capital in the north wall of 'Twelve Acre' Farmhouse, Eynsham.

The excavation also turned up a large scalloped capital from a free-standing pier which probably supported a vault in an undercroft.

There is, as yet, no secure evidence for the piers of the abbey church itself. A number of large semi-circular stones or fragments of stones, about 92cm in diameter, have been found which probably formed parts of columns although perhaps not large enough for the substantial arcades of the nave (Figure 67). A number of smaller half columns or responds, 46cm in diameter, have also been found in the village, both semi-circular and five-sided in plan.

The nave piers were probably constructed of carefully shaped blocks enclosing a rubble infill such as is found in most Norman abbeys. Two apparently reconstructed, or partially reconstructed piers have been found in the village. One is built into the north-east wall

Figure 67. Large half column found in Holewelle Field, now built into its eastern wall.

Figure 68.   Part of a re-constructed pier once in the garden of a house in Acre End Close, Eynsham. Demolished 2016.

of a former shop in Acre End Street and another formed part of a garden wall of a house in Acre End Close (Figure 68) but has recently been demolished by a developer.

Eynsham Abbey's nave arcade may have looked something like that at Southwell Minster (Notts) for example (Figure 69) or the nave of Great Malvern Priory (Worcs).

It would probably have had plain mouldings although some hefty respond columns that have been found (Figure 70), now built into the Abbey Street 'cairn', could originally have been attached to piers. Alternatively, they may have made up quatrefoil columns which would be very unusual.[6] Nine very similar responds to these were found in the 19th century, each 91.5cm wide at the back and 51cm deep from its fillet moulded roll.[7] This latter characteristic would tend to date them to the later 12th or early 13th century. Unfortunately, these latter responds seem to have been reused as building material by the farmer on whose land they were found and have since disappeared.

Returning to Wood's drawing, it will be seen that on the central window of the lower tier of decoration on the north tower he has made an attempt to illustrate that most recognisable of Anglo-Norman motifs – chevron, or zig-zag. (Figure 71). The motif has many possible origins dating back to pre-history but one source may have been from the Middle East and it is interesting that an early 12th century mason known as 'Lalys' was said to have been a Saracen, taken prisoner on Crusade, and ended up as an architect at the court of Henry I.[8] Whatever the truth of the matter, chevron was enthusiastically adopted by British masons from the late 11th century to the early 13th century. Eynsham has a number of different examples of this form of ornamentation and clearly it must have been used extensively on the abbey's voussoirs, wedged-

---

[6]   The nave arcades of St Mary's, Ripple (Worcs) for example, which probably date to the late 12th or early 13th centuries.

[7]   *Bodl. G.A. Oxon c 317 ([20])* Letter from M. Shurlock to Professor J.O. Westwood, April 15 1851.

[8]   Harvey J., *English Medieval Architects*, p. 156, Batsford, 1954.

Figure 69. Southwell Minster (Notts). Nave arcades looking east.

Figure 70. Respond columns now built into Abbey Street 'cairn'.

Figure 72.   *Voussoir with incised chevron.*
Holewelle Field, Eynsham.

Figure 71.   *Detail of the north west tower of Eynsham*
Abbey as drawn by Anthony Wood. The
Bodleian Library, University of Oxford, MS
Wood E1 f. 45R.

Figure 73.   *Pershore Abbey (Worcs). Detail of the south*
west transept.

Figure 74. *Small voussoir with single stranded chevron. Brian Atkins' collection.*

shaped stones which are the components of arches forming doors and windows.

Firstly, there are a number of examples of incised chevron cut into the flat face of stones such as a voussoir from Holewelle field (Figure 72) but also seen elsewhere. This type is actually quite rare and the closest parallels, albeit with beading, are in the south transept of Pershore Abbey (Worcs) (Figure 73) which dates to the early 12th century.[9] It can also be found

Figure 75. *St Peter, Cassington (Oxon). Chancel arch.*

---

[9]   Moss R., *Romanesque Chevron Ornament*, p. 14 note 13, British Archaeological Reports, International Series 1908, Archaeopress, 2009.

on the west doorway of Inishfallen, County Kerry, Ireland, although the Eynsham example is not decorated on the soffit except for a shallow rounded moulding.

Secondly, there is an example of a small voussoir with single stranded chevron (Figure 74). This type of moulding is quite common and can be seen, for example, on the outer order of the chancel arch of Cassington (Figure 75), an Eynsham church, on a band above the blank arcading in the aisles at Malmesbury (Wilts), on the chancel arch of St John's Devizes and on the outer order of the south door at Church Hanborough.

The third type of chevron consists of voussoirs with large flat triangles, either one or two, on a roll moulding. At least 16 of these voussoirs survive rebuilt into both sides of the gateway of the 'White House' in Mill Street (Figure 76). All of them were found in the garden of the house and one of them was given to the 'Queen's Head' pub where it is built into an internal wall (Figure 77). The roll is large, 15cm in diameter, and must have been part of a substantial arch such as one of the main doorways to the abbey church.

Figure 76.   Gateway of the White House, Mill Street, Eynsham.

Figure 77.   Chevron voussoir built into an interior wall of the Queen's Head pub in Queens Street, Eynsham.

*Figure 78.   Chevron voussoir from the collapsed
            Co-op wall in Lombard Street, Eynsham.*

A similar form of chevron, albeit on a
smaller roll, was found in the collapsed
Co-op wall (Figure 78) and a very
battered example in a garden in Mill
Street Mews. This type of chevron can
be shown, for example, on the south
door at Shellingford (Berks) and the
chancel arch at Twyford (Bucks). It
also appears on an outer order of the
north and south doors of Iffley church
as well as some of the interior Norman
windows there (Figure 79).

Figure 79.   St Mary, Iffley (Oxon). North door.

Figure 80.   Large chevron voussoir in a garden in Mill Street. Originally in the possession of Dame Helen Gardner of Myrtle House.

Figure 81.   Chevron voussoir from the collapsed Co-op wall.

Figure 82.   Chevron voussoir. Brian Atkins' collection.

The inner order of this doorway at Iffley contains a more elaborate form of chevron consisting of chevron rolls and there are quite a few examples of this type, of various sizes, consisting of one, two or three rolls and hollows. A large example is privately held by a resident in Mill Street (Figure 80), two are built into a gatepost in Tanners Lane, another is set above the side door to the pottery in Newland Street and another was found in the Co-op Wall (Figure 81). A further example is also held privately (Figure 82). A fragment of such a voussoir was also discovered in the archaeological investigation of 1989-92. Two others were photographed by Bainbridge and originally came from the Nursery Field site. They were taken away by a resident some years ago but one, consisting of three rolls and fillets has recently been returned to the village (Figure 83).[10]

A particularly fine and very unusual example of this lateral face chevron was found in Holewelle field (Figure 84). The voussoir (26cm x 13cm x 9cm) is carved centrifugally so that the 'V's of the chevron point outwards. From the top there is sharp-edged chevron, then a hollow, another sharp-edged chevron with a groove cut in its top edge, a chevron roll and lastly, in the recessed lower spandrel, miniature single stranded chevron with a groove. In common with a few other stones found, there are traces of white pigment which indicates that at some point it was painted. Although chevron decoration in 12th century Norman churches is common, this particular form may be unique. Another example, found close by, consists of a large (15cm) half-roll moulding with zig-zag and a chevron roll in its lower spandrel (Figure 85). Its slightly tilted shape indicates that it may have formed part of a vaulting rib.

---

[10] Another large chevron voussoir (28cms x 18cms) with three rolls has recently (2019) turned up in a rockery at 'The Shrubbery.'

Figure 84.   Chevron voussoir from Holewelle
Field.

Figure 85.   Half roll with chevron in the soffit.
Holewelle Field.

Figure 86.   Point to point chevron.
Originally from the
Vicarage garden. Brian
Atkins' collection.

Figure 87.   Lozenge and roll, possibly part of a door jamb. Brian Atkins' collection.

As the 12th century progressed, masons found ever more elaborate ways to use chevron. One stone from Eynsham (Figure 86) shows point to point chevron and may have been used in a vault like that at Stewkeley (Bucks), as part of a door jamb such as those on the north doorway of Bromyard (Herefs), or part of a blind arcade such as graces the west front of Malmesbury (Wilts).

The stone shows the chevron on one side forming a lozenge shape filled with a raised diamond, a form more common in the second half of the 12th century. There are two

Figure 88.   Chevron with lozenge. Built into a fireplace in a house in Witney Road. Thought to come originally from Nursery Field, Eynsham.

Figure 89.   Voussoir with chevron and lozenge filled with 'grapes'. Found in the excavation of 1989-92 of part of the Abbey site. Now at the MRC, OCMS.

Figure 90.   All Saints, Middleton Stoney (Oxon). South doorway.

other examples in the village (Figures 87 and 88) and another photographed by Bainbridge in the 1980s. A more elaborate version of this motif was found in the excavation. Here the lozenge is filled with grape-like pellets (Figure 89). Grapes were sometimes used as symbols of the Eucharist, the blood of Christ. Both this stone and the previous would have formed part of an elaborate doorway like the south door of Bampton church or the reset south doorway at Middleton Stoney which dates to the third quarter of the 12th century (Figure 90).

The door at Middleton Stoney has jambs with bold chevron mouldings at right angles to the wall and a fragment of something very similar has emerged in Eynsham (Figure

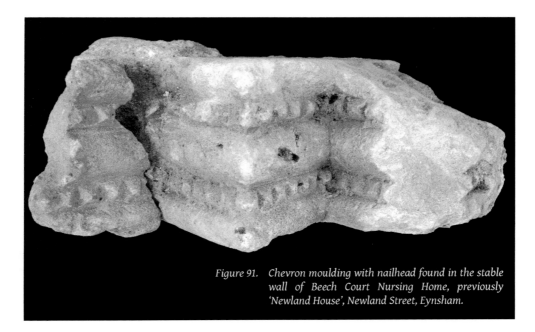

Figure 91.   Chevron moulding with nailhead found in the stable wall of Beech Court Nursing Home, previously 'Newland House', Newland Street, Eynsham.

91). The Eynsham example has rows of nailhead decoration between the chevron rolls and can be paralleled by an example from Reading Abbey now in the gardens at Windsor Castle[11] (Figure 92) and, on a smaller scale, the inner orders of the west door at Iffley. Nailhead decoration can be found on the wall of a house in Mill Street, on a moulded stone originally from a house in the same street but now at Evans Road, on the interior of a house in Acre End Street and another in Newland Street. A small piece of an arch with nailhead was found in the collapsed wall in Lombard Street and another fragment, probably part of a capital, was found in the course of the excavation. It tends to be seen as a late Romanesque ornament which became popular in the Early Gothic period. Nailhead with chevron can be seen locally

Figure 92.   Stone from Reading Abbey in the garden at the base of the round tower, Windsor Castle (Berks).

---

[11] It has been suggested (R. Baxter, *The Royal Abbey of Reading*, The Boydell Press, 2016) that the Romanesque stones at Windsor may not be from Reading Abbey as the stones apparently used at Windsor came from Reading's 14th century Lady Chapel. However, as Barker himself admits, the Romanesque Windsor stones are very similar to others at Reading and it is by no means clear that all the stone brought to Windsor from Reading came exclusively from the Lady Chapel.

on the eastern columns of the chancel arch at Windrush. It is also a feature of Lincoln Cathedral's north doorway on its west front.

Nailhead or pellets with two rows of miniature chevron above also decorate a rectangular panel, just 13cm wide found in a garden in Newland Street (Figure 93). This may have formed part of a frieze like that below the windows of the north and south walls of Stewkley church (Bucks) (Figure 94). Stewkley is one of the most elaborately decorated Norman churches in the country and, in some ways, is reminiscent of Iffley. Parts of the exterior cornice at Kilpeck (Herefs) have a very similar design too.

One form of Norman decoration, which some see as a development from chevron, is known as 'beakhead'. Beakhead has been defined as 'an ornament taking the form of the head of a bird, beast or monster, the beak or jaw of which appears to grip the moulding across which it is carved.'[12] The general idea of heads on arches seems to derive from western France but it was taken up enthusiastically by English masons and came to develop very particular characteristics with roots in Anglo-Saxon models. Over 150 churches in England have forms of this decoration but it was especially popular in Yorkshire and southern counties centring on Oxfordshire. It is doubtful whether such motifs contained any meaningful Christian symbolism which is probably why St Bernard raged against what he called *this deformed beauty and beautiful deformity.*

Figure 93.   Chevron and nailhead panel. Found in Newland Street, Eynsham. Collection of Dr Bryan Hyde.

[12] Zarnecki G. quoting A.W. Clapham, Romanesque Arches decorated with Human and Animal Heads, *Studies in Romanesque Sculpture*, The Dorian Press, London, 1979.

Figure 94.   St Michael, Stewkley (Bucks). Frieze below a window in the nave.

Two examples are known from Eynsham. One is clearly derived from the third type of chevron described above but the point of the triangle has been extended to grip the roll over which it sits (Figure 95). Although lacking any animalistic features it may originally have been painted to give the impression of issuing from a bird or monster head. This example is only known from photographs taken in the 1980s and has since left the village. However, an excellent specimen of a classic form of the genre is held privately in Eynsham and consists of a cat's head with almond-shaped eyes, morphing into a beak which curls around the roll of the voussoir (Figure 96). One of Eynsham Abbey's possessions, St Ebbe's in Oxford, has an inner order of beakheads on its west door.[13] However, the church that has beakhead closest to our example is one where we have already seen parallels with Eynsham, Iffley (Figure 97). The spectacular west doorway there, constructed in the 1170s[14]

Figure 95.   Simple beakhead. Supposedly found in Nursery Field. Photographed by William Bainbridge in the 1980s ©EHG. No longer in the village.

---

[13] The existing arch is a replacement. The original carvings are stored at the Museum Resources Centre at Standlake.

[14] Zarnecki G., English Art Around 1180, *Further Studies in Romanesque Sculpture*, Pindar Press, London, 1992.

has beakhead which is so close to the Eynsham example that it is tempting to believe that the same mason was responsible for both.

Iffley in turn was closely associated with the sculpture at Reading Abbey, one of the grandest monasteries in the country in terms of its decoration and, like Eynsham, a foundation of Henry 1 and dedicated to the Virgin. There are some splendid examples of Reading's decoration in the museum there, including very similar beakhead which, it has been suggested, saw its earliest manifestation at Reading.

It is very likely that at least one of the Reading masons worked in the Eynsham area and therefore possibly at Eynsham itself. Indeed, much of the stone for the main fabric of Reading Abbey was quarried at Taynton, near Burford. The neighbouring churches of South Leigh, Stanton Harcourt and Church Hanborough were all granted to Reading in the 12th century which makes a connection even more feasible. The work of Reading masons can be clearly seen in a number of the county's churches. For example, the capitals to the west door of the chapter house at Christchurch in Oxford and the doorway of Barford St Michael to the north

Figure 96. 'Classic' beakhead. Brian Atkins' collection.

Figure 97. St Mary, Iffley (Oxon). West doorway.

Figure 98. 13th century seal of Eynsham Abbey, The Bodleian Library, University of Oxford, MS DD Queen's 288

of the county. Interestingly, Eynsham, like Reading, seems to have developed the cult of the Virgin. Reading has been credited with producing the first English representation of the Coronation of the Virgin[15] and an early copy of the subject can be found on the tympanum of the south doorway of Quenington church just 20 miles south west of Eynsham. The seal of Eynsham Abbey (Figure 98) dating to the early 13th century, shows the same iconography.[16] Quenington has a beakhead which is identical to one of those at Reading and employs large pellet decoration on its south door, another unusual characteristic of Reading's sculptural motifs. It also has another tympanum with a version of the Harrowing of Hell, a favourite theme of the 'Herefordshire School' of Romanesque sculpture whose links with Reading are substantial.

St Peter and St Paul's in Church Hanborough, just a couple of miles from Eynsham has a tympanum over its north door and the style of the sculpture compares well with one of

Figure 99. St Peter and St Paul, Church Hanborough (Oxon). Tympanum over the north door.

---

[15] Zarnecki G., The Coronation of the Virgin on a Capital at Reading Abbey, *Studies in Romanesque Sculpture*, The Dorian Press, London, 1979.

[16] *Bodl. MS DD Queen's 288* April 6 1255, Eynsham quitclaims Drowda Hall to the Priory of Monk Sherborne. Two abbey seals and reverse seals attached.

Figure 100. Reading Abbey. Cloister capital, Reading Museum.

the capitals from Reading Abbey cloister. The carving of St. Peter (Figure 99) like the figures representing the Trinity from Reading[17] (Figure 100) has heavy jowls and eyebrows, garments hatched with parallel lines and a doll-like pose. Interestingly, the Hanborough tympanum also contains an image of the Agnus Dei.

Another unusual stone from Eynsham may also have a connection with Iffley and Reading (Figure 101). Possibly part of a door jamb it has a unique form of decoration – a cog-wheel

Figure 101. Door jamb with cog-wheel strap moulding. Found in Holewelle Field.

---

[17] Baxter identifies the figures as Saints. However, the figure on the right appears to clutch a bird to his chest with his left arm. This detail makes it almost certain that this composition was meant to represent the Trinity, with the Lord as Good Shepherd holding the dove of the Holy Spirit. A very similar iconography, and style, can be found in an early 12th century Lincoln manuscript, *Lincoln Cath. Lib. A.3.17 f142*, although there the dove of the Holy Spirit descends between the two figures.

Figure 102. St Mary, Iffley (Oxon). South doorway.

strap around a roll moulding or possibly a strap bordered with nailhead.

This could be seen as a mutation from beakhead and it bears some resemblance to the more geometric forms of the motif found on the south doorway of the west front of Lincoln Cathedral. Bands on a roll can be found on stones originally from Reading Abbey but now at Windsor[18] but the closest parallel to the form of the Eynsham straps, although without the crenelated edging, would seem to be on the outer label of the south door at Iffley (Figure 102).

The middle order of the south door at Iffley is supported on the east by a shaft with diaper patterning with flowers and a similar piece of column, with lozenges created by three-stranded interlacing bands, has been found in Eynsham (Figure 103). However, the closest parallels to the Eynsham plaits are to be found on churches of the 'Herefordshire School' (e.g., Kilpeck in Herefordshire and Ribbesford in Worcestershire) and, as already noted, there are undoubted links between the School and Reading. The south door at Iffley has a capital on its east side which is sculpted with Samson and the lion. This was a distinctive motif of the 'Herefordshire School' and provides yet another connection between it and Iffley.

Another shaft found in the village has decoration which may be unique (Figure 104). It is three-quarter sculpted with panels of saltire crosses in squares. Saltire crosses are not uncommon in Romanesque sculpture but this type of carving is particularly prevalent in the churches of the 'Herefordshire School'. The form of decoration can also be found in some churches in Western France which provided much of the inspiration for Reading and the Herefordshire School. However, its use in England on a column such as the Eynsham example would appear to be unusual. A fragment built into a wall on the site of Reading Abbey may

[18] Parrinder S., Romanesque Sculpture from Reading Abbey, Unpublished MA dissertation, Birkbeck College, University of London, 1982.

Figure 103. Sculpted Romanesque column.
Dr Bryan Hyde collection.

Figure 104. Sculpted Romanesque column.
From a house in Mill Street,
Eynsham.

Figure 105. Stone fragment from Reading Abbey,
built into the Forbury garden wall.

be part of a similar respond (Figure 105) and one of the shafts on the external arcade of the south-east transept of Canterbury Cathedral shares some of its characteristics.[19] The inspiration for the decoration of these shafts may well have come from the border panels of illuminated manuscripts, like those in the mid-12th century Psalter from Winchester.[20]

A further moulding for an arch of which a couple of examples have been found in Eynsham, is the fret or crenellation (Figure 106). The motif is quite rare in England and tends to be found on larger churches, abbeys and cathedrals. For example, it is used on the arch and jambs of the central doorway of the west front at Lincoln; on the eastern dado above the southern arcade of the nave at Malmesbury and on the west doorway of the parish church at Kenilworth (Warks) (Figure 107). The latter doorway has been re-set from the Augustinian Priory church there and in addition contains beakhead very similar to the Eynsham example. Interestingly, Iffley church was given to Kenilworth Priory by Julian de St Remigio in the 12th century. Fret and beakhead also once adorned Dorchester Abbey and fragments of the fret design appear on Reading Abbey stones at Windsor Castle. It tends to be used most frequently as the outer order of an arch and, given the moulding at the head of the Eynsham example, this would appear to be the case here too.

Figure 106. Stone with fret moulding from a garden
in Acre End Street, Eynsham.

---

[19] Kahn D., *Canterbury Cathedral and its Romanesque Sculpture*, Illustration 143. University of Texas Press, 1991.
[20] *British Library Cotton Nero C. IV.*, e.g. folios 37 and 38.

Figure 107.   Kenilworth Priory doorway re-set in the west front of St Nicholas, Kenilworth (Warks).

Not all of the doorways at Eynsham were so elaborate, as demonstrated by a Norman voussoir found in the grounds of 'The Gables' and now built into the wall facing onto Newland Street (Figure 108). It consists of a squared moulding and a roll with a keel moulding between, such as that on the arch of the south doorway of St Peter and St Paul at Church Hanborough. Similar doorways can be found at Langford and Barnsley (Gloucs) (Figure 109).

A very unusual motif which may have been part of a frieze is now built into a house in Oxford Road, Eynsham (Figure 110). It consists

Figure 108.   Voussoir found in the grounds of 'The Gables' and now acting as a support for a lintel over a gateway into Newland Street, Eynsham.

Figure 109. St Mary, Barnsley (Gloucs). South doorway.

of two adjoining four-sided, roughly square figures whose sides curve at each end to create a sort of 'ravioli' shape. The basic form is similar to ones found at Gloucester Cathedral, Old Sarum, Winchester Cathedral, Romsey Abbey, and Reading Abbey amongst others and seems to occur on buildings associated with royal patronage.[21] However, the Eynsham examples are not set within circles and lack the central hollow of those cited above. Rather, they are identical to those re-set in the exterior north wall of the nave of Portchester Priory, also founded by King Henry I. A stone built into a house wall in Newland Street has the same 'ravioli' shape but with a four-petalled flower set within it (Figure 111), a flower similar to those on a Reading Abbey arch at Windsor.

Figure 110. Block with 'ravioli' motif built into the east wall of 'The Elms', Eynsham.

---

[21] Thurlby M., *The Herefordshire School of Romanesque Sculpture*, p. 139/40, Logaston Press, 1999.

Figure 111. Stone with 'ravioli' motif enclosing a four-petalled flower. Built into the interior wall of a house in Newland Street, Eynsham.

Figure 112. Curved panel with linked roundels enclosing flower motifs. Built into a barn wall in Paddock's Close, off Mill Street, Eynsham.

Figure 113. St Mary Priory, Tutbury (Staffs). Panel on the west front.

Another distinctive Romanesque panel is built into a wall in a Close off Mill Street (Figure 112). Roughly 40cm x 10cm it has four apparently linked roundels with decorative elements including a multi-petalled rosette. Given that the stone is clearly curved, it may have formed an outer label framing a large doorway.

Roundels or medallions with a variety of motifs can be found in many places including, for example, on a reset frieze in the western gable at Iffley, on the outer label of the south door

Figure 114. Corbels built into the wall of the vestibule between St Peter's RC church and the Tolkein Room, Eynsham. Originally in the Vicarage garden.

Figure 115. Corbel built into the Abbey Street 'cairn', Eynsham.

at Harlington (Middx), on the soffits of voussoirs at Reading and the tympanum and lintel of the south doorway at Great Rollright.

However, in most cases these roundels are beaded whereas the Eynsham examples are not and the closest parallels are the circles on the middle order of the west doorway at Porchester and the panels on the west front of the highly ornate Priory church at Tutbury, (Staffs), although the latter are set within squares rather than being linked (Figure 113).

There are a number of other Eynsham stones from the Norman period which were used as corbels supporting a parapet or a beam. Two are now built into the wall of the lobby between St Peter's church and the Tolkein room (Figure 114). Another, a monster head, can be found in the Abbey Street 'cairn' (Figure 115) and a further example is now in the Museum

Figure 116. Corbel. Part of the Margaret Foote collection, now at the MRC, OCMS.

Figure 117. Corbel built into the wall of a garage in The Bitterell.

Figure 118. Corbel. Photographed by W. Bainbridge in the 1980s ©EHG. Now built into a patio wall of a house in Clover Place, Eynsham.

Resources Centre at Standlake (Figure 116). A number of others have been found over the years, e.g. Figure 118, and these may have formed part of a corbel table such as appears around many Norman churches such as nearby Cassington and abbeys such as Pershore (Worcs). One grotesque head (Figure 117) built into a wall in the Bitterell, has drilled goggle eyes and is very similar to a corbel from the Romanesque church at Glastonbury, now in the Abbey Museum there. Although corbels of such types are common it is interesting that several, particularly that of Figure 115, are identical to ones at Reading.

Another corbel on a flat rectangular base has recently been discovered (Figure 119). The male head has clearly defined almond-shaped eyes and a twisted moustache above sculpted lips. It bears comparison with some of the exterior corbels of the famous Herefordshire church of Kilpeck (Figure 120) and the heads of sculpted human figures which can be found in other contexts in churches from the same 'School' (e.g. fonts at Eardisley and Castle Frome, pillars at Shobdon and Kilpeck and capitals at Leominster). Moustachioed heads also decorate the south door and

Figure 119. Corbel, found in Acre End Street, Eynsham.

Figure 120. St Mary and St David, Kilpeck (Herefs). Exterior corbel on north of nave.

Figure 121. Head of a cross or grave marker. Once built into a wall in the Vicarage garden. Brian Atkins' collection.

inner chancel arch at Iffley. However, they are not exclusive to the Herefordshire School as a very similar corbel at St Mary Magdalene, Castle Ashby (Northants) demonstrates.

A very intriguing sculpted piece is a small stone (25cm x 20cm x 8cm) decorated with a foliated cross (Figure 121). Originally it seems to have been carved on both sides but one side is much worn. It may have been the head of a free standing cross or a grave marker. The design is similar to, but cruder than, the decoration on a much larger 12th century tomb slab from Eynsham now in the Museum Resources Centre (Figure 122). The leaf terminals of the cross, bear comparison with the

Figure 122. *Grave slab with foliate motif. Once in St Leonard's church, then the Vicarage and now at the MRC, OCMS.*

foliage on a relief on a respond shaft at Steyning (Sussex) which has been dated to about 1120[22] and to the tympanum at Coleshill (Figure 59).

One of the most important finds in Eynsham in recent years was discovered in Tanner's Lane. Roughly 20cm long it shows the lower part of a man on a horse with a hunting dog at his feet (Figure 123). It is very similar to the depiction in the Bayeux Tapestry of Earl Harold carrying a falcon whilst riding to Bosham (Sussex), before embarking on his fateful journey

Figure 123. *Fragment of stone, possibly part of a capital, with the bottom half of a man on a horse with his hunting dog. Found in Tanner's Lane, Eynsham.*

[22] Zarnecki G., *English Romanesque Sculpture 1066-1140*, London, 1951.

Figure 124. Harold Godwinson with hunting dogs. From a copy of the Bayeux Tapestry now in the Reading Museum.

to Normandy (Figure 124).[23] The motif is singularly appropriate given Eynsham's proximity to the Royal hunting lodge at Woodstock.

However, this is more likely to be a depiction of one of the Labours of the Months, humankind's response to God's ordering of the Universe, in which particular activities are ascribed to certain times in the year. Popular in manuscripts, the theme is very rare in surviving English Romanesque sculpture. The motif is found on the outer order of the south door at Barfreston (Kent), carved *c.* 1180, and there are fragments at Barton-le-street and Alne, both in Yorkshire. It is thought that the western entrance to Malmesbury Abbey, also about 1180, once had Labours of the Months and Signs of the Zodiac in the arch medallions, but less than half of the doorway survives and it is in a very poor state. Three examples occur on fonts, one of which, that at Brookland, Kent, has May/June represented by a man hawking (Figure 125).[24] The font is thought to date to the end of the 12th century.[25]

---

[23] The image is from the copy of the 'Tapestry' now in Reading Museum.
[24] The other examples are at Thorpe Salvin (West Yorks) where Autumn is represented by riding and hunting, and Burnham Deepdale in North Norfolk.
[25] Pevsner N. (ed.), *The Buildings of England, West Kent and the Weald*, Penguin Books, 1976.

Figure 125. St Augustine, Brookland (Kent). Font with Signs of the Zodiac and Labours of the Months. Detail of May, hawking.

It isn't easy to determine the function of the Eynsham stone but it was possibly part of a capital or a frieze like that which once adorned the Great Hall at Wallingford Castle (Berks). In that case the panels, dating to the 1120s, illustrated the signs of the zodiac which often accompanied depictions of the Labours of the Months. Another tiny fragment from Eynsham, showing the bottom of a woman's dress with a dog at her feet may have been part of the same scheme (Figure 126). It was found in a garden in Queens Lane some 25 years ago but is now in Scotland.[26] A drawing was made of it at the time and the Ashmolean declared it to be medieval. These pieces show again the precociousness of some of the masons working at the abbey.

---

[26] Brasier A., A Medieval Artifact, *ER* 7, 1990.

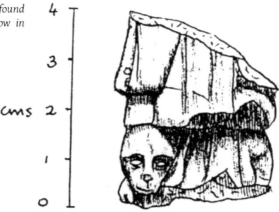

Figure 126. Drawing of a fragment of stone found in Queen's Lane. The stone is now in Scotland.

Some other tantalising fragments have been found in the village. One, from the garden of a house in Oxford Road which is largely built of abbey stones, is a rectangular block which appears to show the hind quarters and feet of a lion or possibly a griffin (Figure 127). The lion is a symbol of St Mark but is also associated with the Resurrection as medieval legend had it that lion cubs were born dead but came to life three days after birth when breathed on by their father. The griffin is a mythical animal with the head and wings of an eagle and the body of a lion. Griffins can be seen on the very unusual tympanum at Charney Bassett which supposedly illustrates part of the legend of Alexander the Great who was carried into the heavens by griffins, another type of the Resurrection. Both lions and griffins are also found on the outer label of the central west door at Iffley and again the similarity between those carvings and Reading has been noted.

Figure 127. Large rectangular stone block showing the hind quarters of an animal. Possibly a lion or a griffin. Garden of 'The Elms', Eynsham.

A further discovery also appears, superficially, to represent the claw of a lion but more likely forms part of a scallop-like shell (Figure 128). Scallop shells are often associated with cleansing or anointing with water and also with the idea of rebirth. They feature, for example, on a number of Romanesque fonts such as those at Beverley Minster (Yorks), Dunstable Priory (Beds) and Westwell in Oxfordshire.

The hole in the base of the Eynsham fragment indicates that it was attached to another stone and that it may have been part of a shelf or possibly formed a section of a bowl or stoup. It has similarities to the decoration of the lavabo at Much Wenlock Priory[27] (Figure 129) and could conceivably have formed a section of a fountain in Eynsham's lavatorium.

---

[27] Zarnecki G. and Holt J. and Holland T. (eds), *English Romanesque Art 1066-1200*, p. 202, Arts Council of Great Britain, 1984

Figure 128. Stone fragment with scalloped shell decoration. Brian Atkins' collection.

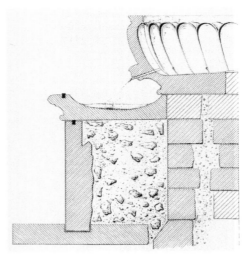

Figure 129. Part of a drawing by J.C. Thorn of the elevation of the lavabo at Much Wenlock Priory (Shropshire). ©Arts Council of Great Britain 1984.

Figure 130. St Mary, Iffley (Oxon). Carving of a small bird and nest in the hollow between clustered shafts on the south-west bay of the chancel.

Another fragment that has been found in the village may also demonstrate links with a mason who worked at Iffley. One of the most celebrated reliefs there is of a small bird carved on the angle shaft of the chancel arch (Figure 130) and Eynsham might also have had a panel with a similar motif (Figure 131).

The archaeological excavation of 1989-92 did not turn up a great deal of Norman work other than what has been mentioned above and a fragment of string course with indented chevron such as can be seen on many Norman churches. However, the most interesting finds were a group of three flat-backed monolithic shafts, one with a capital decorated with upright leaves (Figure 132). This is an unusual form but can also be found on a number of the capitals of the clearly Transitional north doorway of St Mary Magdalene church at Castle Ashby (Northants) (Figure 133), on the abaci of the south door capitals at Dinton, on the capital of the western respond of the south aisle at Chalgrove and on the inner jambs of the north doorway at Quenington.

Figure 131. Fragment of stone with a carving of a bird. W. Bainbridge ©EHG. Once at 58 Acre End Street, Eynsham. Current whereabouts unknown.

Figure 132. Flat-backed shaft with capital found in the archaeological excavation of 1989-92. Now in the MRC, OCMS.

The Eynsham example was dated to between 1180 and 1200 or even later and the three shafts were thought to have been part of a domestic range. Another piece was a cross-shaped finial decorated with early stiff-leafed foliage, perhaps from the gable of a large building (Figure 134). These fragments show that although the bulk of the abbey complex must have been completed by the 1180s, construction activity continued and in fact was probably a constant in the life of the abbey in the medieval era.

Precise dating of the development of the Norman abbey is difficult, owing to the absence of documentary evidence, and, as we have seen, must depend for the most part on stylistic assessments, comparisons with other buildings and with the 'minor' arts, notably illuminated manuscripts. Pattern books and collections of sketches, of which a few survive, also provided a path for the transmission of designs to and between masons.[28] Even so, there is plenty of room for disagreement amongst art historians, especially as the remains of Eynsham are so fragmentary. It should also be stressed that, despite the number of surviving pieces, it is quite probable that we do not have examples of all the motifs and styles which were part of the original decoration of the abbey.

---

[28] Kahn, op. cit., p. 68.

Figure 133. St Mary Magdalene, Castle Ashby (Northants). Detail of the north doorway.

Figure 134. Cross-shaped finial found in the excavation of 1989-92. Now in the MRC, OCMS.

Nevertheless, enough has been revealed to suggest that Eynsham's abbey was a grander and more highly ornamented building than its complete disappearance would lead one to assume. In part perhaps this must be due to the fact of royal patronage but also to the connections between Eynsham and Iffley, and through it to Reading and the Herefordshire School. In addition, despite the foundation date of 1109, most of the indications are that the abbey was not completed until the second half of the 12th century. The delay may have been the result of the 19 year political and civil crisis created by the rivalry for the throne between Stephen and Matilda and it is possible that the existing Saxon abbey remained at the centre of the new foundation for longer than one might have thought. Interestingly, the only 12th century coins so far found in the abbey precinct are two silver halfpennies from the reign of Henry II (1154-89) which might be an indication of increased activity on the site at that time.[29]

On the other hand, it would be wise to remember the cautionary words of A. Kingsley Porter who warned against the tendency of architectural historians to date Romanesque work later than seemed reasonable. He was especially critical of the 'Darwinian' approach to architectural sculpture, the idea that sophistication of technique or form necessarily developed in a linear way. Simplicity of motifs and methods do not always denote an early date, nor are works of significant sculptural merit exclusive to a later period.[30] In short, despite most of what has been said above, Eynsham abbey could have been completed in the first half of the 12th century rather than the second, although current received wisdom would suggest otherwise.

---

[29] One was found in the excavation of 1989-92 and another more recently by a metal detectorist in Holewelle field, Eynsham.

[30] Kingsley Porter A., *Romanesque Sculpture of the Pilgrimage Roads*, Hacker Art Books, 1966. Reprint of the original. Vol. 1.

Chapter 5

Fame and Ambition

Adam was but human – this explains it all.[1]

The most important figure in the history of Eynsham Abbey in the late 12th and early 13th centuries was Adam, a monk during the long incumbency of Abbot Godfrey (1150/1-1195). He had two brothers and his father was probably Edmundus Medicus, a prominent citizen of Oxford. Adam was well educated, a man of considerable talent and intellect and was made sub-prior of Eynsham abbey. Between 1196 and 1197 he wrote, in Latin, the *Vision of the Monk of Eynsham*, the story of a near-death revelatory journey to purgatory and the gates of heaven, experienced and told to him by his own younger brother Edmund, a novitiate at the abbey.[2]

Like other such works that appeared at the time, the *Visio* was in part a devotional work and in part a warning to sinners of the pains they would have to bear in the afterlife. It was probably intended for monastic audiences and attained such fame that the manuscript was copied many times. Some 34 versions of it survive and at least ten others are known to have existed. It was translated into French verse and German prose and an English translation, the *Revelation of the monk of Eynsham,* was one of the first books to be produced when the printing press was introduced to England in the late 15th century.[3] The work is said to have influenced Dante although, unlike the *Visio,* Dante's *Commedia* sees purgatory as an 'ante-room of heaven', a place of hope and potential grace rather than 'an out-patient department of Hell.'[4]

According to Adam, his brother Edmund had been very ill and sometimes close to death for over a year when, in the early hours of Good Friday 1196, he was found by his fellow monks lying unconscious in the chapter house. He remained insensible until the evening of Easter Saturday after which he gradually recovered. Reluctantly, and bit by bit, Edmund began to tell of his experiences whilst in his coma. It seems that his brother Adam was encouraged by Hugh, Bishop of Lincoln, to write Edmund's words down although it is clear this process took many months and possibly over a year.

Edmund explained that he was guided on his passage to the other world by St Nicholas. Along the way he met an assortment of the souls of the departed in purgatory. Amongst them were: a prostitute; an alcoholic goldsmith; homosexuals; abbots; an anchoress; bishops who had forgotten their vows and corruptly misused their power; a poor man's wife; monks and nuns who had abandoned the strictures of their vocation; a knight who had broken his oath to go on Crusade and another that was overly fond of hawking. There were highwaymen;

---

[1]   Mark Twain, *Pudd'nhead Wilson*, heading of Ch. 2, Harper, New York, 2010. Originally published in 1894. The section in this chapter on The Vision of the monk of Eynsham was published by the author in the *Eynsham Record* 33, 2016.

[2]   Salter H.E., *Eynsham Cartulary,* Vol. 2, Oxford Historical Society, Clarendon Press, 1908.

[3]   Easting R. (ed.), *The Revelation of the Monk of Eynsham,* Oxford University Press, 2002. NB When the Vision was translated into English, 'Eynsham' was mistakenly transcribed as 'Evesham'.

[4]   Duffy E., *The Stripping of the Altars, Traditional Religion in England 1400-1580,* Yale University Press, 1992.

murderers; adulterers; poisoners; usurers; abortionists; apostates; an abbess; two young nuns who were lepers; a knight that was guilty of simony; and a learned clerk who, before he took up holy orders, had wealth but had behaved harshly to poor people.

Edmund described in vivid detail the torments that awaited some people in the afterlife. Portraying the first place of torture in purgatory he described the *Infinite kinds and variety of pains that I saw there. Some of the sinners were roasted by the fire and some were fried in a pan. Some were slashed to pieces down to their bones and their joints pulled from the sockets. Some were boiled in baths of pitch and brimstone with a horrible stench...Some were chewed by the venomous teeth of incredible worms. Some were piled in heaps and impaled with fiery sharp stakes and poles. Some were hanging on gallows, others were pulled apart with hooks and others were beaten raw with whips and ripped to pieces.*[5] The second and third places of pains, piled on the horrors, so none would be in any doubt as to the consequences of their wickedness in this life. The severity and duration of torments each suffered depended on the nature of the sins they had committed although Edmund was assured that most were ultimately destined for salvation, particularly if they were contrite and, importantly, their souls were prayed for by the living. Edmund's narrative would have found an echo in the 'Doom' paintings that adorned most parish churches and probably the chancel arch of Eynsham Abbey too. In St Laurence, Combe, one of Eynsham Abbey's churches, Satan crouches in the mouth of hell as devils usher sinners to their fate (Figure 135).

Some distinguished figures of the day also appear in Edmund's account and though he does not name them specifically they are readily identifiable by some of the details given about their lives. For example, there is Baldwin, Archbishop of Canterbury who had acquired a reputation for piety and devout conduct in his younger days but who, once appointed to the archbishopric had become obsessed with power and abandoned the spiritual health of the people. He had *unwisely promoted unsuitable men to church benefices and he feared to properly enforce church law in case he angered the king who had appointed him to his position.* Nevertheless, his torments were not as great as they might have been due to the intercession of Thomas Becket. Baldwin had founded a hospital for pilgrims in the Holy Land which he named for the Saint. Baldwin indeed never returned from his pilgrimage, dying in Acre in 1190. Edmund and Adam's father had also died in Palestine which, at least partially, accounts for the inclusion of the knight who failed to fulfil his vow to go there.

A certain King of England was also encountered *who in his lifetime had been amongst the most powerful princes of this world.* This was clearly King Henry II who had died in 1189. Completely clothed in fiery-hot armour *he sat on a horse that blew out of its mouth and nose a flame as black as pitch mixed with the smoke and stench of hell...The saddle that he sat on was stuck through on both sides with fiery skewers and nails which pierced his bowels.* These cruel punishments were for *the unjust shedding of men's blood and for the foul sin of adultery,* a reference to his role in Becket's martyrdom and his notorious affair with Rosamund de Clifford at Woodstock.[6] However, it was the King's harsh

---

[5] A modern rendering by the author of the Middle English Revelation in Easting op. cit. Unless otherwise noted the same is true of all further italicised extracts.

[6] She was buried before the high altar of the abbey of nearby Godstow where a cult of 'Fair Rosamund' quickly developed. Her body was later removed from its tomb there at the insistence of Bishop Hugh of Lincoln and reburied in the cemetery.

forest laws that had a particular resonance for Eynsham given its proximity to the royal hunting grounds and the forest of Wychwood, the exact southern limits of which were disputed by the abbey. Thus, Edmund has the king's *cruel tormentors, wicked fiends, scornfully reproaching him for his vengeful treatment of those who had killed his game, his hart and hind, his buck and does and such like which by natural moral law ought to be allowed to all.* The king had killed some and maimed others and had never done full penance for his brutality.

Henry's constant quarrels with his sons were notorious and he complained to Edmund that despite all he had done for them to make them *rich and mighty,* they and others that he had raised up forgot about him after his death and failed to do anything that might relieve him of his pains or shorten his time in purgatory. Nevertheless, Henry's case was far from hopeless as his pains were somewhat eased by *the prayers of religious men, to whom he had frequently been very generous.* This may refer to the king's establishment of the Carthusian house at Witham in Somerset, to which he had appointed Hugh of Avalon prior in 1179. Equally though, it could refer to the special rights and privileges he had conferred on Eynsham, including a fair twice a year and free passage throughout the land for all food

Figure 135. St Laurence, Combe (Oxon). Detail of the 'Doom' painting over the chancel arch.

Figure 136. St Albans Abbey (Herts). North arcade of the nave.

and clothing for the monks.[7] One of the fairs coincided with the Pentecost processions and thereby attracted large crowds to the town and prosperity to the monastery. The king certainly hoped for Salvation and Edmund gave him credit for his sorrow at having *oppressed the people with undue taxes.*

Many of the characters that the monk Edmund encountered on his progress relate to people he and his brother Adam had encountered visiting the abbey and *had often seen.* Both Henry II and Baldwin had of course been at Eynsham with other dignitaries for the council that was held at the abbey there in 1186 to elect the new Bishop of Lincoln, Hugh of Avalon. Others that appear were clearly fellow monks such as the *sexton* (i.e. sacristan) of the abbey church. In telling his story, Edmund describes the interior of the church where there were *three or four representations of our blessed lady Saint Mary, having on her lap our Saviour Jesus Christ in the form of a little baby. They were positioned at every altar and beautifully painted in gold and various other colours to stimulate devotion by those who saw them. Before every image hung a lamp which, according to the custom of that church was always lit on every major Saint's feast, throughout the year, day and night from the first to the second evensong. Similar lamps lit the whole church.* Given the dedication of the abbey to St Mary and the writer's knowledge of the practices of the abbey it would seem reasonable to suggest that Edmund was describing what he was familiar with at Eynsham. The disposition of the murals may have been similar to the painted Norman nave piers of the north arcade of St Albans abbey church (Figure

[7]   Gordon E., *Eynsham Abbey 1005-1228 A Small Window into a Large Room*, Phillimore & Co. Ltd., 1990.

Figure 137. Illustration of the Virgin and Child from a book once in Eynsham Abbey's library. The Bodleian Library, University of Oxford, MS. 269, f. iii.

136) which also originally had altars below them.[8] The western faces have Crucifixions above and scenes from the life of the Virgin in the lower register.

A manuscript, known to have been part of Eynsham Abbey's library, survives in the Bodleian. It contains a famous painted drawing of the Virgin Mary (Figure 137) that has been described as 'one of the most imposing examples of English Romanesque art.'[9] Although it is not known whether the work was actually executed at Eynsham, the image of Saint Mary would have provided inspiration to the monks in the same way as the paintings in the church. Indeed, the representation may well have provided a model for the murals in the abbey. The unusual fretwork frame, which appears unfinished, bears comparison with a full-page miniature in the St Albans Psalter depicting the Annunciation. It might also have served as an example of the sculpted motif which, as we have seen, adorned at least one of the arches in the abbey.

The reference to the hanging lamps which illuminated the altars dedicated to Saint Mary and the rest of the monastic church is interesting. Much of the rest of the abbey complex was probably lit with small stone oil lamps, many examples of which have been found around the village such as the examples below (Figure 138), and in the course of archaeological investigations.

Another of the personages that Edmund conversed with in purgatory was a *rector* of a religious house, an abbot who had recently died and *who to his own great cost, as also to his flock's, had held his charge of souls too long.*[10] This must be Abbot Godfrey, who had managed Eynsham Abbey's affairs for 44 years from 1151. According to Edmund, the abbot *was in*

[8] Pevsner N. and Cherry B., *The Buildings of England – Hertfordshire*, Penguin Books, 1977.
[9] Kauffmann C.M., *Romanesque Manuscripts 1066-1190*, p. 86, Harvey Miller, London, 1975.
[10] Gordon, op.cit., p. 118.

Figure 138. Two oil lamps. Once in a house in Church Street, Eynsham.

very great and sore torments, and suffered very grievous pains, sometimes in fire and sometimes in stinking baths of brimstone and pitch. The reason for his harsh punishment was his idleness, his worldliness, his love of empty amusements, his pride and his desire to curry favour by recklessly giving gifts from the monastery to his friends. In particular, there was his anxiety to secure church positions and wealth for his relatives regardless of their ability or piety. Two of Godfrey's 'nephews' indeed, Bartholomew and Ralph, were in possession of Mickelton and Souldern, amongst the most profitable of Eynsham's ecclesiastical livings.[11]

In addition, Godfrey failed to control and discipline the monks of his own house so that he allowed them *to play silly games, to babble about trivia, to tell childish jokes and to wander idly outside the abbey.* Taking advantage of his laxity, some were led into wicked ways and committed dreadful acts including *that foul and abominable sin that should not be named* – i.e. homosexual intercourse or sodomy. Interestingly, Edmund was somewhat taken aback to learn of lesbianism for *I never heard before or previously suspected that certain women were also depraved and despoiled by such a foul sin.* Edmund stated that there were four monks in particular (he doesn't name them) that Godfrey picked out as being *obstinate* and *incorrigible* and who, *by their wickedness, have infected and almost ruined the whole monastery.* This latter quote echoes the words of St Benedict who urged that obdurate monks should be driven out, *for fear that one diseased sheep may infect the whole flock.[12]*

It is clear from such details that the *Vision* emerged, in part at least, as a result of an internecine struggle at the monastery between those who represented the old order, like Godfrey and his cronies, and a reformist element, led by Adam. Adam indeed puts into the mouth of the suffering Godfrey a sorrowful admission that when alive he had failed to help those *that were good religious men full of zeal and burning with love for the order.* Instead Godfrey confessed that he had done his best to undermine them by a whispering campaign against

---

[11] Salter H.E., *Eynsham Cartulary*, Vol. 1: p. xv, Oxford Historical Society, Clarendon Press, 1907. The term 'nephew' was sometimes used as a euphemism for the son of a religious figure who theoretically was pledged to celibacy.
[12] Abbot Parry and Esther de Waal, *The Rule of Saint Benedict*, p. 51, Gracewing, 2003.

their piety *for I was hostile to their reforms, and hindered them: and obstructed all they did, and all they tried to do*.[13] Edmund's narrative of what he saw must have stirred up controversy within the abbey and probably led some monks to openly doubt its veracity, particularly those who recognised themselves as the targets of Godfrey's attacks. Quite consciously therefore, Adam was meticulous in detailing the exact sequence of events that led to his brother's vision, his recovery from illness and especially the healing of an open ulcer on Edmund's leg. All of *which prove that it is not a product of man's conceit but utterly of the will of God.*

It was once claimed that Eynsham's monk Edmund and Edmund le Rich, later Archbishop of Canterbury and canonized in 1246, were one and the same. However, this hypothesis was effectively demolished by H.E. Salter although it is believed that St Edmund's father, Reginald le Rich, had ended his days as a monk at Eynsham. No more is known of our Edmund but his remarkable *Vision* and *Revelation* ensured that he would never be forgotten.[14]

After Abbot Godfrey died, about May 1195, a dispute arose with King Richard I as to who Godfrey's successor should be. Bishop Hugh had sent one of his clerks to take possession of Eynsham and to administer its secular properties and revenues with the help of the monks until an election for a new abbot could be held according to ecclesiastical rules. However, the king was overseas at the time fighting the King of France, and Richard's justiciar, or regent, did his best to challenge Hugh's right to determine who should be the next abbot. As a result, the abbacy was vacant for two and a half years. It was at this time that the *Eynsham Cartulary*, a collection of documents relating to Eynsham's rights, privileges and land holdings, first appears. Starting with the foundation charter, the bulk of the first part of the *Cartulary* is in one hand, probably Adam's, and stresses the abbey's ancient roots, property and special status, being the possession of the Bishops of Lincoln who exercised the right of appointing its abbots – useful evidence for the case that Hugh was pursuing to protect his right of patronage.[15] It has also been suggested that Adam's homilies and Biblical references about good kingship in the *Vision* were prompted by the bishop's quarrel with the king.

Against the odds, Hugh won his case although some monarchs continued to claim rights over the abbey for years thereafter.[16] Following his victory, Hugh paid a personal visit to Eynsham and spent eight days with the monks *refreshing them greatly by the wine of his good humour and the excellent fare of his kindliness* whilst they elected their future abbot.[17] Neighbouring abbots were invited to witness the presentation by the monks of the abbot elect, Robert of Dover, to Bishop Hugh, after which they all repaired to Lincoln where the new abbot received his formal blessing.

---

[13] Gordon, op.cit.
[14] Edmund re-appears in Adam's *Vita Hugonis* as the anonymous clerk, given to seeing visions.
[15] Eynsham was one of only two abbeys (the other was Selby in Yorkshire) which was the property of the bishop rather than the king. Knowles D., *The Monastic Order in England 940-1216*, Cambridge University Press, 1963.
[16] Salter, *Cartulary*, Vol. 1 op. cit.: p. 309.
[17] Douie D.L. and Farmer H. (eds), *Magna Vita Sancti Hugonis,* Vol. 2: p. 42, Nelson's Medieval Texts, Thomas Nelson and Sons Ltd, 1961.

It is hard to avoid the conclusion that a degree of manipulation of Eynsham's documents had taken place, particularly as Adam was then promoted to prior, effectively second-in-command of the abbey. One charter in the *Cartulary*, which appears to be a papal endorsement of lands given to Stow Minster, has been described as 'clearly spurious.' Popes did not confirm monastic charters and the grants of property not only conflict with the evidence contained in Domesday Book, but the charter contains the name of an Archbishop of Canterbury who didn't exist.[18] Doubts have been raised about the authenticity of other early Eynsham charters too, particularly in light of their rather peculiar arrangement and chronologically odd insertions.[19]

Bishop Hugh was certainly grateful for the support of Eynsham and *showered favours on the house under his rule, and enriched it by his gifts.*[20] The new abbot was given a crosier inlaid with silver and ivory and a richly decorated chalice. Hugh confirmed Eynsham's existing possessions and allowed the abbey a 'pension' of 20 shillings per annum from the church of Lower Heyford and a payment of four shillings annually from South Newington. At the same time the abbey was permitted to appropriate Cassington church. Appropriation meant that the abbey became the rector of the church, appointing a vicar to perform the parochial duties in return for a fixed salary or the receipt of smaller tithes, usually a third of the value of the benefice.[21] Smaller tithes were more onerous to collect and included garden crops, animal products, poultry and timber. On the other hand, the abbey took the more valuable greater tithes, those levied on grain and other field crops including hay and wool from sheep. In return, the rector usually assumed responsibility for the repair and maintenance of the chancel of the church whereas the parish continued to look after the nave and its associated structures. The revenue from appropriated churches became an increasingly important part of a monastery's income. Sometimes, though prohibited by Canon Law, monasteries staffed their appropriated benefices with monks in order to avoid paying for the services of a vicar but whether Eynsham was guilty of such practices is unclear.[22]

Shortly after his success, the bishop, recognising his talents, took Adam from the monastery to become his personal chaplain in Lincoln. Adam accompanied Hugh on many of his travels and remained his close friend and confessor until Hugh died in 1200. Adam may have remained in Lincoln until 1209 but then went into exile in France; perhaps in the company of the new Bishop of Lincoln, Hugh of Wells who left England after King John had been excommunicated by Pope Innocent III. An Interdict was placed on England which suspended church services and the administration of all sacraments except baptism, confession and the last rites. Hugh of Wells remained abroad until 1213 when King John submitted to the pope and his excommunication was lifted. However, Adam appears to have returned by 1212 when his 'Life' of Hugh of Avalon, the *Vita Hugonis* was completed. He had been asked by the monks of Witham to write this in about 1206 and he may have used his time in France to do some research there about Hugh's earlier career at the

---

[18] Salter, *Cartulary*, Vol. 1, op. cit., p. 31.
[19] Gordon, op. cit., Chapters 14 & 28.
[20] Douie, op. cit.
[21] Pounds N.J.G., *A History of the English Parish*, Cambridge University Press, 2000.
[22] But see Appendix 1 and Abbot William Walwayn 1469-97.

monastery of Grande Chartreuse. The *Vita* was widely copied across Europe, especially in the Charterhouses as Hugh became the first Carthusian saint.

Like all biographies, the *Vita* is necessarily selective and incomplete and says little about Hugh's great learning, skills as an administrator or his role in the rebuilding of the Cathedral after its 'collapse' in 1185.[23] Adam was aware of some of its limitations and excused himself by stating that others had already written about many of Hugh's achievements. One of these previous biographers must have been the Welsh scholar Giraldus Cambrensis who focussed on those aspects of the bishop's life not covered by Adam, especially Hugh's creation of a famous theological school at Lincoln. Instead, Adam's 'Life' is deeply personal and vivid, based on his intimacy with Hugh in the last three years of his life. Although it would be an exaggeration to describe it as a 'warts and all' portrayal it is considered more accurate than most hagiography. Adam includes instances of Hugh's irritability and the carnal temptations that had sometimes beset him, but Adam's great admiration and affection for the man is also clear. Hugh's pastoral zeal, his campaigns against ecclesiastical corruption and his protection of the rights and privileges of the Church brought him enormous esteem as did his personal qualities. Adam described Hugh as *a man of utter integrity and candour, of charm and holiness and of remarkable and outstanding moral and intellectual eminence.* Hugh's affability and accessibility, perhaps surprisingly for a man in his position, also extended to women who he treated with great respect as representatives of the sex to which Mary, Mother of the Lord, had belonged. Even more unusual was his personal protection of lepers and Jews, the latter during the anti-semitic riots in Lincoln in 1190.

Hugh was very stern with sinners including those of the highest rank. He didn't hesitate for example, to excommunicate the king's chief forester who, it was claimed, had acted tyrannically. Nevertheless, Hugh and Henry II seemed to have had a good relationship. There was a genuine affection between the two men which may explain Adam's references to Henry's generosity to churches and monasteries and Adam's omission of any direct attribution of blame to Henry for his role in the murder of Becket. Adam of course, was writing during the reign of the infamous King John about whom he has nothing good to say. By comparison with John, his father Henry must have seemed both heroic and truly spiritual.

As a result of his *Vita* and his close connections with the bishop, Adam was called to give evidence in 1219 to the commission appointed by Pope Honorius III to enquire into Hugh's life and miracles. Apart from providing details of Hugh's saintly character, Adam claimed to have personally witnessed Hugh' s miraculous cure of a violent lunatic called Roger Colhoppe at Cheshunt (Herts) in 1199. His account was confirmed by the Abbot of Waltham and the disturbed man's neighbours. Many other miracles attributed to Hugh were described, including the cure of the illnesses of those who visited his tomb in Lincoln Cathedral. Hugh was canonised in 1220. By this time, Adam too had been elevated to greater things as he had been appointed Abbot of Eynsham by Bishop Hugh of Wells in 1213.

Adam entered into an unenviable inheritance, particularly as the abbacy of Eynsham had been vacant for five years due to the dispute between King John and the papacy. In addition,

---

[23] Farmer D.H., *Saint Hugh of Lincoln*, Darnton Longman & Todd, 1985.

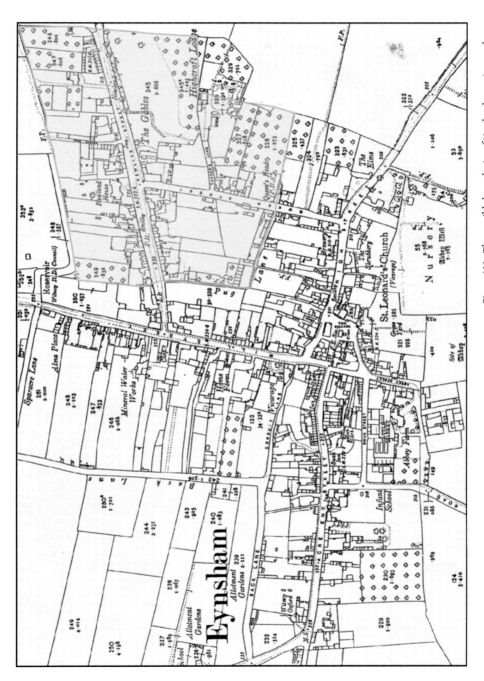

Figure 139. The possible boundaries of Newland superimposed on a 1913 Ordnance Survey map of Eynsham. Paul Hughes.

it seems that Adam may not have been able to escape entirely the unhealthy climate created by his much criticised predecessor Godfrey. Adam was very ambitious for his monastery and initiated several schemes designed to enlarge the fortunes of Eynsham Abbey. First, in 1215, there was in effect an attempt to create a new town out of the northern part of the manor, to provide rental income for the monastery. It became known as Newland. Figure 139 shows the possible boundaries of Newland superimposed on a 1910 Ordnance Survey map of Eynsham.

Newland consisted of approximately 20 acres of land let at four shillings an acre. Tenants were not liable for feudal service or dues and could will or sell their property for a fee. It had its own court to settle disputes and elect officers, probably held at what is now the 'White Hart' in Newland Street, and fines were paid to the abbot. In 1442 these amounted to only six shillings and the whole enterprise never really took off, partly perhaps due to the growth of Oxford.[24] St Leonard's church in the old village continued to serve both communities.

Secondly, in 1217 Adam decided to quadruple the size of the abbey precinct and build a flight of five large ponds to provide freshwater fish, particularly pike, for the abbot and the abbey's frequent distinguished guests (Figure 140). Ordinary monks were reliant on salted herring that were transported by barge to Henley and thence by road.[25]

This project involved securing a licence from the king, buying out a number of landowners, diverting a river, closing the main road to Stanton Harcourt which ran in front of the abbey and building a new road, with a bridge over the river Chilbrook, along the western boundary of the new precinct of the abbey, now Station Road. The enterprise would also have necessitated the building of walls around the precinct, a standard feature of English monasteries by this time. A later source described the *high great walls being ditched 15 feet broad.*[26] The ponds were fed in part from a stream emanating from a spring known as the Holewelle. It is possible that some of this work could have been supervised by a certain Ralph of Northampton, an Augustinian canon of St James, who was employed by Henry III to repair his fishponds at Woodstock Palace in 1227.[27] The project could be regarded as an expensive luxury and incurred on-going costs for maintenance. In 1390 for example, £5-6s-3d was spent on the cleaning of ditches and fishponds.

Within the newly created precinct to the west of the abbey was a large courtyard with barns for grain and for housing oxen, cows, sheep and other animals. There may also have been a slaughterhouse or at least a store for carcasses.[28] The existing Abbey Farm Barns seem to have been built, at least partially, on the medieval footprint, and cobbled roads between them, a metre below the current ground level, were revealed in the archaeological watching brief during the site's recent development.[29] It was from this home farm that

---

[24] Gordon E., Eynsham Charters, ER 2, 1985.
[25] Salter H.E., *Medieval Oxford*, Clarendon Press for the Oxford Historical Society, 1936.
[26] Select Cases in the Star Chamber 1477-1509. Selden Soc. Xvi, 1902, pp. 137-62. Quoted in Townley S., 'Riottes, Extorcions and Inuries' A 16th century affray in Eynsham, ER 6, 1989.
[27] Harvey J., *English Medieval Architects*, Batsford, 1954.
[28] Salter, *Eynsham Cartulary*, Vol. 2: Charter 607.
[29] Moore J. Heritage Services, *An Archaeological Watching Brief at Abbey Farm Barns, Station Road, Eynsham, Oxfordshire, February 2013.* See also Chapter 14.

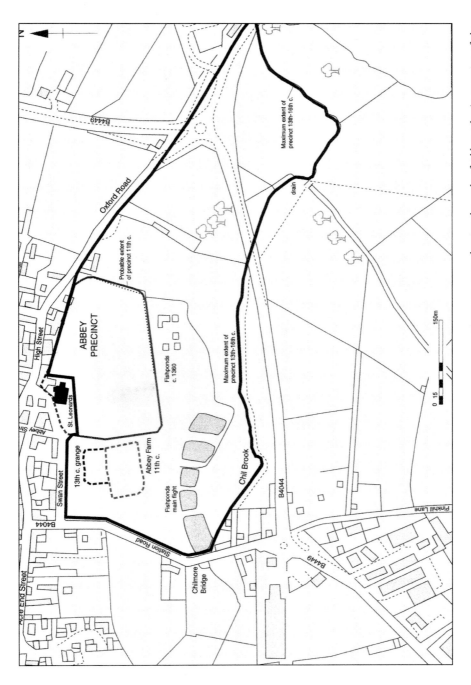

Figure 140. Map showing the scale of Abbot Adam's extension of the Abbey precinct. From Hardy A., et.al., Aelfric's Abbey, p. 6, with modifications by the author. © Oxford Archaeology.

Figure 141. 'Smokehole' from a demolished barn (Seaney's) off Thames Street. Now at the MRC (1986 223.1), OCMS. Photo ©Sue Chapman.

the abbey's own estate or 'demesne' was run. The demesne was large, as indicated by the labour force retained by the abbey. In 1316 it was made up of a bailiff or farm manager, 18 ploughmen, two full-time and three part-time shepherds to care for the abbey's flock of between 800 and 1000 sheep, a pig-man, a dairyman, a forester, a gardener and a miller. A wood-cutter was also employed on a temporary basis.[30] Much of the everyday labour of course came from those tenants of the abbey who owed services as their rent.

In addition to these works there seems to have been some major alterations to the abbey's domestic range possibly because of a partial collapse of the structure which had been built over a prehistoric enclosure ditch. A small kitchen was also added to its north-west corner. A smokehole found in the village (Figure 141) may be related to these developments and might have served the same function as that of the chimney of the 13th century Chequer, one of the surviving ranges of buildings of Abingdon Abbey (Figure 142).

Other works were undertaken too as two fifths of all the Gothic 'type-stones' from the archaeological investigation

---

[30] Hardy A. and Dodd A. and Keevill G.D. et al., *Aelfric's Abbey - Excavations at Eynsham Abbey, Oxfordshire, 1989-92*, English Heritage. Published by Oxford University School of Archaeology, 2003.

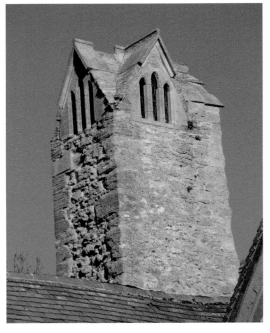

Figure 142. Chimney of the 13th century 'Chequer' of Abingdon Abbey.

Figure 143. Large chamfered stone from an arch. Discovered in a garden in Merton Close.

of 1989-92 derive from the Early English period, roughly *c.* 1180 to *c.* 1260. This style of architecture is characterised by the use of pointed arches and a number of large single chamfered stones have been found in the village which clearly made up a gothic arch or arches. One example is shown here from Merton Close (Figure 143) but identical pieces have turned up elsewhere.

Early English Gothic also featured plate tracery, compound piers, waterleaf and bell-shaped capitals, 'dogtooth' decoration, ornamental label stops and plain stone-ribbed vaults. Elaborate roll mouldings and columns with 'fillets' became fashionable as did so-called 'water-holding' bases. Good examples of many of these have been found in the village. Figures 144 and 145 show a bell-shaped capital and a water holding base and Figure 146 a fragment of filleted column. An example of a 'filleted' column set in a water holding base

Figure 144. Early English Gothic capital. Once in the Vicarage garden. Brian Atkins' collection.

Figure 145. 'Water holding' base. Found in Nursery field, now in a garden in Acre End Street.

Figure 146. Fragment of a filleted column. Found at Abbey Farm, Eynsham.

Figure 147. Detail of the south side of the chancel arch, St Michael, Stanton Harcourt (Oxon).

Figure 148. Part of a jamb or mullion with a filleted moulding. Found in a collapsed wall in Conduit Lane in 2014.

can be seen on the chancel arch of the nearby church at Stanton Harcourt (Figure 147).

Two further stones found in the village have examples of fillet mouldings. One, found in a collapsed wall in Conduit Lane may have been part of a door jamb (Figure 148). The other, unusually, has many fillets and may have been part of a free-standing column from the cloister (Figure 149).

One stone, which dates to the early 13th century, again demonstrates that some of Eynsham Abbey's architectural sculpture was out of the ordinary. This is part of a capital decorated with bunched foliage and star-like flowers or ivy (Figure 150). In general form, though not in detail, the closest to this motif is found on one of the capitals on the south door to

Figure 149. *Part of a column with multiple fillets in a garden in Tanners Lane, Eynsham.*

Figure 150. *Part of an Early English Gothic capital with stiff-leafed foliage and bunched leaves. Once in the Vicarage garden. Brian Atkins' collection.*

Figure 151. *St Peter, Hook Norton (Oxon). Capital of the south door.*

Figure 152. *Stiff-leaved foliage capital. W. Bainbridge ©EHG. Once in the Vicarage garden. Whereabouts unknown.*

Figure 153. Part of a vaulting rib. Brian Atkins' collection.

Hook Norton church (Figure 151) and the capitals of the arcaded porch at Bishop's Cleeve (Gloucs).

An example of a similar capital (Figure 152) is known to have existed in the 1980s when it was recorded by Bainbridge.

There are also examples of vaulting ribs found in the village, some of which have been built into the 'cairns' and others held privately (Figure 153). These latter specimens share, for example, the characteristics of the 13th century vaulting from Hailes Abbey now displayed in the museum there (Figure 154) and to the 13th century vaulted passage from

Figure 154.   Vaulting on display at Hailes Abbey (Gloucs) 'cloister' museum.

Figure 155. Fragment of a chamfered vault rib. Found in Holewelle field.

the cloister to the infirmary at Gloucester Cathedral.

In addition, there are a few examples of plain chamfered vault ribs which are identical to some of those also on display at Hailes. (Figures 155 and 156)

Apart from the expense involved in all these enterprises, Eynsham's Abbot Adam became involved in a number of damaging legal cases resulting from his attempts to increase the abbey's revenues and influence.[31] Indeed, disputes over land and privileges between Eynsham's abbots and neighbouring landowners, including other abbeys like Abingdon, seem to have been a regular feature of the monastery's existence in the medieval era. In addition, for reasons that are not clear, Adam took on a penalty that had been imposed on Oxford town in 1213 for the lynching of certain students. This amounted to £3-8s-8d annually for the benefit of poor scholars and was still being

Figure 156. Reconstructed vaulting at Hailes Abbey museum.

---

[31] Gordon E., Eynsham Charters, *ER* 5, 1988.

paid by the abbey at the Dissolution.[32] It has been suggested that Eynsham took on this obligation in return for an immediate lump sum to help alleviate its financial problems. Perhaps, as has been observed, Adam's time with the famously energetic and financially liberal Hugh of Lincoln provided not the best model for the administrator of the somewhat smaller religious house at Eynsham.[33]

By 1227, the abbey had accumulated large debts, including £152-15s which it owed to David the Jew of Lincoln, and later Oxford, and 168 marks, approximately £112, which it owed to the bishop. These alone probably represented about 50% of its annual income. Bishop Hugh of Wells visited Eynsham Abbey in 1227 and Adam was dismissed from his post by him the following year for serious mismanagement of the monastery's property and perjury. Perjury was a serious charge but it has been suggested that this simply referred to Adam's inability to fulfil his appointment oaths to administer the abbey's affairs properly. However, it may not be a coincidence that at the same time the chapter of Eynsham Abbey laid down new procedures for applying the abbey's official seals to documents, suggesting that Abbot Adam had sometimes acted in an arbitrary manner.[34] Indeed, new seals were ordered and made in the year of Adam's dismissal.[35] Not long afterwards, an Eynsham monk, John of Wood Eaton, compiled the *Customary* which detailed the regular practices of the abbey and how monks should behave.

Adam may have continued to live at the abbey for a while but is thought to have retired to one of the abbey's properties, the manor of Little Rollright where he died sometime after 1233.

---

[32] Henry VIII insisted that the university should continue to receive Eynsham's payment from general revenues and the Vice-Chancellor accepted £2-18s-6d for poor scholars from the Paymaster General until 1984.
[33] Douie, op. cit.
[34] Gordon, *Eynsham Abbey,* op. cit., p. 133.
[35] Salter, *Cartulary,* Vol. 2, op. cit., p. 176.

Chapter 6

The Shrine of St Andrew

But with thise relikes, whan that he fond
A povre person dwellyng upon lond,
Upon a day he gat him moore moneye
Than that the person gat in monthes tweye.[1]

A few years later, during the abbacy of John de Douor of Eynsham (1239-41), the annals of Tewkesbury Abbey for 1240 tell us that *there were many miracles at Eynsham at the arm of St Andrew which had been brought thither from Jerusalem.[2]* St Andrew was the brother of Simon Peter and one of Christ's leading apostles. Some medieval legends refer to him as the founder of the Church of Constantinople whilst others include a journey to Ethiopia. It was thought that he was martyred in Greece and his relics were supposedly taken to Constantinople. After the fall of that city in 1204, Crusaders eventually took his body to Amalfi. His head was sent to Rome where it was revered and treasured until 1964 when it was returned to Constantinople (Istanbul) by Pope Paul VI. One legend has it that his relics were translated to Scotland in the eighth century which is why he was adopted as their patron saint. [3]

Apart from the X-shaped cross on which he was supposedly crucified, his other attribute is a fishing-net with which he plied his trade, both literally and, like his brother Simon Peter, as a 'fisher of men.' His image has been found at Durham Cathedral, Lacock Abbey and Norwich Cathedral as well parish churches such as Combe which was owned by Eynsham Abbey (Figure 157). There, to demonstrate his importance to the abbey, he was placed next to the central figure of Christ. The normal practice was for St Peter to be placed on Christ's right hand.

The cult of Saints and veneration of their relics had a long history and Eynsham's first Benedictine abbot, Aelfric, had himself written *Lives of the Saints* and made reference in his *Customary* to the relics of Saints kept at Eynsham.[4] Abbot Adam of course had written a biography of Hugh of Lincoln, later known as the *Magna Vita Sancti Hugonis.* According to Adam, Bishop Hugh had been an assiduous collector of relics. Amongst his most treasured possessions, which Adam was charged with caring for, was a tooth and part of the shroud of St Benedict, given to him by the monastery at Fleury, St-Benoît-sur-Loire. Sometimes however, Hugh's enthusiasm could result in rather surprising behaviour. On a visit to Fécamp to view the relic of *the most blessed lover of Christ, Mary Magdalen,* Hugh

---

[1] Chaucer G., *Canterbury Tales.* Prologue, The Pardoner. Folio, 2008.
[2] Salter H.E., *Eynsham Cartulary,* Vol. 1: p. xxi, Oxford Historical Society, Clarendon Press, 1907.
[3] Farmer D.H., *The Oxford Dictionary of Saints,* Clarendon Press, Oxford, 1980.
[4] Jones C.A., *Aelfric's Letter to the Monks of Eynsham,* p. 115 and p.123, Cambridge University Press, 2006. During the excavation of part of the abbey site (1989-92), a small, half-fashioned ivory figure of St John the Evangelist was discovered which Graham Keevill thought might have once decorated a Saxon reliquary. *ER* 10 p.9, 1993.

Figure 157. St Laurence, Combe (Oxon). Detail of the 'Doom' painting above the chancel arch showing Christ in judgement with St Andrew at his right hand.

surreptitiously tried to break off a bit of her arm bone with his fingers. When that failed, to the horror of the monks, he used his teeth to extract two fragments which he gave to Adam for safekeeping. On another occasion, at Peterborough Abbey, Hugh cut off a surviving sinew from the still incorrupt arm of St Oswald, King of Northumbria and Martyr.[5]

The passion for accumulating such tokens of Christian heritage is amply demonstrated by those possessed by Eynsham's great rival, Abingdon. An early 12th century inventory claimed that the abbey there had a piece of the True Cross, a nail from the Crucifixion of Christ, a drop of the sweat of Our Lord, a fragment from the table of the Last Supper and one of the rocks with which St Stephen was stoned to death. In addition, there were body parts: teeth, hair, arms, ribs, hips, fingers and skull fragments from at least 62 apostles, martyrs and fathers of the early church.[6] Not to be outdone, Reading Abbey had a spectacular collection of 234 relics including the hand of St James, the head of St Philip and the one part of Christ's body which did not ascend to heaven, his foreskin. There were at least nine other such prepuces of Our Lord in European churches.[7]

This was not just a case of collecting mementos for their own sake. It was widely believed that Saints were able to intercede in Heaven on behalf of those who prayed to them and it was thought that relics retained the supernatural powers of their source. They were regarded as a fount of healing and protection and, in an era when medical knowledge was limited,

[5] Douie D.L. and Farmer H. (eds), *Magna Vita Sancti Hugonis*, Vol. 2: p. 169-70, Nelson's Medieval Texts, Thomas Nelson and Sons Ltd, 1961.

[6] Nash Ford D., *Royal County of Berkshire History*, Nash Ford Publishing, 2001.

[7] Baxter R., *The Royal Abbey of Reading*, The Boydell Press, 2016.

Figure 158. Part of a 13th century reliquary found by a metal detectorist in a field adjoining Twelve Acre Farm, Eynsham.

many of the incurably ill sought relief from pain and possible cures by visiting the shrines set up to house their remains. The acquisition of the arm of St Andrew would have certainly added to the spiritual aura of Eynsham. In addition, the income potential of subsequent pilgrimages to the abbey, the sale of badges and other souvenirs, the giving of bequests, would not have been lost on the monks and possibly helped to relieve the financial difficulties resulting from Abbot Adam's incumbency. Interestingly, in 1993, a small stylised figure (5cm x 2.5cm) with traces of gold and green enamel and a tiny piece of blue stone or glass representing its right eye was discovered in the village (Figure 158).

It was dated by the Ashmolean to the 12th or 13th century who considered that it may once have been one of a row of such figures attached to a reliquary box as the two holes indicate. Probably made in Limoges, it could have contained what was said to be the Apostle's limb.[8] The Ashmolean has two almost identical figures in its collection and a very similar piece was found in an archaeological investigation of one of the manors at Chalgrove in the late 1970s.[9] Beautiful reliquaries of gold, enamel and precious stones reminded pilgrims of the value of the relic and acted as prompts to the wealthy to make gifts worthy of it.

The possession of the relic may also have provided an opportunity to build a structure to display the sacred artefact to best advantage or remodel part of the existing abbey church in the same way that the east end of Canterbury Cathedral had been rebuilt to house the remains of the martyred and canonised Thomas Becket which had previously been placed in the crypt. Similarly, St Hugh's shrine was re-housed in the famous Angel Choir at Lincoln, built in the third quarter of the 13th century and probably designed by the mason Simon de Tresk.[10] Lincoln became in effect a second Canterbury and attracted many pilgrims. Such a building may well have provided inspiration for changes to the east end of Eynsham Abbey particularly as the Bishop of Lincoln at the time, Richard de Gravesend (1258-80), apparently had a strong relationship with Eynsham's Abbot John of Oxford (1268-81).

[8]   *ER* 11, 1994, editor's note p. 9.
[9]   The Ashmolean examples were found in Bury St Edmunds and Fairford.
[10] Harvey J., *English Medieval Architects*, Batsford, 1954.

Entries in the Eynsham *Cartulary* for 1258 and the mid-1260s refer to donations for *the light before St Andrew's altar*. They imply the existence of at least a side-chapel, possibly recently built, with a continually burning oil lamp dedicated to the Saint.[11] Special vigils for St Andrew are referred to in the *Customary* written by an Eynsham monk, John of Wood Eaton, in the second quarter of the 13th century.[12] This also supports the idea of a separate chapel. Fragments of glass found in the course of the archaeological investigation between 1989 and 1992, included one with the painted head of St Andrew, thought to be 13th century, which may have come from such a building (Figure 159). [13]

Figure 159. Fragment of stained glass showing the head of St Andrew. Found in the excavation of 1989-92, Photo © Oxford Archaeological Unit. Now at the MRC, OCMS.

In terms of painting style there are links between Eynsham's glass and Lincoln Cathedral's 13th century north transept rose window known as the Dean's Eye. It has been suggested that given the range of pictorial glass found, Eynsham must have been rich in figurative or narrative windows and that most of it was fitted in the 13th century.[14] The abbey must have glowed with coloured light, creating an awe-inspiring spectacle.

Another find, dating to the mid-13th century, was a wavy six-armed lead ceiling boss with a beaded edge which would originally have been gilded with gold leaf. Comparable stars have been found elsewhere including the roof of the Guardian Angels Chapel at Winchester Cathedral which dates to *c.* 1240. It seems clear therefore that the possession of the relic of St Andrew prompted another burst of building activity at the abbey. Perhaps, as with other pilgrimage centres, the abbey church was provided with an ambulatory to facilitate the circulation of large numbers of pilgrims around a shrine as was the case at Lincoln. However, an investigation of the east end of the abbey church which lies in part in St Leonard's graveyard and in part beneath the adjoining Nursery field, has not yet been possible. Nevertheless, this idea is supported by the archaeological excavation of part of the abbey site between 1989 and 1992 which concluded that there was evidence of a 'substantial building of national importance underway at the abbey in the third quarter of

[11] Salter, op.cit., charters 313 and 338.
[12] Gransden A., The Customary of the Benedictine Abbey of Eynsham in Oxfordshire p. 127, *Corpus Consuetudinum Monasticarum*, Franciscum Schmitt – Sieburg, 1963.
[13] Hardy A. and Dodd A. and Keevill G.D. et al., *Aelfric's Abbey – Excavations at Eynsham Abbey, Oxfordshire, 1989-92*, p. 336. English Heritage. Published by Oxford University School of Archaeology, 2003.
[14] Hardy et al., p. 335.

Figure 160. Salisbury Cathedral (Wilts). Chapter house from the east.

the 13th century.' This period saw the development of the Decorated Gothic style, regarded by some as 'the first flowering of English Medieval Art.'[15]

One of the most significant discoveries was a collection of early bar tracery window pieces with rebates to fix the glass such as was used in the cloisters and chapter house at Salisbury in the 1260s (Figure 160). The Salisbury chapter house windows are of four lights with two quatrefoil circles and a large octofoil circle above.

Given their size and shape, the Eynsham tracery would have been part of one or more three-light lancet windows with three round windows, oculi, above. These may have come from an aisle of the church or chapel attached to it. Bainbridge photographed an oculus built into a wall (Figure 161) probably originally from a monument or shrine.

---

[15] Harvey, op. cit., p. 5.

Figure 161. Oculus with cusping built into a wall, possibly in the old Vicarage garden before 1985. See the drawing by Alfred Cobb in 1870 of one of the gateways in the Vicarage garden (Figure 270). W. Bainbridge ©EHG. Possibly at the MRC, OCMS.

Figure 162. Part of an oculus in a house in Acre End Street, Eynsham.

However, several other fragments of windows have been found in the village, including the example here which would have been fitted at the point where one of the oculi joined the window frame (Figure 162). A similar piece was found in the course of the excavation.

Another larger, more elaborate window or windows has been inferred from other stones found in the village. One of these is a mullion photographed by Bainbridge in the 1980s (Figure 163) and other such mullions can be found built into several of the 'cairns' in the Eynsham Heritage trail.

Figure 163. Mullion. W. Bainbridge ©EHG. Once built into the 'cairn' in the recreation ground. Now 'lost'.

Another fragment of tracery (Figure 164) with cusping detail came from a collapsed wall in the village.

The use of glazing slots rather than rebates in these stones would tend to date the structure/s to the late 1260s or 1270s. Nevertheless, they probably belong to the same building phase as the other bar tracery windows and have features which also link them to Salisbury's cloisters. Likewise, a large voussoir, 35.5cm x 25.5cm on its top and bottom edges (Figure 165), with filleted rolls and deep-cut hollows would seem to be part of this constructional programme. Found within the abbey precinct north of the fishponds it may have formed part of an important entrance to the church such as a processional door for pilgrims to view the relic of St Andrew. It bears comparison with the profile of voussoirs in the Angel choir at Lincoln.

Several other stones characterised by the same type of mouldings were unearthed in the archaeological investigation and arches with similar voussoirs dating to the mid to late 13th century can be found in a number of Oxfordshire churches such as the south doorway at Broughton and the porch doorway at Ducklington.

Figure 164. Fragment of tracery found in the Co-op wall in 2014.

Figure 165. 13th century voussoir found in a collapsed wall in Holewelle field.

In addition to the above, some fragments of small quatrefoil columns of blue/grey freshwater limestone from Purbeck in Dorset have been found in the village (Figure 166) and others were discovered in the course of the excavations of 1971 and 1989-92. Several other pieces of small single columns of darker Purbeck stone are built into the garden wall of a house in Clover Place. This type of stone is harder to work but polishes up like marble. As such it tended to be used on monuments or shrines and it is just possible it might have formed part of the fitments to display the arm of St Andrew. Interestingly, a mason called John of Gloucester is recorded as having inspected a consignment of Purbeck marble purchased for Westminster Abbey in the mid-13th century. John worked at Westminster and Gloucester in the 1250s and 1260s but he also worked on the royal properties at Windsor and Woodstock. The latter of course is but a few miles from Eynsham and it is possible that John may have been involved in some way in building developments at the

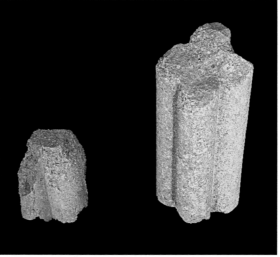

Figure 166. Fragments of quatrefoil columns of Purbeck marble. Co-op wall and Brian Atkins' collection.

abbey. His connections with Oxfordshire are confirmed by the fact that he was granted an estate at Bletchingdon and two houses in Oxford for his services.[16]

The excavation of 1989-92 turned up a small limestone capital whose base fits the profile of the clustered columns as does another capital with acanthus leaves, now built into the St Peter's 'cairn' (Figure 167).

---

[16] Harvey, op. cit.

Figure 167. Small capital with acanthus leaves. Built into St Peter's 'cairn'.

The same 'cairn' incorporates a small base stone of clustered half columns sandwiched between two flat surfaces one of which has a slightly sculpted top edge to take a quatrefoil column. A very similar stone, found in Newland Street (Figure 168) has been put together with a Purbeck column here, to demonstrate its possible original appearance (Figure 169). A fragment of another such base and a larger version of the same have also been found in the village.

The shrine of St Frideswide in Christchurch cathedral in Oxford, dating to the late 13th century, has similar clustered columns fashioned from the same stone as those at Eynsham and bases of the same general form although in marble (Figure 170). Likewise, the shrine of St Edburga,

Figure 168. Small base with quatrefoil top found in Newland Street. Dr Bryan Hyde collection.

Figure 169. Reconstruction of base with quatrefoil column.

once at Bicester Priory and now in the chancel of Stanton Harcourt employs comparable miniature Purbeck columns.

On the other hand, it has been suggested that these stones may have been part of a pulpitum screen or, more likely, a canopied tomb of an abbot, like that of Bishop Bridport (d. 1262) at Salisbury Cathedral. If this is the case then either Gilbert of Gloucester (d. 1264) or John of Oxford (resigned 1281), both long serving Eynsham Abbots, are possible candidates. In addition to the use of Purbeck marble, there have been found some fine-grained, brilliant white stones which may have been

Figure 170. The shrine of St Frideswide in Christchurch cathedral, Oxford.

imported from Caen in Normandy. Caen stone was particularly prized in the medieval era as in its 'raw' state it was easy to cut and was ideal for fine mouldings. When exposed to air it progressively hardened and was good at resisting weathering.

Around the base of St Frideswide's shrine are pierced rectangular panels of quatrefoil tracery. A similar panel has been found in Eynsham (Figure 171) and, like the Purbeck columns may have been part of a shrine or monument, possibly to enable pilgrims to view the relic.[17] Alternatively, very similar window panels adorn the chapel at Clevedon Court, Somerset, which dates to the early 14th century.[18] The Eynsham example, photographed by Bainbridge, still had traces of blue paint adhering to it and there are slots for glass.

The excavation identified another monument, wall fitting or sedilia on the basis of pieces of small openwork tracery and vaulting ribs. Comparisons were drawn with the chapel of Broughton Castle and the shrine base of St Alban at St Albans Cathedral which would date the Eynsham fragments to between 1290 and 1320.

A large number of fragmentary floor tiles, of the 'Stabbed Wessex' type, were also found in the excavation consisting of 18 different designs. This type of tile in Oxfordshire is also usually dated to the late 13th to early 14th century and the Eynsham examples bear

---

[17] The 'screen' was built into the west end of a barn in Mill Street belonging to a Mr Arnatt in the early 19th century and was remarked on by the Reverend Thomas Symonds, vicar of Eynsham, who thought it could have belonged to a shrine, *Bodleian MS Top Oxon b 275*. The barn was demolished in 1962.
[18] Wood M., *The English Mediaeval House*, Ferndale Editions, 1981.

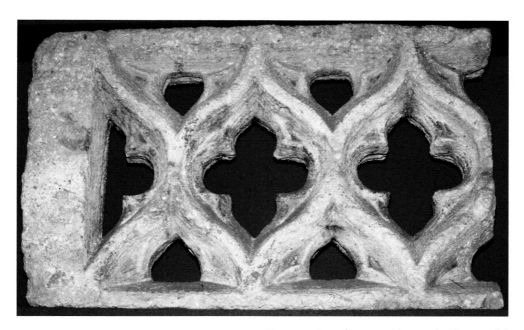

Figure 171. Part of a rectangular panel with quatrefoil tracery from a demolished barn in Mill Street, Eynsham. W. Bainbridge ©EHG. Now in the MRC, OCMS.

comparison with those in the Latin Chapel of St Frideswide's Priory (now Christchurch) in Oxford. It has been suggested that the floor there dates to 1289 and that the Eynsham tiles were from the same period.

In addition to extensions to the abbey church there was considerable re-modelling of the claustral facilities including major alterations to the domestic range. It is also possible that the re-building of St Leonard's parish church in this period was related to the increased traffic of pilgrims to the town and may reflect the architectural preferences of the abbey whose church it was (Figure 172). The south aisle for example contains two windows with Y-shaped tracery and two with curvilinear tracery, all of which would date this part of the church to the late 13th century.

At this time a mason called John of Christchurch was under contract at Eynsham and in 1281 the abbey granted him a lifetime allowance for his *faithful and laudable services*. This consisted of *a daily supply of one monk's bread, one servant's bread and a gallon and a half of best beer. In addition, an outer garment in time for Christmas consisting of a clerk's suit with fur, and for all other necessities 40 shillings annually to be paid in instalments quarterly.*[19] Even if John became infirm or too weak to work further, all the above allowances would be retained and a decent room within the monastery provided for him. John was clearly a man of some standing

---

[19] Salter, *Cartulary*, op. cit. From the Latin of Charter 496.

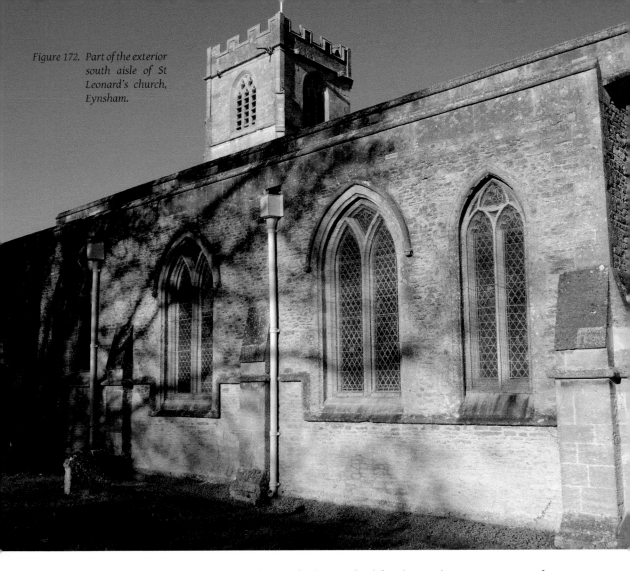

Figure 172. Part of the exterior south aisle of St Leonard's church, Eynsham.

and the award of a furred robe annually was fairly standard for those who were Masters of Works and/or in the employ of the king.[20]

As a master mason he was in part an architect responsible for design but he was also a craftsman who made the moulds and the templates for other masons to shape stone. In addition, he would probably have been responsible for procuring stone from local quarries or even from overseas. It is certain that his services were valued and that the abbey was anxious to retain them. Indeed, the charter makes it clear that *he will not be allowed to serve anyone else or bind himself to service without a special licence from the abbot or his successors.* The allowances given to John suggest a long standing relationship with the abbey and a significant constructional programme for him to supervise. His reputation was such that the abbey did agree to his employment at Exeter between 1301 and 1302 at the time that the new east end of the cathedral there was being constructed.[21] He died in 1307. His career

[20] Harvey, op. cit., p. 328.
[21] Hamilton Thompson A., Historical Revisions – Cathedral Builders, *History* Vol 10 No. 38, July 1925, Historical Association.

certainly seems to coincide with the great rise in building activity of quality at Eynsham which, the archaeology concluded, was particularly evident between *c.* 1260 and *c.* 1280.

It is also possible that Master Henry of Eynsham who operated on a number of Royal projects in the early 14th century, including Caernarvon Castle, Wales, and Clarendon Palace near Salisbury, may have worked at the abbey at some point in his career. The work at Caernarvon must have been substantial as according to his petition to Parliament in 1303 he was still owed the sum of £19-5s-¼d for his time there, probably more than a year's remuneration. It is known too that he was responsible for building a great tower at Pontefract Castle and that he was wealthy enough to grant a large estate to the nearby Priory of Monk Bretton in West Yorkshire to pray for his soul. He spent many years engaged in construction at Spalding Priory (Lincs).[22] Most people's surnames were just evolving in the 13th and 14th centuries and it may be that his second name arose because of the work he was involved in at Eynsham in the early 1290s. Given his work for the Crown and the close relationship between Eynsham Abbey and royal residences nearby at Woodstock and Oxford, a connection between Master Henry and the abbey would not be surprising.

Such building works may have been possible because of the increase in pilgrims visiting the monastery. The abbey would also have benefited from the grant by Henry III of a weekly market and annual fair to its manor of Charlbury in 1256 and land given in the same parish by the Grant family and John Heynon before 1264. Further donations of property in Gloucester, Milcombe, Nether Worton, Shifford, Wyck Rissington and Goring were made in the mid-13th century. Eynsham had also appropriated the church of Whitfield (Northants) in 1240 and the churches of Brize Norton and Histon (Cambs) in 1268. The latter two, the abbey claimed, was partly necessitated by the immense damage done to their properties during the war between the barons and King Henry III but would also have provided long term monies for construction work.[23]

Nevertheless, the financial situation of the abbey may have been stretched, at least in the short term, as indicated perhaps by a loan of ten marks to the abbey by a certain Nigel de Tyllebroc in 1268. Another possible sign of the need to tighten belts was demonstrated by the visit of the Archbishop of Canterbury, John Peckham in November 1284, after which he ordered that the overly generous allowances granted to Abbot John of Oxford, who had resigned but continued to live lavishly at the abbey, should be considerably reduced. His daily allowance of 64 pints of beer was reduced to a mere 32 which would have to suffice for his companion monk as well. In addition, the abbey was urged to monitor more closely official expenses outside the monastery.[24] There is also a reference in the *Cartulary* for the need to raise a loan.

The situation may have been partly relieved by the appropriation of Charlbury church in 1293.[25] However, the abbey was quite relaxed about spending such a windfall. In an ordinance of 1296 concerning the new revenue stream, allowances for the monks were

---

[22] Harvey, op. cit., p. 103.
[23] Salter, *Cartulary*, op. cit. p. xxii.
[24] For a translation of charter 452 and Peckham's letters, see Gordon *ER* 3, pp. 6-11, 1986.
[25] Salter H.E., *Eynsham Cartulary* Vol. 2: p. xxxi, Oxford Historical Society, Clarendon Press, 1908.

increased so that *they would not have their attention diverted from spiritual things by the need to focus on their temporal well-being.* Ten pounds was granted to the prior to facilitate the celebration of certain works of piety and anniversaries. The former included *eight marks to the guardian of the altar of Our Lady.* The latter included 30 shillings for an annual 'foundation' feast of three tables laden with food and plenty of wine *according to the normal practice.* St Benedict's warnings to monks to *take care that your hearts are not weighed down by over-eating* appear to have been largely ignored.[26] In addition, the pensions, allowances and gifts given by the abbot and his monks seem to increase significantly thereafter.[27]

Provision for the poor and pilgrims was not entirely forgotten. 30 pence was given to Eynsham paupers and seven shillings and six pence annually to support 60 poor people in the parish of Charlbury. The dismembered St Andrew, who was especially remembered for his share in the feeding of the 5000, must have been turning in his grave – wherever that was.

In the late 13th century, about 1290, the new road created by Abbot Adam between what is now Abbey Street and Station Road was closed as a public thoroughfare, partly no doubt because it impractically bisected the Abbey Grange and the Abbey Barton. The increase in the number of pilgrims to the abbey would have exacerbated this inconvenience. The road that replaced it ran along what is now Swan Street or possibly Acre End Street.[28] As a way of further separating itself from the affairs of the parish however, Adam's road seems to have been retained for the exclusive use of the abbey, providing convenient access from the outer precinct to its farmland. Later in the medieval era an imposing outer gateway was constructed at its west end. [29]

---

[26] Abbot Parry and Esther de Waal, *The Rule of Saint Benedict*, p. 67, Gracewing, 2003.
[27] On the other hand, it is possible that in some cases Eynsham may not have had a choice in the matter. For example, Dugdale refers to the abbey's previous grant of £5 per annum to Alfonsus de Sienna to enable him to support his studies at Oxford, which was made at the insistence of the papal legate to England.
[28] Bond J., The Fishponds of Eynsham Abbey, *ER* 9, 1992.
[29] Parrinder S., Thomas Hearn's Eynsham, *ER* 33, 2016.

Chapter 7

The Oxfordshire School

God is in the details.[1]

In the second quarter of the 14th century a school of mason sculptors flourished in the north and west of Oxfordshire. Possibly based in Banbury,[2] they specialized in cornices or friezes bearing lively figures playing musical instruments, composite grotesques with human heads and animal bodies, fantastical dragons and other beasts, all put together with no discernible theme or intellectual purpose. Also characteristic of the school are: capitals made up of crouching figures with arms interlinked; exuberant curvilinear tracery and the extensive use of ballflower and rosette decoration, particularly in the ornamentation of canopied niches and tomb recesses. Their work can be seen at Adderbury, Alkerton, Bloxham and Hanwell in the north of the county and at Bampton, Cogges, Ducklington and Witney in the west.[3] The elaborate spire of St Mary's, Oxford, has also been identified as the work of these masons in what the art historian Lawrence Stone has called the Age of the Decorator and his 'triumph over the architect'.[4]

At Eynsham, evidence was uncovered by the archaeologists for continued building activity at this time which may have been influenced by this school even if a direct connection with it is not yet provable. One piece of stone from the excavation of 1989-92, a fragment of voussoir or rib (Figure 173) has a rose tendril motif on the soffit with a small ballflower on the side. Another, smaller stone from the excavation, also in storage at the MRC, has an identical rosette, possibly part of the decoration of a cornice.

A very similar piece to that illustrated, though on a smaller scale, was found in a garden in Newland Street (Figure 174).

Figure 173. Part of a voussoir or rib with ballflower and rose tendril. Found in the excavation of 1989-92. Now stored at the MRC, OCMS.

---

[1] Mies van der Rohe in the *New York Times*, 19 August, 1969.
[2] Pevsner N. and Sherwood J., *The Buildings of England - Oxfordshire*, p. 357, Penguin Books, 1974.
[3] Two loose stones at St James, Somerton, also show the influence of the school. One has a headless figure playing the bagpipes, the other a grotesque. The church largely dates to the 14th century.
[4] Stone L., *Sculpture in Britain - The Middle Ages*, Penguin Books, 1972.

Figure 174. *Fragment of stone with rose tendril motif. Dr Bryan Hyde collection.*

Figure 175. *St Mary, Bloxham (Oxon). Part of the west doorway.*

Figure 176. *14th century miniature arcading built into a wall in Eynsham Vicarage garden. Photographed by Bainbridge before it was removed in 1986 ©EHG. Current whereabouts unknown.*

The style of decoration, flowers linked by sinuous stems, compares well with that on the middle order of the west door at Bloxham (Figure 175), one of the key exemplars of the work of the school.

The Bainbridge collection includes another stone (Figure 176) in the form of miniature arcading which is also decorated with rosettes very similar to those on the soffits of windows in the north chapel at Cogges. The Eynsham stone may have formed part of a shrine, monument or niche canopy for a statue.

Bainbridge also recorded a stone (Figure 177) with a row of tiny ballflowers, curved as if part of an arch. Rosettes and ballflower were used to decorate the west door at Bampton (Figure 178).

Another moulded stone (Figure 179) with a small, exquisitely carved ballflower in a hollow, like that on Figure 173, was excavated from the infill layers of the old stable wall in

Figure 177. Stone fragment with small ballflowers set in a concave moulding. W. Bainbridge ©EHG. Currently in a garden in Newland Street, Eynsham.

Figure 178. St Mary, Bampton (Oxon). Part of the west doorway.

Figure 179. Stone with small ballflower. Found in the wall of the stable block of Beech Court House, Newland Street, Eynsham.

Beech Court House, Newland Street. Such miniature ballflower decoration can be found on the elaborate tomb recesses in the north transept chantry chapel at Witney (Figure 180). The Eynsham example may have served a similar purpose.

Figure 180. St Mary, Witney (Oxon). North transept tomb recess of the unknown patron of the chapel.

Figure 181. St Bartholomew, Ducklington (Oxon). North aisle stringcourse with ballflower.

Ducklington church nearby, contains in its north aisle a continuous string course with large ballflower around both the aisle and above the windows (Figure 181).

There is evidence from a garden in Newland Street (Figure 182) for a similar feature at Eynsham.

Figure 182. Part of a possible stringcourse with ballflower built into the wall of a garden in Newland Street. W. Bainbridge ©EHG.

A piece of an arch (Figure 183) with a shallow rib and two grooves with rows of pellets or ballflower, probably also belongs to this early 14th century building campaign at Eynsham, by or influenced by this Oxfordshire group of masons.

Figure 183. Part of an arch with pellets or ballflower. From Eynsham Vicarage garden. Now at the MRC, OCMS. Donated by the vicar in 1974.

Figure 184. Sculpted female head label stop. Originally in the possession of Dame Helen Gardner of Myrtle House. Now in the garden of a house in Mill Street, Eynsham.

Figure 185. Sculpted male head label stop. As 184.

A couple of finely modelled stone heads (Figures 184 and 185), label stops, can be attributed to this period of building too and are similar to those on the west door at Bloxham, though less badly weathered.

It has to be admitted that the evidence for a direct connection between the Oxfordshire school of masons and Eynsham is fragmentary and inconclusive, especially as no larger scale sculpture has been found.[5] Nevertheless, such a kite is worth flying and may be supported by further finds in future years.

---

5   There are weathered and damaged stones which could be fragments of such sculptures, notably one in a garden in Evans Road which is chamfered on four sides and may depict an animal playing an instrument but such an interpretation is difficult to be sure of.

Chapter 8

The Wrath of God

A voice in Rama has been heard, much weeping and crying has sounded throughout the various countries of the globe. Nations...have already been stripped of their population by the calamity of the said pestilence, more cruel than any two-edged sword. And into these said places now none dare enter but fly far from them as from the dens of wild beasts...They have become abodes of horror and a very wilderness.[1]

The 12th and early 13th centuries in England were marked by an economic boom and population growth, to about 5 million from 1.5 million at the time of Domesday. However, the late 13th and early 14th centuries saw a series of disastrous harvests and subsequent famine and malnutrition which severely weakened the health of the nation. This was the context for an outbreak of bubonic and pneumonic plague, the 'Great Mortality' which seemed to threaten the very existence of Christendom and usher in the 'Last Days'. Probably the worst natural disaster in human history, it was later referred to as the Black Death and was responsible for the demise of between a third and a half of the population of Europe. The pandemic, which killed its victims in days and sometimes hours, was terrifying both for its dreadful symptoms and its incomprehensible causes.

Originating in Central Asia, it first arrived in the West Country from France in the summer of 1348 and spread from there eastwards, hitting Oxfordshire particularly hard in the spring of 1349. In Oxford, 43% of the clergy died, in Woodstock deanery 42%, and in Bicester 40%.[2] The impact on ordinary people, particularly the poor living in dirty and insanitary hovels favoured by the rats that carried the disease, was probably even worse. In Witney, for example, one historian has concluded, two thirds of the entire population were wiped out.[3] In Oxford, according to Anthony Wood, those who were rich enough to do so retired to their country estates whilst *those that were left behind were almost totally swept away. The school doors were shut, colleges and halls relinquished and none scarce left to keep possession, or make up a competent number to bury the dead.*[4] The chancellor of Oxford appealed to the King for help as *the university is ruined and enfeebled by the pestilence and...its estate can hardly be maintained or protected.*

The problem of the disposal of so many bodies was very real as churchyards in some places became overcrowded, new cemeteries had to be consecrated and large plague pits dug. One contemporary chronicler described how *the plague carried off so vast a multitude of people of both sexes that nobody could be found who would bear the corpses to the grave. Men and women*

---

[1] Extract from a letter from the Bishop of Winchester warning the clergy of his diocese of impending calamity. October 1348. Quoted in Ziegler P., *The Black Death*, p. 121, Folio Society, London, 1997. The Bishop's opening phrase is from the prophet Jeremiah (31:15) and recalled by Matthew (2:18) when describing the Massacre of the Innocents. A shorter version of this chapter was published in the *Eynsham Record* 35, 2018.

[2] Ziegler P., *The Black Death*, p. 116, Folio Society, London, 1997.

[3] Chambers E., *Eynsham Under the Monks*, p. 34, Oxfordshire Record Society, Oxford, 1936.

[4] Zeigler, op. cit., p. 118. Much of the ensuing discussion is based on this source.

carried their own children on their shoulders to the church and threw them into a common pit. From these pits such an appalling stench was given off that scarcely anyone dared even to walk beside the cemeteries.[5] It is sometimes claimed that the Litchfield in Eynsham, west of Station Road, served as an overspill churchyard for plague victims but apart from the name – lich or lych is an Old English word for a dead body – there is, as yet, no other evidence to support the contention. On the other hand, given the close proximity of the abbey church and the parish church in Eynsham, with little room in the cemetery between them, the idea would not be unreasonable.

We can but guess how Eynsham's villagers were affected for one of the curious aspects of the epidemic was the apparent randomness with which it impacted on communities. One village might be utterly devastated whilst another, just a few miles away might be hardly touched. Initially perhaps, Eynsham's residents may not have been bothered by the news from the continent or even from Dorset, it was all so far away. But as the disease spread inexorably eastwards, their growing awareness of their vulnerability may have resulted in penitential processions, like those ordered by several bishops, *to beg God to protect the people from the pestilence.* In some places villagers were urged to walk, in bare feet and with bowed heads, around market places and churchyards reciting the litany. Later, when the plague was at its height, the Bishop of Bath and Wells, aware of the fact that many priests in his diocese had died or had fled their communities, was prepared to countenance the last Sacrament of Penance being heard by one of the laity and *if no man is present, then even to a woman.* The situation must indeed have been desperate for the Church to accept that it could no longer cope without the daughters of Eve.

There are no figures for Eynsham's mortality but if it was consistent with the general trends around the country, about two hundred people in the village might have died of the plague. Some historians have suggested that because death was such a commonplace occurrence in the past, people must have been desensitised to it – that it meant less to them in the same way that we in the West today tend to assume it means less to people in the developing world. The limited evidence from Chroniclers that we have, would seem to give the lie to this generalisation and behind all the bare statistics there must have been a myriad of heart-breaking personal stories. Nevertheless, despite the horrors which all must have experienced directly or indirectly, despite the barren fields, the neglected livestock, the ruinous houses, the broken-down mills and especially the gruesome deaths of family and friends, communal life for the most part seems to have survived in the long term.

Monasteries of course were particularly susceptible to the Black Death as groups of people living in close proximity enabled the plague to spread more easily. For example, the great Abbey of Westminster saw its abbot and 27 of its monks carried away. At St Albans, the abbot and 47 monks out of a complement of 100 were struck down. In the small Priory of Mickelham in Sussex only five of the convent of 13 survived and Battle Abbey in the same county lost over 50% of its inmates. Across the country nearly a half of all monks and nuns perished and numbers were never again to reach the levels that they had in the

---

5   William of Dene, a monk of Rochester. Quoted in Zeigler, op. cit., pp. 138/9.

early medieval period. In addition, some monasteries, like that at Rochester, lost so many of their labourers that the monks ran short of food and were forced to mill their own flour or go without bread.

Eynsham's monastery was affected in a variety of different ways. First, it further complicated a major crisis in the abbey started by the deposition in 1344 of Abbot Nicholas de Upton who was relieved of his responsibilities by the Bishop of Lincoln for some unknown offence. The bishop installed William de Staunford in his place in May 1344 but William clearly felt insecure as records show that he deposited a chest with the Abbot of Oseney for safekeeping. Two monks indeed abandoned Eynsham Abbey, presumably in fear of their lives, and became vagrants. They were right to feel uneasy as Nicholas de Upton returned to Eynsham shortly after with 1500 armed men, according to his enemies, and violently expelled William along with his supporters. Five of the monks travelled to Avignon to petition the pope. Nine others were temporarily dispersed and one, John de Nony, was allowed to remain at Glastonbury to which he had fled to escape the bloodshed.[6] St Benedict's injunctions that monks were not to engage in physical violence were largely forgotten.

Nicholas de Upton seems to have antagonised some of the abbey's tenants as well for in 1345, 12 of them asserted at the Court of King's Bench that the abbot was imposing illegal demands on them in the form of excessive labour services. In addition, the abbot was exacting arbitrary and exorbitant fees and taxes.[7] The case was apparently not pursued but the fact that it was brought at all may provide a further insight into the character of Nicholas de Upton. Nicholas remained in control of the monastery until the autumn of 1348 when he was attacked by *certain secular men*. However, he was not immediately restored to his full powers by the bishop, who appointed two monks, Robert de Chinnor and Giles de Tewkesbury, to administer the abbey's affairs, indicating perhaps that the bishop was not entirely unaware of the identification of those 'secular men' as he seemed to be.

In May 1349, whilst the plague was at its height in Oxfordshire, two monks arrived in Lincoln from Eynsham to inform the bishop that one of his temporary administrators had died and that the other was unlikely to survive. The two messengers, brothers Valentine and Walter de Bredon were themselves given the responsibility for Eynsham's management but they too were struck down before they could return to the abbey. They may indeed have contributed unwittingly to the spread of the epidemic to the north of England. The bishop, probably reluctantly, had no alternative but to re-instate Nicholas to his full powers and he remained in office until late 1351 or early 1352 when he resigned. He apparently continued to live at the abbey when he was replaced by Geoffrey de Lambourne – ironically, one of the monks who had fled the abbey in the face of Nicholas' violent return in 1344. Nicholas was granted the profits of the manor of Mickelton for his maintenance and continued to exercise influence over the business of the abbey for many years thereafter. Abbot Lambourne does not seem to have been a significant improvement on his predecessor. He was criticised by an Episcopal inspection of the abbey between 1363 and 1366 for letting valuable books go

[6]   Salter H.E., *Eynsham Cartulary*, Vol. 1: p. xxv, Oxford Historical Society, Clarendon Press, 1907.
[7]   Chambers, op. cit., p. 21.

missing from the abbey's library. Instead of accepting that he was ultimately responsible, Geoffrey blamed abbey officials and even a previous Bishop of Lincoln.[8]

The Black Death impacted on Eynsham Abbey in other ways too. Paradoxically perhaps, the high death rate initially meant increased income for the abbey for fines paid on the estates of the deceased and fees for burial. However, the longer term economic consequences for the abbey were not so favourable. One of its manors, the large and reasonably prosperous hamlet of Tilgarsley to the north west of the village, seems to have been completely wiped out by the plague. This is confirmed by the fact that in 1359, the tax collectors declared that they were unable to collect the lay subsidy as the hamlet had been deserted since 1350.[9] Tilgarsley's lands were thereafter directly controlled by the abbot who enclosed most of its open fields and its few remaining inhabitants apparently decamped to Eynsham proper. Despite popular tradition about the reasons for the lost villages of England, such a total and sudden abandonment of a medieval settlement as a direct result of the plague is rare.

So complete was the destruction of the hamlet, that the exact whereabouts of Tilgarsley was not known definitively for a long time, although the area around Bowles Farm to the north west was suggested. The antiquarian Thomas Hearne, wrote on 26 April 1721 that he had *been told today of a Place, a little beyond Eynsham in Oxfordsh., called Tylgardsley, where they say there hath been a Church, and they call the grounds surrounding the Place the 'Bowles'.*[10] Thomas Symonds, vicar of Eynsham in the early 19th century, also claimed that *stones and bones* were often found there in a field called the Church yard although there is no evidence to suggest that the hamlet ever had its own chapel.[11] One explanation for the finds Symonds referred to may be that the plague victims were buried in the hamlet itself rather than being taken to Eynsham's graveyard, possibly as a way of containing the outbreak.[12] However, more recently, the County archaeologist has stated that, based on Lidar images and some earthworks, the hamlet of Tilgarsley lay just south of the northern parish boundary and east of the medieval track, a possible old saltway which might have brought the valuable mineral from Droitwich in Worcestershire to Eynsham wharf and thence to Oxford and London.[13] The identification of Tilgarsley would appear confirmed by the medieval ridge and furrow strip system surrounding the site (Figure 186).

The presumed saltway (shown in red) runs diagonally from top centre left of the pre-by-pass map to where it runs on to the present A40 next to the garage. It is thought that it originally continued along what is now Spareacre Lane, then north of Newland turning south to Eynsham Wharf near the Talbot and thence to the Thames.[14] A stream forming the parish boundary runs across the top of the map and Tilgarsley (marked with a star) can be seen below it and east of the saltway. The medieval open field system can be seen to its east

---

[8] Hardy A. and Dodd A. and Keevill G.D. et al, *Aelfric's Abbey – Excavations at Eynsham Abbey, Oxfordshire, 1989-92*, p. 12, English Heritage. Published by Oxford University School of Archaeology, 2003.

[9] Salter H.E., *Eynsham Cartulary*, Vol. 2: p. 69, Oxford Historical Society, Clarendon Press, 1908.

[10] Hearne T., *Remarks and Collections*, printed for the Oxford Historical Society at the Clarendon Press, 1906. Vol VII (1719-22), reprinted by BiblioLife.

[11] *Bodl. MS Top Oxon b 275*, Rev Thomas Symonds Collection, p. 13.

[12] Chance E., Tilgarsley, ER 34, 2017.

[13] E-mail from Hugh Coddington to Councillor Charles Mathew, 8 June 2016. Lidar stands for Light Detection and Ranging. (NGR SP 4222 1105)

[14] Parrinder S., Eynsham – Worth its Salt, ER 36, 2019

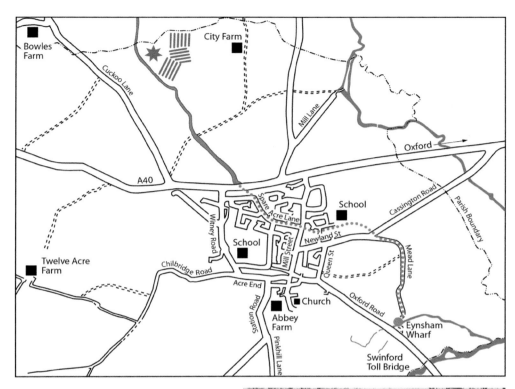

Figure 186. Sketch map of the northern part of Eynsham Parish showing the presumed saltway and the position of Tilgarsley DMV. Paul Hughes

and south. The southern boundary of Tilgarsley would seem to be the east-west ditch which crosses the saltway, marked on the Corpus Christi estate map of 1615 as Torres Grave Mere.[15] Part of the southern course of the saltway leading down to Eynsham is shown here (Figure 187).

Figure 187. The southern part of the saltway near the A40.

---

[15] Atkins B., 'Tar's Grave', *ER* 13, 1996.

Another Eynsham manor, that of Wood Eaton, nearly suffered the same fate as Tilgarsley, as the *Cartulary* explained. *In the time of the mortality of men or pestilence which befell in the year of our Lord 1349, scarce two tenants remained in the manor and they would have departed had not Brother Nicholas of Upton, then Abbot...made an agreement with them and the other tenants who came in afterwards.*[16] Villeins were now in a stronger position and, despite laws restricting their mobility, as befitted their tied status, were prepared to risk going elsewhere to other landlords to get more favourable conditions or better lands.

The problem of disappearing tenants continued throughout the 14th century as the manorial court-rolls make clear. In April 1382, the issue of several escaped villeins from the abbey's property at Brookend (Chastleton) was brought before the court. In one case the father of an individual and in other cases the jury were commanded to ensure their return. Similar injunctions were made at every court thereafter until 1469. Despite such orders and the threat of hefty fines it seems that nothing was done even though in many cases it was known where the culprits had gone to. Nor were fellow landlords cooperative as they were anxious to hang onto the new labour they had acquired in a time of shortage. The abbot could have resorted to obtaining a royal writ to secure the return of his villeins but it seems that this was more expensive than it was worth. Apart from his labour, a villein was only of value occasionally as when his daughter was to wed an outsider or his son went into holy orders. Fines would then be levied but were difficult to enforce if the individuals concerned had moved away. Sometimes indeed, members of the jury, who were theoretically responsible for enforcing the will of the court, themselves did moonlight flits to a nearby village, escaping the abbot's jurisdiction.[17]

The deal which the abbot struck with the surviving Wood Eaton tenants was that they could be relieved of most of their customary feudal services in return for paying a slightly higher rent. Even so, the abbot's concessions met with limited success and six cottages were still unoccupied as late as 1366. The case is an interesting example of the trend towards money rents rather than service rents, a trend which accelerated thereafter and ultimately resulted in the disappearance of feudal services altogether. Attempts to resist this change by landlords and their representatives in government created increasing resentment amongst the peasant class and were a contributory factor in the Peasant's Revolt in 1381.

Even before this indeed, the trauma of the Black Death may have been a factor in a violent affray in Eynsham just a year after the plague had ravaged the neighbourhood. Bewilderment and grief were succeeded by anger, suspicion and a determination by the inhabitants to hang onto what little they had left; to resist attempts by those with power who seemingly wished to take advantage of their situation. *Like madmen*, a number of Eynsham peasants attacked the magistrate, Thomas Langley, who as royal forester was trying to assert that Tilgarsley's now deserted lands were part of the Wychwood.[18] The fury may have been related to an old custom whereby parishioners on Whit Monday were allowed to keep what timber they could cut and drag to the abbey yard, as long as they

---

[16] Ziegler, op. cit., p. 117.
[17] Salter, *Cartulary* 2, op. cit., pp. xxvi-xviii.
[18] Crossley A., *Victoria History of the County of Oxford*, Vol. XII: p. 108, OUP 1990. University of London Institute of Historical Research.

could resist attempts by the abbey's servants to prevent them taking it away. The tradition seems to have lasted into the late 17th century but was discontinued, presumably because it created a public disturbance but also because of deforestation. Tilgarsley adjoined or may have been part of what was later known as Eynsham Heath, an area much prized for its 'furze'. The rights of Eynsham tenants here included not just the prerogative of taking wood for fuel or repairs but the right to graze pigs in the woods for which they paid an annual fee or pannage. This was not the only instance of disturbances created by attempts to dispossess Eynsham residents of their customary rights there.[19]

In Little Rollright, which also belonged to the abbey, eight out of twelve of the lesser peasants died during the plague and their land, like that of Tilgarsley was subsumed into the demesne. Part of the land was still not cultivated 14 years later and the income of the manor had shrunk by a quarter.[20] Another hamlet, Hamstall, to the south-west of Eynsham, where all the land was held by the abbey, was also severely depopulated by the plague and eventually disappeared. All that remains now is 'a mound of stones in the middle of the field to the south of the track approaching the "Nunnery"'.[21] The hamlet also shows up on Lidar images.

The value of the abbey's properties in general fell as the prices of agricultural produce declined and income from rents diminished. This was the case, for example, of one of the abbey's properties in Somerton whose value fell by a third between 1291 and 1390. In addition, the cost of hiring labour to replace what had previously been expected of feudal services rose, despite government statutes to prevent it. This in turn encouraged the process of converting arable land to pasture which was less labour intensive but necessitated enclosure. With manorial incomes shrinking and tithes left unpaid in some instances, monastic finances became more precarious and debts accumulated. For example, in 1353 Eynsham Abbey owed one man, Edmund de Bereford, the vast sum of £1000[22] and four years later the abbey asked the bishop if it could appropriate the church of Merton as the abbey's income had shrunk because of the plague.[23] The appropriation by the monastery, of Mickelton church in 1351 and Tetbury church, Gloucestershire, in or just before 1361, may also be associated with the Eynsham's financial difficulties at this time. Likewise, the grant by Edward III in 1353 of the tithes of the wild beasts and other animals in Cornbury Park in Charlbury may reflect Royal concern about the abbey's problems. These problems were exacerbated by a murrain in 1366 which killed half of the abbey's flock of 800 sheep, a significant economic asset.[24]

In the short term the lack of money and skilled labour, may have halted any major building plans that the abbey had in mind, in the same way that the Bishop of Winchester's grandiose schemes to re-model the Cathedral there had to be put on hold. Some historians indeed, have credited the Black Death for the abandonment of the lavish Decorated Gothic style

[19] Parrinder S., Eynsham Abbey – The Final Accounts, ER 32, 2015.
[20] Salter, Cartulary 2, op. cit., p. lxiv.
[21] Weedon J., Hamstall's Trace, ER 6, 1989.
[22] Page W. (ed.), Houses of Benedictine Monks: The abbey of Eynsham. The Victoria County History of Oxford, Vol 2, London, 1907.
[23] Salter, Cartulary 2, op. cit., Charter 671.
[24] Hardy et al., op. cit.

and its replacement by the less complicated and therefore cheaper Perpendicular Gothic style. Such was certainly true when work on the choir at York Minster was resumed in 1361. The problem with this argument is that the transition to the Perpendicular preceded the plague as evidenced by the significant work at Gloucester Cathedral which dates to the 1330s. At Eynsham, money may have been an issue but there is a reference in the *Cartulary* to the construction of another flight of fishponds or hatcheries, *recently dug* in 1360. In addition, the monks at Eynsham continued to spend quite lavishly on personal items, as will be seen, and resources were found to renovate and up-date many of the churches under their control.

It should be admitted that even before the Black Death, there were signs that Eynsham was in economic decline by the early 14th century but the process seems to have been exacerbated by the plague. The poll tax returns for 1377 show that it was amongst the least of market towns in the county and by the late medieval period the village was largely made up of small farmers, agricultural labourers and abbey servants rather than traders.[25] Nor was the Great Mortality of 1349 the last of the plague as there were further outbreaks in the 1360s, 70s, 90s and 1405. It would take several centuries for the population of England to recover and some of the changes instigated or accelerated by the pestilence would have a permanent effect on the nature of society, religion and politics.

An interesting abbey stone, possibly part of a door jamb has recently turned up within the abbey precinct (Figure 188). It contains a bit of graffiti, a fine compass-drawn daisy wheel design which is relatively common in medieval churches, tithe barns and some large houses across Europe. Indeed, there is a virtually identical one on the western jamb of the tower arch inside St Leonard's parish church although the abbey example is set within a double circle like those on a sculpted panel in the porch of Upper Slaughter church (Gloucs).

It used to be thought that these were used by masons to instruct their apprentices in the principles of geometry. Others have seen them as consecration crosses or even 'badges of a religious or knightly order.'[26] However, the current thinking is that the majority of these apotropaic markings were intended to protect people from malign forces. It has been suggested that the complex structure was designed to trap the demons that roamed the world in the same way that an intricate and symmetrical spider's web trapped flies. Perhaps therefore, they might also ensnare the evil spirits that inhabited the plague.[27]

[25] Crossley, op. cit., p. 104.
[26] Pritchard V., *English Medieval Graffiti*, Cambridge University Press, 1967.
[27] Parrinder S., Graffiti in St Leonard's Church, *ER* 32, 2015.

Figure 188. Stone jamb with a medieval 'daisy wheel' apotropaic motif. Holewelle Field.

Chapter 9

Visions of Heaven and Hell

Within my parish-cloister I behold
A painted Heaven where lutes and harps adore
And eke an Hell whose damned souls seethe full sore:
One bringeth fear, the other joy to me.[1]

One of the psychological impacts of the Black Death was a certain neuroticism, an all-pervading gloom and fear of the coming apocalypse. This may account for the increasing popularity of manuscripts such as the *Vision of the monk of Eynsham* but it also found expression in much of the art of the period. Murals had been standard in ecclesiastical establishments from Saxon times and served a dual purpose. To the more educated they would have been an aid to devotion and a reverential tribute to Christian tradition and belief. Whereas, to the majority of the population who were illiterate, they were visual reminders of familiar scriptural and apocryphal stories as well as moral teachings – a poor man's Bible. After the plague, depictions of the Day of Judgement, the Seven Deadly Sins, the Dance of Death and in particular the warnings of the story of the Three Living and the Three Dead, seem to have become more common. In the latter, three kings encounter three skeletons whose message was that however wealthy and important you think you are, in the end you must die like everybody else and your death may come sooner than you think.[2] There were warnings too against blasphemy, against Sabbath-breakers and against idle gossip.[3]

Of Eynsham Abbey's wall paintings little survives although the 12th century *Vision of the Monk of Eynsham* possibly gives clues to some of the early decoration as we have seen. As a consequence of the archaeological investigation of part of the abbey site between 1989 and 1992 a limited number of plaster fragments were subjected to analysis. This revealed the use of yellow and red ochre pigments mixed with different quantities of chalk to give a range of colours and black pigment 'applied in a line.' Some of these were employed in the form of a geometric design.[4] In addition, quite a few abbey stones that have been found in the village contain fragments of whitewash and colour wash. One had a simulated masonry joint painted in red and a 13th/14th century tracery panel now in the Museum Resources Centre had quatrefoils picked out in blue (Figure 171).[5] Extensive traces of green, red, blue and gold pigment have been found at other cathedrals and abbeys, including Lincoln, Wells and Salisbury so it is reasonable to assume that the whole of the interior of Eynsham's abbey church would have been painted and probably some of the exterior too. Many abbey

---

[1] From a Ballade by the 15th century French poet François Villon. Quoted in E.C. Rouse *Medieval Wall Paintings*, Shire Publications, 1996. A shorter version of this chapter was published in the *Eynsham Record* 34, 2017.
[2] A local example of this theme can be found in the isolated church at Widford (Oxon). An extensive scheme of the 'Danse Macabre' adorns the Gild Chapel in Stratford-on-Avon.
[3] Rosewell R., *Medieval Wall Paintings*, Boydell Press, 2008.
[4] Hardy A. and Dodd A. and Keevill G.D. et al, *Aelfric's Abbey - Excavations at Eynsham Abbey, Oxfordshire, 1989-92*, English Heritage. Published by Oxford University School of Archaeology, 2003.
[5] Both stones were photographed by Bainbridge. The painted line is on slide 54.

Figure 189. St Laurence, Combe (Oxon). Doom painting above the chancel arch.

stones, ashlar blocks, have clearly been prepared to make them more receptive to plaster, the preferred medium for wall paintings.

There is but one reference in the *Cartulary* to a possible mural at Eynsham Abbey when, in 1390, a certain William Burdon was paid 6s-8d for the cost of painting a picture to be located above the high altar.[6] He may have carried out other commissions for the abbey but its records are far from complete. It is unusual for a medieval artist to be named and it may be an indication of his status. He may in fact be the same William Burdon (or his father) who 20 years earlier had been paid the enormous fee of £40 'for the painting of a tablet in the canon's chapel, and of a reredos in the upper chapel at Windsor.'[7] This would have been the building which preceded the present St George's chapel and on which Edward III had spent the incredible sum of £50,000, nearly £20 million in today's money. Families of painters are not unknown in the middle ages. Indeed, the remarkable artistic polymath Matthew Paris, working in the 13th century, had a brother and a nephew who were also painters with him at St Albans. In addition, there were clearly bands of travelling artists with distinctive styles, like the so-called Lewes Group who decorated at least five churches in Sussex around 1100.

The theme of Burdon's composition at Eynsham and whether it was actually a mural or altar retable is impossible to tell. However, there are a number of Eynsham's churches where wall paintings have partially survived the activities of iconoclasts and the plaster-stripping obsessions of later generations. These may help to inform us of the nature of the murals that once decorated the abbey. For example, St Laurence church in Combe Longa has quite extensive and well preserved paintings which provide useful insights into late medieval spirituality. Combe was granted to Eynsham Abbey in 1141/2 and extensively re-built by it in the 14th and early 15th centuries, to which period most of the paintings date.

The most impressive is a Last Judgement on the east wall of the nave, although the top parts are partially obscured by the insertion of a roof truss in the early 17th century (Figure 189). Unlike earlier representations, which frequently portrayed Christ in Majesty above the chancel arch, this imagery is very much about Judgement, the promise of Heaven to the

[6]   Salter H.E., *Eynsham Cartulary*, Vol. 2: p. lxxviii, Oxford Historical Society, Clarendon Press, 1908. A *Reginaldo the painter* appears as a witness to Charter 221 (1213-28) in the *Cartulary* Vol. 1, but it is not known that he worked at Eynsham Abbey.

[7]   Cheetham F., *English Medieval Alabasters*, Phaidon Press, 1984.

Blessed and especially the Torments of Hell for the Damned. At the centre of the 'Doom', Christ is seated on a rainbow, a symbol of God's salvation of humanity after the Flood and a prefiguration of Christ's salvation of mankind. It is also an echo of the Revelation of St John (4:2/3) which describes *a throne...set in heaven, and one sat on the throne...and there was a rainbow round about the throne*. Christ's robe is open to the waist to show the gash in his side made by the spear of the Roman soldier Longinus and blood pours from the wounds in his hands. His right hand is raised in blessing and his open left palm is held up in judgement.

On either side of Christ, somewhat unusually, are the apostles, most of whom are identifiable by the symbols of their martyrdom or objects associated with their legends. To His left is St Paul carrying the sword with which he was beheaded and a book, representing his epistles. There follows St James the Great, apostle, clutching a staff and in the garb of a pilgrim, symbolising his pilgrimage to Spain and Compostella. He was venerated throughout western Christendom for his apparent help in expelling Islamic invaders from the Iberian Peninsula. Then comes St Luke with his gospel and a paintbrush indicating one of his professions; St James the Less holding the club with which he was beaten to death; St Thomas with a builder's rule, a reference to the palace that he was asked to build for the King of India, and St Bartholomew carrying the knife with which he was flayed alive.[8]

To Christ's right is St Andrew with the X-shaped cross on which he was crucified. The prominence given to this saint is a reminder of the fact that Eynsham had acquired the reputed arm of St Andrew in the 13th century (Figure 157). After him, St Matthew with a purse, a reference to his one-time job as a tax collector and St John the Evangelist with a poisoned chalice and a snake, which relate to an attempt on his life by the Emperor Domitian. There follow two unidentified figures, one of which may be a female donor, and lastly St Peter with the keys to Heaven and wearing a white vestment and a richly embroidered cope, symbolic perhaps of his role as the first Bishop of Rome. St Peter's right hand is assisting one of the naked souls of the Blessed to rise from her coffin to enter the Kingdom of Heaven.

On the other side of the chancel arch, the damned are being pulled into the mouth of hell by ugly red devils with horns (Figure 135). The sinners include a priest, prostitutes with naked breasts and a miller, presumably guilty of giving short measures or adulterated flour. At the church in Wood Eaton, one of Eynsham's manors north east of Oxford, the message is clearly spelt out in Latin on the beam below and translates as 'The Blessed come to my Father, the sinners go to eternal fire.'[9] The colours of Coombe's mural are varied and bright which suggests that the artist used more expensive oil-based pigments.

On the north-east wall of the nave is a painting of the Passion with the crucified Christ flanked by the Virgin Mary and St John, 'the disciple whom Jesus loved' and into whose care he entrusted his mother (Figure 190). This is the image of the suffering Christ, his face wracked with pain, whose blood pours from the wounds in His hands and feet and the gash in his side made by the centurion Longinus. It recalls the Eynsham monk Edmund's words

---

[8]   Farmer D.H., *The Oxford Dictionary of Saints*, Clarendon Press, Oxford 1980.
[9]   Rosewell, op. cit.

Figure 190. St Laurence, Combe. Crucifixion painting on the north-east wall of the nave.

when he *behylde the right side of the ymage of oure Lordis body, and hit wellid oute of blode, as a mannys flesh is wont to blede whenne hit is cuppid.*[10] The whole composition is framed by a border of stylized clouds like an illuminated manuscript, which may indeed have provided the inspiration. The image appears to have been painted over a previous depiction of the same theme and may have served as a reredos for an altar.

At the east end of the south wall of the nave is a fragment of the Annunciation (Figure 191). Only the face and part of the wing of the Angel Gabriel survive, the remains of a scroll with the text *AVE MARIA GRACIA PLENA DOMINUS TECUM* (Hail Mary, full of grace, the Lord is with you), and the hand of God above. The Angel faces a niche in the chancel wall which may once have contained a statue of the Virgin Mary.

Further west, above the south door, facing the entering worshipper or traveller, is a damaged painting of the legend of St Christopher. His image was thought to protect anyone who saw it from dying that day without benefit of the final sacraments as is made clear by a previously visible text which accompanied his image at Wood Eaton. At Combe, the figure of the Saint himself was destroyed in the 16th century when it was over-painted by the text of the Ten Commandments

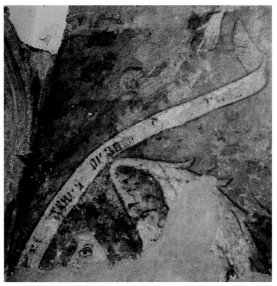

Figure 191. St Laurence, Combe. Annunciation painting on the south-east wall of the nave.

---

[10] Easting R. (ed.), *The Revelation of the Monk of Eynsham*, Oxford University Press, 2002.

Figure 192. St Peter ad Vincula, South Newington (Oxon). Scenes of Christ's Passion on the south face of the north arcade of the nave.

flanked by Moses and Aaron. However, the creatures of the river that Christopher forded with the Christ child can still be made out. They include a shark, part of an otter and a mermaid, the latter being a medieval symbol of carnal vanity.[11] An excellent and largely complete image of the Saint can be found in the church at Horley, in the north of the county.

Opposite, either side of the main entrance of Combe church, are the very faded images of St Margaret of Antioch killing the Devil, in the form of a dragon, with a spear. As the patron Saint of pregnant women, the siting of this painting must have been deliberate as the church porch would have been the venue for marriages and the 'churching' of women after childbirth. On the right hand side stands St Catherine of Alexandria under a canopy, holding in her right hand the sword with which she was beheaded. Originally she had a wheel on her left arm but this is no longer visible. St Margaret and St Catherine are often paired together in this way.

Despite the poor state and partial nature of some of these paintings it is clear that these finely drawn works were not those of a rustic amateur but probably the products of a peripatetic craftsman or group of artists that the abbey employed. The distinction between the works of a country painter and a professional can be clearly seen in another church in the possession of Eynsham Abbey, South Newington, whose murals have been described as the finest in Oxfordshire.[12] The more primitive paintings, executed in an archaic style in ochre, are in a cartoon-like frieze of 15 scenes above the north arcade of the nave and date to the late 15th century (Figure 192).

[11] Clarke D.T. and D., *St Laurence, Combe Longa*, Parochial Church Council of Combe Longa, 1994.
[12] Pevsner N. and Sherwood J., *The Buildings of England – Oxfordshire*, Penguin Books 1974.

Figure 193. South Newington. Scenes of Christ's Passion. Entry into Jerusalem. Garden of Gethsemane. Christ before Pilate or Caiaphas.

They depict the story of the Passion and the identifiable scenes begin with Christ's Entry into Jerusalem with palm fronds being thrown from the city walls. Next is Christ's Agony in the Garden of Gethsemane as his disciples slept, a goblet representing Jesus' plea to his father to 'let this cup pass from me' and also of course a symbol of the Eucharist (Figure 193).

Then follows Christ before Caiaphas or Pontius Pilate, The Scourging of Christ and The Road to Calvary, with Simon of Cyrene who, according to the synoptic gospels, was compelled to bear the Cross which Christ was struggling under. The Crucifixion is shown with the three Marys at Christ's feet and Stephaton assuaging his thirst with a sponge soaked in vinegar, placed on a reed and held to Jesus' mouth (Figure 194).

Figure 194. South Newington. Scenes of Christ's Passion. Scourging. Carrying the Cross. Crucifixion.

Figure 195. South Newington. Scenes of Christ's Passion. Resurrection.

The last scene which is discernible (Figure 195) depicts Christ climbing out of his grave carrying the banner of the Resurrection and the soldiers sent to guard the tomb lying insensible on the ground.

The adjoining panel probably represents his first appearance to Mary Magdalene in the garden but is incomplete. Below, in the spandrels of the arcades are shields with the instruments of the Passion imposed on 'Trees of Life' or 'Trinity Trees'. The central one displays the Crown of Thorns, nails, pincers and a hammer surrounding the Cross (Figure 196).

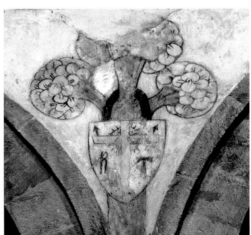

Figure 196. South Newington. Tree of Life or Trinity Tree.

The paintings in the north aisle are altogether different, not least because they were painted in the unusual medium of oil on plaster rather than using water-based pigments, another sign that they were made by an expert painter with access to a broader palette. Professor Tristram, writing in 1933, dated these to *c.* 1330 and considered them to be 'of a nature seldom found in a parish church,' a statement which would perhaps support the idea that they were specially commissioned by Eynsham Abbey or a distinguished patron of the church.

This latter view is supported by the fact that the donors kneeling before the image of the Virgin and Child on the south east wall of the aisle have been identified from the heraldry as Thomas Gifford and his wife Margaret Mortayne (Figure 197). The continuing close connection between Eynsham and the Gifford family is demonstrated by the fact that just before the Dissolution, in 1537, the abbey granted George Gifford an exceptional lease of the rectory of South Newington, for 90 years for £8 per annum.[13] It is however impossible to know whether the donors paid for the whole scheme of paintings here or just those in which they appear. On the other hand, it is clear that it was the donors not the artists who would decide the subject matter of paintings. The wealthier the donor, whether Eynsham Abbey or the Gifford family, the more elaborate and richly decorated the image.

The Virgin is crowned, clothed in red and green robes and stands

Figure 197. South Newington. North aisle paintings of the Annunciation and Virgin and Child.

'in a languid Gothic pose' against a floriated background under an ogee arch. 'A highly ornamental figure' she holds a lily in her left hand, a symbol of purity and of the Advent of Christ. The lily is a fleur-de-lis, an emblem of royalty and was given to Mary as Queen of Heaven. In the crook of her right arm sits the Christ Child who holds a fruit in his right hand to signify that he was the fruit of Mary's womb and/or that he was the fruit of the vine which expressed the new relationship between God and man. 'The whole is courtly and polished and can be compared with the finest miniatures of this date.'[14]

It is worth remembering that Eynsham Abbey was dedicated to St Mary and, according to the monk Edmund, had similar representations, albeit from an earlier time. In the adjoining splay of the north-east window an upper scene shows the Annunciation with a lily in a vase between the Virgin and the Announcing Angel. Below, a faded St James the Great with a black pilgrim's hat, a staff in his right hand and originally a scallop shell in his right.[15] He is accompanied by a kneeling donor, perhaps a recognition that Thomas Gifford had made or would make a pilgrimage to Compostella.

[13] Salter, op. cit.
[14] Pevsner, op. cit.
[15] Long E.T., Medieval Wall Paintings in Oxfordshire Churches, *Oxoniensia*, Vol. XXXVII, 1972.

Figure 198. South Newington. Paintings of the murder of Thomas Becket and Thomas Lancaster.

Over the north doorway in the aisle is a very accomplished version of the martyrdom of Thomas Becket (Figure 198), kneeling in prayer before the altar in Canterbury Cathedral. This has been described by E.T. Long as 'probably the finest surviving example of the subject in England.'

The knights are equipped with contemporary armour and the movement and drama of the scene comes across forcibly as one knight draws his sword and another slices off the top of Becket's skull. In the background the appropriately named chaplain, Grim, is trying to protect Becket. To its east is another 'martyrdom' which has been identified as the execution of Thomas Lancaster in 1322, a unique depiction. He had led a revolt against the unpopular King Edward II and his favourite Piers Gaveston. Miracles were said to have taken place at Pontefract where Thomas Lancaster was buried and attempts were made by his supporters to persuade the pope to declare him a Saint. The Gifford family may have been among these which would explain his presence here and of course both Becket and Lancaster have the first name of the donor Thomas Gifford. [16]

Figure 199. South Newington. Painting of St Margaret and the dragon.

---

[16] Pevsner, op. cit.

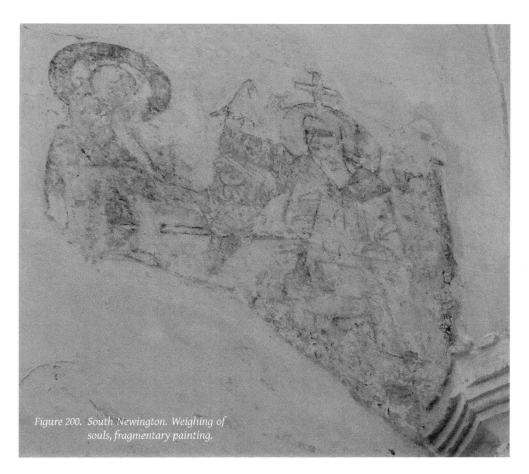

Figure 200. South Newington. Weighing of souls, fragmentary painting.

One real Saint that is depicted is that of St Margaret and the Dragon on the south side of the east window. Again, this is an appropriate image as her namesake was Margaret Mortayne (Figure 199). St Margaret holds a lance in her right hand and a book in her left hand.

Above the chancel arch is a fragmentary and barely discernible Last Judgement. Adjoining it, at the eastern end of the north wall of the nave arcade, is part of a representation of the Weighing of Souls with the Archangel St Michael on the right, with a crown, and the Virgin interceding on the left (Figure 200).

Another of Eynsham's churches which has some interesting examples of medieval art and unusual iconography is the small aisleless building at Shorthampton, once a dependant chapel of Charlbury. Not all the images here are readily identifiable and some are disputed by art historians. On the west wall, just a wing of a large dragon survives and it is assumed to have belonged to a 15th century version of the legend of St George. On the north wall the figure of St Leonard, according to Pevsner, or St Anne educating the Virgin, according to Rosewell. St Leonard was a popular Saint of Benedictine orders like Eynsham and the parish church built by the abbey was dedicated to him. Moreover, St Leonard was the patron Saint

*Figure 201. All Saints, Shorthampton (Oxon).
Portrait of a bishop or Saint.*

of captives and the image does appear to show him offering a cup to a figure kneeling at his feet. On the other hand, the mural has also been interpreted as a seated woman teaching a child to read, with an ox nearby, which E.T. Long believed was St Frideswide who is depicted in the same way in a copy of the Gospels at Magdalen College, Oxford.[17]

Further along is an early 14th century image of a 'bishop' wearing a pallium ornamented with black crosses and a plain white mitre as worn by abbots (Figure 201). The figure holds a cross-headed staff or crozier in its left hand and is making the sign of blessing with its right. Rosewell does not identify the 'bishop' but Long believes that it is probably St Thomas of Canterbury. On the other hand, the vestment may be a dalmatic, one of the attributes of both St Stephen and St Lawrence.[18]

Figure 202. Shorthampton. Painting of the Miracle of the clay birds.

Over the exceptionally tiny chancel arch is a fragmentary Last Judgement which extends to the adjoining south wall. A beast with a crown and a devil with horns are amongst the only things discernible and possibly the damned in a large cauldron. On the south respond of the chancel arch is the Virgin and Child and the apocryphal Miracle of the Clay Birds which the infant Jesus modelled and then brought to life for his companions, a rare subject

---

[17] Long, op. cit.
[18] Ferguson G., *Signs and Symbols in Christian Art*, Oxford University Press, 1980.

Figure 203. Shorthampton. Painting of St Zita.

(Figure 202). The other child depicted may be his cousin, St John the Baptist. Originally another child could be seen.[19]

Further south on the east wall of the nave, a largely unreadable Passion sequence with drops of blood. On the window splay in the south wall is the figure of the 13th century St Zita or Sitha whose cult was popular in the late Middle Ages but who was not formally canonized until the 18th century (Figure 203). She was invoked by housewives and domestic servants and one of her symbols was a bread basket, a reference to the story that angels baked her loaves whilst she was rapt in ecstasy. She is an uncommon subject but also appears in another Oxfordshire church, St Etheldreda, Horley.

On the south wall of the nave is another very unusual scene, the Miracle of St Eligius or Eloi and the horse (Figure 204). A seventh century French bishop, famous as a founder of monasteries and for his sermons against pagan superstitions, St Eloi's cult attained its widest popularity in the later medieval period. Before he became a priest he had been a metalworker and was the patron of goldsmiths, blacksmiths and farriers. His main emblem is a horseshoe, a reference to the legend that he once shoed a restless horse after removing its leg which he then restored.[20] Here, a man with his horse approaches from the left and St Eloi stands by his forge on the right. The horse appears to be supported in a wooden frame to secure him and calm him down. Horseshoes can be seen on the forge's hood.

A few other Eynsham churches have fragmentary wall paintings but are badly damaged and difficult to decipher. Cassington has the remains of a 14th century Doom above the chancel arch, with traces of Christ's rainbow seat in Heaven and the lower parts of naked souls that

[19] Long, op. cit.
[20] Ferguson, op. cit.

Figure 204. Shorthampton. Painting of St Eloi.

have emerged from their graves. Faint outlines of an early 15th century St Catherine and another of St Margaret are depicted under fictive canopies on window splays on north and south windows. At Yarnton there is what might be part of a Passion cycle to the south of the chancel arch and facing the entrance to Souldern church was once a large St Christopher which is now little more than a dirty smudge. Of the rest, some churches, like Tetbury and Sarsden, were entirely rebuilt in the post-medieval era or so insensitively treated by later generations that little or no trace of their original pictorial schemes have been preserved.

An example of the latter is the church of St Leonard's, Eynsham, which the abbey had provided for the parish. It once had some fragmentary late 13th or early 14th century wall paintings in the chancel which were discovered in 1936. At that time, although much mutilated it was still possible to determine the original decorative design and they were described in some detail by the architectural historian E.T. Long. In the sanctuary there was 'a wide dado round the lower parts of the walls, consisting of a trellis-pattern in buff, with a red fleurs-de-lys in each diamond shaped section. Above this on the north and south walls are three tiers of subjects divided by a band of pink. The space above the subjects and over the windows was decorated with simple masonry-pattern, but only a portion of that on the north wall has survived.' The scheme on the north wall was better preserved and depicted the legend of St Catherine. The wheel on which she was tortured and her decapitation were 'easily discernible'. The south wall probably depicted the story of St Margaret and her slaying of the dragon but was 'almost indecipherable'. There were fragments of subjects on either side of the east window and the canopied niche to its north was also painted 'with green foliage and white flowers on a red ground and a barber's pole design on the angle shafts'. The north and south lateral windows had masonry patterns on their splays and red rosettes and chevrons around the edge of the arch and on their mullions.

Despite their poor state of preservation Long believed that what remained showed 'the accomplished nature of the figure drawing and the delicacy of the colour scheme, which betray a master hand.' Furthermore, he felt it was 'fairly safe to attribute them to some craftsman connected with the adjacent monastery.'[21] As mentioned above, the fleur-de-lys motif was associated with St Mary to whom the abbey was dedicated so Long's conclusions may be supportable. Likewise, six-petalled red rosettes were said to stand for the six attributes of the Virgin, namely 'holiness and purity of body, purity of heart, meekness, fear of God, austerity of life and steadfastness.'[22] Unfortunately, most of these paintings in St Leonard's were covered in whitewash in the 1980s and only that of St Catherine remains, with traces of the dado trellis and decoration below, but is very difficult to make out. Nearby Kidlington church once had some 'indescribably' graphic depictions of the Seven Deadly Sins which were also attributed to 'a famous monk of Eynsham Abbey' although the church was never actually in the abbey's possession. The paintings were covered up in the late 19th century as it was said that they offended the delicate sensibilities of the congregation.[23]

In fact, the assumption that most painters of murals were monks is probably over stated, although it is quite possible that young people who showed artistic talent may well have received some of their training in monastic scriptoria. The great majority of painters seem to have been lay professionals, from particular workshops based in major towns and religious centres, who spent their lives travelling around their regions carrying out commissions. As we have seen at South Newington, these could be part of an elite group of craftsmen under a Master, who moved in court circles and were employed by wealthy individual or institutional patrons. On the other hand, there were the provincial jobbing artisans who accepted smaller and less well remunerated assignments.

So, what can we deduce about the decoration of Eynsham Abbey? Apart from the paintings of the Virgin and Child in the abbey church, referred to in Edmund's *Vision* in the late 12th

---

[21] Long E.T., Mural Paintings in Eynsham Church, *Oxoniensia*, Vol.II, 1937.
[22] Heath-Whyte R.W., *An Illustrated Guide to the Medieval Wall Paintings in the Church of Saint Mary the Virgin at Chalgrove in the County of Oxfordshire*, Parochial Church Council of St Mary's Church, 2003. Carved, six-petalled rosettes were also part of the ornament on Eynsham's market cross erected by the abbey.
[23] Weedon J., Church Medieval Wall Paintings, ER 23, 2006.

century, it would be legitimate to suggest that the abbey, dedicated to St Mary, would also have had scenes from the Biblical and Apocryphal Life of the Virgin. These would include The Annunciation, The Nativity and The Adoration of the Magi and after, the Virgin's Death, Funeral, Entombment, Assumption and Coronation. All these are found in the church of St Mary, Chalgrove, in the same county and a representation of the Coronation of the Virgin can be seen at St Mary, Black Bourton, ten miles west of Eynsham.

Eynsham would surely have also possessed a representation of St Christopher to give succour and inspiration to the pilgrims that made their way from far and wide to view the relic of St Andrew. Depictions of St Christopher are amongst the most common of wall paintings and apart from Coombe, examples in Oxfordshire can be found at Black Bourton, Bloxham, Dorchester Abbey, Kirtlington, Horley and Wood Eaton amongst others. Given the focus of pilgrimage to Eynsham it would be reasonable to suppose that paintings relating to the life of Saint Andrew would also be found here.

The *Vision* of 1197 refers to a chapel, within the abbey church, dedicated to St Lawrence and all the martyrs. Although it is not possible to say exactly where this was, it would not be overly speculative to assume that above and about the altar in this chapel would have been depictions of this Saint. He was an archdeacon of the Church in Rome in the third century and was executed both for his beliefs and for defying the city's prefect by distributing the Church's treasures to the poor. His special symbol is the grid iron on which he was supposedly martyred and sometimes he carries a dish of gold and silver coins or purse with reference to his almsgiving. A particularly well preserved image of the Saint can be seen in a side chapel in Westminster Abbey.

In the *Vision* Edmund also mentions other Saints on his journey: St Margaret, St Michael the Archangel, St John the Evangelist, St Gregory and *the gloryus martir and archebishoppe of Englonde, Sent Thomas of Canturbery.* Becket had only recently (1173) been canonized but, as we have seen at South Newington, his martyrdom was a popular subject for artists and their patrons throughout the medieval period. Becket's shrine was a magnet for those wishing to show their devotion to the Saint or to plea for his intercession on their behalf. Eynsham was no exception and one of the few surviving accounts of the abbey's expenditure, the Roll of the chamberlain or steward of 1404, refers to the expenses incurred by two monks, Thomas Meritone and John Cirencester, whilst making their pilgrimage to Canterbury.[24] In the course of the excavations on part of the abbey site (1989-92), a lead pilgrim plaque was discovered with the mitred figure of St Thomas riding a horse, a memento perhaps, brought back to Eynsham by one of the monks.

Edmund of course was guided to the world hereafter by St Nicholas, for whom he seems to have had a special affection. This may be down to the fact that both Edmund and his brother Adam probably grew up at Osney Abbey where there was a separate chapel dedicated to St Nicholas. On the other hand, Eynsham Abbey may have had a particular affinity to St Nicholas. Either way, the legends and miracles associated with the Saint were very popular in the art of the Middle Ages. He was usually portrayed as a bishop and his main attribute was three

---

[24] Salter, op. cit., p. xciv

purses or balls, symbols of his charitable giving. He is the patron Saint of children and sailors and because of the latter he was frequently painted with an anchor or ship. Painted images of the Saint can be seen at Haddon Hall chapel (Derbys), Norwich Cathedral and Romsey Abbey (Hants) as well as a number of parish churches. Above the arch of the central crossing in the abbey one might expect a Last Judgement, a pictorial representation perhaps of the words of Eynsham's monk Edmund, who described in vivid detail the torments that awaited some people in the afterlife although, given the revelations in Chapter 12, it is debateable as to the impact that it actually had on many monks' behaviour.

Not only the abbey church but other conventual buildings would have been painted too. Scenes of the Last Supper sometimes decorated monastic refectories such as St Thomas' Hospital in Canterbury and St Martin's Priory Dover, now lost. A well-preserved example of a refectory embellished in this way is at the monastery of Santa Croce in Florence, Italy (Figure 205). The fresco, painted by Taddeo Gaddi in the 14th century, depicts the Last Supper below a Tree of Life, with the crucified Christ surrounded by the four evangelists and 12 prophets. This was to remind the monks that when they broke bread and drank wine, they were revisiting the sacrifice of Christ's body and blood on the Cross which Jesus himself had referred to at table before his betrayal. Three of the four smaller scenes either side appropriately relate to meal taking as well. A contemporary copy of Leonardo da Vinci's famous version of the mural in the refectory of Santa Maria delle Grazie in Milan, dating to the late 15th century, can be seen in Magdalen College Chapel in Oxford.

Chapter Houses were also invariably painted too. That at Worcester has traces of painted drapery and angels in its bays and fragments of a Tree of Jesse or genealogy of Christ curling around its central pillar. That at Westminster still contains extensive and well preserved scenes illustrating the Revelation to St John and the Apocalypse. This seems to have been a popular theme for chapter houses and it has been suggested that those which used to be in the chapter house of St Mary's Priory in Coventry acted as an aide-memoire for the monks who were expected to recite the text at Sunday services. At Cleeve Abbey in Somerset, even the abbot's private reception room contained paintings, including an allegorical scene of a man trapped between the temptations of the flesh and the Devil and angelic offerings of eternal life in the hereafter.

As alluded to above, the exterior of the abbey church may well have been painted too and, given the effect of weathering, would probably have been renewed on a regular basis. At Worcester Cathedral, Norwich and York Minster, at least parts of the buildings were whitewashed and decorated with patterns to imitate masonry. The central western portal of Salisbury Cathedral was known as the 'Blue Porch', at Ely Cathedral the Lady Chapel was painted with red lozenges and circles whilst at Wells the nearly 400 statues on the west front were brightly coloured. From the career of the mid-15th century sculptor John Massingham junior it is clear that this was not exceptional as he not only painted his own work but that of fellow carvers too.[25] The medieval taste would seem garish to modern eyes and at odds with our preference for bare stone as a recent experiment projecting colour onto the west front of Amiens Cathedral in France demonstrated.

---

[25] Harvey J., *English Medieval Architects*, Batsford, 1954.

*Figure 205. Santa Croce, Florence, Italy. Painting of the
Last Supper in the refectory.*

Lastly, it is worth remembering that the paintings in Eynsham Abbey would have been complemented by extensive panels of stained glass windows such as can still be found in the parish church at Fairford (Gloucs). The abbey would have glowed with colour and vibrancy promoting a sense of wonder and of the sacred. To fully appreciate the overall effect this would have had necessitates a great leap in imagination. A number of churches in England, Kempley (Gloucs), Hardham (Sussex) and Chalgrove (Oxon) for example, do have extensive schemes of paintings. But, finding an English church whose paintings are still as bright and sharp as they would originally have been, is virtually impossible, as is one unaffected by war, the forces of nature, the prejudices of Protestant iconoclasts or the efforts of Victorian 'restorers'.

Chapter 10

Keeping up Appearances

When we build, let us think that we build for ever.[1]

Despite the financial difficulties we have noted in Chapter 7, the abbey continued to spend money on updating its facilities. The archaeological excavation of 1989-92 indicated that the late 14th and early 15th centuries saw the demolition and re-building of the kitchen, garderobe and lavatorium as well as the re-building of the cloister arcade and possibly the chapter house.[2] William Alnwick, Bishop of Lincoln (1436-1450) made an official visitation to Eynsham in 1445 which was held in the refectory rather than the chapter house.[3] This might indicate that the latter was unavailable due to re-building or repairs. Some years before, in 1389, a certain John Spillesbury, mason, had been paid 18s-8d for work on the *new chapel* at the abbey. In the same year, £44-9s-0d was paid for repairs and building work at Eynsham and Charlbury and included the wages of carpenters, masons and thatchers.[4] The greater portion of this money must have been spent on the abbey. This may be related to the fact that King Richard II, a patron of the arts, visited the abbey in 1389 – possibly to inaugurate the new building which may have been the *curious Chapelle* later remarked on by John Aubrey.

John Spillesbury was a well-respected mason/architect and may have originally derived from Spelsbury, a village north of Charlbury (Oxon). Like the painter John Burdon, he had also worked at Windsor. Spillesbury was employed for 80 days there in 1362-3 under the famous head mason William Wynford, presumably on the extension to the original St George's chapel. Wynford in turn had worked with Henry Yevele, regarded by some as the greatest English medieval architect and responsible for perfecting the Perpendicular Gothic style. Spillesbury was employed intermittently by William Wykeham, Bishop of Winchester and worked on the Episcopal manor of Highclere in Hampshire between 1370 and 1397 for a yearly retainer of £1 and wages of 6d daily. In 1370 for example, he spent 142 days cutting limestone for two windows for the bishop's chamber and quoins for the angles of the wall.[5]

Spillesbury seems to have been part of a 'school' of masons and carpenters, headed by Wynford and including several named figures who worked together on a number of different projects such as Highclere and New College, Oxford. They included William Brown, a mason from Oxford; Hugh Herland, master carpenter; and William Ickenham senior and junior, also carpenters. This team and their apprentices and journeymen could well have been employed at Eynsham as well. Nevertheless, being part of such a 'school' was not necessarily restrictive and Spillesbury clearly had time and freedom to take on other projects. He has, for example,

---

[1] John Ruskin, *The Seven Lamps of Architecture*, Ch. 6. Forgotten Books, 2012.
[2] Hardy A. and Dodd A. and Keevill G.D. et al, *Aelfric's Abbey – Excavations at Eynsham Abbey, Oxfordshire, 1989-92*, English Heritage. Published by Oxford University School of Archaeology, 2003.
[3] Thompson A.H. (ed.), Visitations of Religious Houses in the Diocese of Lincoln Vol. 2 1436-1449, *Lincoln Record Society*, Vol. 8, 1919.
[4] Salter H.E., *Eynsham Cartulary*, Vol. 2: p. lxxviii, Oxford Historical Society, Clarendon Press, 1908.
[5] Harvey J., *English Medieval Architects*, p. 248, Batsford, 1954.

Figure 206. 14th/15th century stone carved angel with heraldic shield probably the support for a vaulting springer. First noted by Thomas Hearne in the 18th century and later relocated to the Vicarage garden where it was drawn by A.F. Cobb c. 1870 (Figure 270). Currently stored at the MRC, OCMS.

been identified as the architect who worked on the cloisters of Worcester Cathedral Priory in 1395-6, a fact that may be pertinent to developments at Eynsham.

One of the stones from Eynsham Abbey is the figure of an angel holding a shield which was clearly made to slot into a wall and to support a structure springing from its back (Figure 206). Although such motifs were not uncommon in late 14th and 15th century ecclesiastical structures, particularly large churches, abbeys and cathedrals, the Eynsham sculpture closely resembles that on the north wall of the cloister at Worcester cathedral which supports a vaulting springer (Figure 207). The Eynsham angel may well have performed the same function when the abbey cloister was rebuilt or remodelled.

A number of springers for such vaults can be found around the village, most obviously in the 'cairns' in Market Square (Figure 208), Abbey Street and the Recreation Ground.

Three large stone roof bosses with distinctive rib profiles would also support the suggestion that the cloisters and/or chapter house were updated at this time when such remodelling was particularly in vogue.

Figure 207. Worcester Cathedral. North wall of the cloister showing an angel supporting a vaulting springer.

Figure 208. Vaulting springer in the Market Square 'cairn', Eynsham.

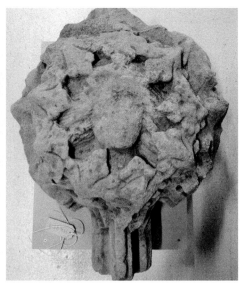

Figure 209. Stone roof boss. Originally in the Vicarage garden. Now stored at the MRC, OCMS.

Figure 210. Vaulting boss. Originally in the Vicarage garden. Now at the MRC, OCMS.

The largest (51cm x 51cm), originally at the junction of six ribs, has a face surrounded by three-lobed leaves (Figure 209). These foliate heads are not unusual and occur in many vaulted abbeys and cathedrals like Gloucester and Worcester.

Another boss has a twisted rope motif, possibly a symbol of Christ's Passion, and what may be the letters IHS or IHC, the first three letters of Ihsus, or Ihuc, the name of Jesus in Greek (Figure 210).

On the other hand, the motif might be a rebus, something which conveys a message by means of an image, usually a pun on a name. In which case it might represent one of the abbots or a patron of the abbey. A third boss (Figure 211), though badly weathered, has a rose with large outer petals and is similar to one of those in the north walk of the cloister at Worcester [6] and others in the cloister at Wells, the porch at Gloucester, the west end of the nave there and the vaulting of the crossing at Tewkesbury. There are also two bosses

---

[6]   Cave C.J.P., *Roof Bosses in Medieval Churches*, Cambridge University Press, 1948.

Figure 211. Vaulting boss. Originally in the Vicarage garden. Now at the MRC, OCMS.

in the nave at Winchester with the same design which date to the early years of the 15th century.[7] All three Eynsham bosses are currently stored at the Museum Resources Centre (MRC). Originally, these bosses, like most of the other abbey stones, would have been brightly painted such as the example from York Minster below (Figure 212).

Another stone, found in a garden in Mill Street, may belong to the same construction programme (Figure 213). It forms the junction point of six vaulting ribs whose profile is different from those referred to so far. There is no boss, which either indicates that it was hacked off at some point, never existed in the first place or had some other form of decoration. The first of these suggestions seems preferable as there are faint signs of a possible heraldic motif like the second of the three bosses from the MRC.

In addition to the above, two small, cast-lead ceiling bosses were found in the excavation of 1989-92. The sixteen-pointed stars would have

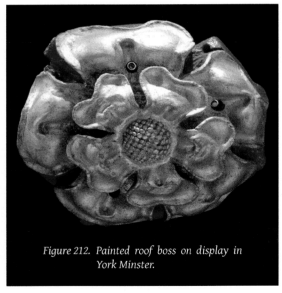

Figure 212. Painted roof boss on display in York Minster.

been gilded originally and, combined with the stone bosses, may have looked something like the lierne vaulting of the crossing at Tewkesbury which dates to the late 14th century (Figure 214). Similar gilded stars once decorated the ceiling of the Augustinian Abbey of St Mary at Cirencester, designed to replicate the heavens, and painted versions of the same type adorn the 15th century pulpit in the parish church there.

---

[7] Smith A., *Roof Bosses of Winchester Cathedral*, Friends of Winchester Cathedral, 1996.

Figure 213. Damaged roof boss in a garden in Mill Street, Eynsham.

Not all the roof bosses were quite so elaborate and one stone found in the village has a simple stone star at the junction of several ribs (Figure 215).

Another unusual lead survival, found in the excavation, were parts of a small, detailed, scale representation of a three-tiered four-light window, the bottom and central tiers separated by a course of plain panels (Figure 216).[8] Similar lead 'came' models have been found at Rievaulx and Fountains Abbeys.[9] It is thought that they were ventilators that would have been set into windows and may indeed have been representative of the architectural scheme of such windows. The Eynsham example is similar to the elaborate cloister windows

Figure 214. Tewkesbury Abbey (Gloucs). Vaulting of the crossing.

8   Hardy et al., op. cit., pp. 270/71.
9   Barber T. and Boldrick S. (eds), *Art Under Attack – Histories of British Iconoclasm*, p. 37, Tate Publishing, 2013.

Figure 215. Simple roof boss built into a wall in a garden in the Bitterell.

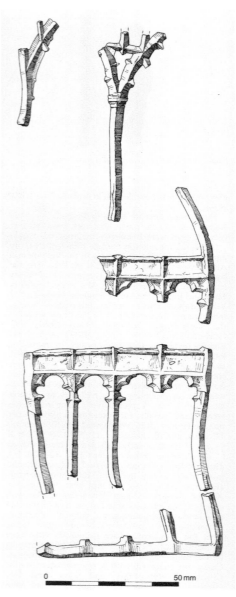

of the east walk at Gloucester which dates to the third quarter of the 14th century (Figure 217).

Several stone pieces of cusped tracery with horizontal bar headings like those at Gloucester have been found in the village and probably belong to the same building programme. Two of these are built into the gable ends of a barn in Aelfric Court, Oxford Road, whilst another, possibly part of a blank panel (Figure 218), is now built into an interior wall of a house in Thames Street.

Another stone in the village, built into a house in Acre End street, provides further evidence of constructional activity in the late 14th and early 15th centuries (Figure 219). This corbel head may have supported a roof beam or vaulting in the 'new chapel' referred to above. Two other corbel heads would seem to belong to the same period (Figures 220 and 221).

Figure 216. Fragments of a lead window 'ventilator' found in the excavation of 1989-92 ©Oxford Archaeological Unit. Now at the MRC, OCMS.

Figure 217. Gloucester Cathedral. East walk of the cloister.

Figure 218. Blank stone tracery built into the interior wall of a house in Thames Street, Eynsham.

Figure 219. Corbel head built into the back wall of 100 Acre End Street, Eynsham.

Figure 220. Corbel head. W. Bainbridge ©EHG. Supposedly at the MRC but thought to be 'lost'.

Figure 221. Corbel head. W. Bainbridge ©EHG. Formerly in the Vicarage garden. Now built into the passage wall between St Peter's Catholic church, Eynsham, and the adjoining Tolkein Room.

The chapel may also have sported the two gargoyles or water spouts which survive, one in the shape of a dog's head (Figure 222) and another with the head of a ram.

The archaeological report drew parallels between the fragments found at Eynsham during the excavation and the 15th century Beauchamp Chapel at St Mary's, Warwick. It focussed attention on a vault rib 'of distinctive design that mirrors the exterior profile of the chapel's mullions.'[10] As already stated, the rib attached to the roof boss above shares the same design and another piece of vaulting stone in Eynsham has an identical moulding (Figure 223). Several other stones found in gardens in Acre End Street, others at 'The Shrubbery' and another built into a garden wall in the Bitterell share the same characteristics. All of which would tend

---

[10] Hardy et al., op. cit., p. 230

Figure 222. Dog's head gargoyle formerly in the Vicarage Garden. Now at the MRC, OCMS.

Figure 223. Portion of rib vaulting found in Holewelle field.

to date the Eynsham programme of improvements to the first half of the 15th century.

These building works would have been helped by the continued bequests left to the abbey in wills. One such was that made in 1393 by a certain William de Horbury, clerk of the King's Chancery, which provides an interesting insight into the rituals at the abbey and the sort of benefits that rich donors felt they were entitled to expect from the monastery. He wished to be buried in the abbey church, next to the late Abbot Godfrey, and for *an honest priest to celebrate divine service there for three years after my death for the health of my soul and of my benefactors' souls. To the abbot and convent, a cup called Le Grypeskeye with cover, and every day when they sing Laetabundus in the hall after grace, all in the hall shall drink from the said cup and say De Profundis with the Lord's Prayer for the soul of the said William Horbury...To the said abbot and convent of Eynsham, £30 to pray for my soul and for my benefactors and all faithful departed, and 10 marks for a marble stone to be placed upon my grave in the said abbey...I will that forty pounds of wax burn around my body in the vigil and on the day of my burial.*[11]

The executor of the will was Nicholas Babworth, Treasurer of England, who ended his career as Bishop of Bath and Wells. Clearly a man of some substance, William Horbury appears several times in the documentary records of the time of King Richard II. For example, it is known that he was Master of the hospital and patron of the Chapel of St Leonard, Towcester and that he had granted land to the abbot and convent of Kirkstall in Yorkshire. Horbury may well have accompanied the king on his visit to Eynsham in 1389 although his desire to rest next to Abbot Godfrey, who died in 1388, indicates perhaps that he had a longer acquaintance with the abbey.[12]

---

[11] Cited in Richards P., *Eynsham: A Chronicle*, Eynsham History Group, Robert Boyd Publications 2005 (Prerogative Court of Canterbury, Rous 9).
[12] Two other later wills are known which refer to the abbey, that of Elyoner Martyn, from an important Eynsham family, made in February 1503/4 and that of John Burge made in 1508. Both stipulate that they were to be buried within the abbey church of St Mary. Weaver J.R.H. and Beardwood A. (eds), *Some Oxfordshire Wills proved in the Prerogative Court of Canterbury, Oxfordshire Record Society* Vol. 39, 1958.

Chapter 11

Laying up Treasures on Earth

Refrain from frivolous curiosities such as niches for statues...casements and fillets and other idle quaintnesses. They lead...to too great and sumptuous expense.[1]

Although the archaeology seemed to point to a decline in constructional activity in the late Gothic period[2], this may only have been a reflection of the necessarily limited spatial scale of the excavation. Some of the other evidence would seem to point in a different direction. We are told for example, that in 1471 the abbey spent £30-12s-1d on building works.[3] For comparison, in 1475, the famous master mason/architect William Orchard was paid just £13 6s 8d for designing and making the seven-light great west window of the chapel at Magdalen College, Oxford.[4] The sum paid by the abbey may therefore include the insertion of a new large window in the gable of Eynsham's west front as shown in the Wood drawing. As well as Magdalen's chapel, Orchard was responsible

Figure 224. Mason's mark on a column of the north aisle of St Leonard's church, Eynsham.

for the building of the cloisters there for which he was paid 6s-8d for each window and door.[5] Some of the mason's marks found there have also been found in the north aisle of the parish church of St Leonard's, Eynsham, which dates to the late 15th century (Figure 224).[6] If, as seems likely, Orchard's masons worked at the parish church, it would be but a short step, literally, for them to have worked on the abbey buildings as well, especially as St Leonard's belonged to the abbey.

This hypothesis is perhaps supported by another mason's mark found on a stone believed to have come from the abbey and now built into a wall in the Bitterell (Figure 225). In the shape of a bow it is similar to one found at Magdalen. The Eynsham example differs only

---

[1] Instructions to the master mason of Oxford University in 1439. Quoted in Davis R.H.C., The Chronology of Perpendicular Architecture in Oxford, *Oxoniensia*, Vol. XI/XII 1947, pp. 75-89.

[2] Hardy A. and Dodd A. and Keevill G.D. et al., *Aelfric's Abbey - Excavations at Eynsham Abbey, Oxfordshire, 1989-92*, p. 234, English Heritage. Published by Oxford University School of Archaeology, 2003.

[3] Salter H.E., *Eynsham Cartulary*, Vol. 2: p. lxxxix, Oxford Historical Society, Clarendon Press, 1908

[4] Harvey J., *English Medieval Architects*, p. 199, Batsford, 1954. Orchard (c. 1450-1504) was probably the most important local mason of his time and had a hand in most new building in Oxford in the late 15th century. His most famous work was the vaulting of the Divinity School there.

[5] Gee E.A., Oxford Masons 1370-1530, *Archaeological Journal* CIX, 1953, pp. 54-131.

[6] Davis R.H.C., A Catalogue of Mason's Marks as an Aid to Architectural History, *Journal of the British Archaeological Association*, 1954, 3rd Series xvii, pp. 43-76.

Figure 225. Mason's mark on a voussoir above a gate in the Bitterell, Eynsham.

Figure 226. Mason's mark on a stone found in Holewelle field.

in having an extra line across the centre which could be explained by the fact that some masons seem to have adopted the mark of their father but with a small difference. It is possible that a father and son may have worked at Eynsham as part of the same team of masons. Another mason's mark has been found on a stone from a field once part of the abbey precinct (Figure 226). Although it cannot yet be attributed to any mason or group of masons, it is worth recording, especially as it seems to be quite an unusual mark. Most of the other marks found have been simple crosses which can be found in many buildings nationwide.

One of the great imponderables about such marks is that not every medieval church with ashlar masonry contains them whereas the church at Witney, for example, has many hundreds of them. This may be partially explained by the Victorian passion for scraping church walls to reveal the bare stone beneath layers of paint and plaster. However, it has also been suggested by R.H.C. Davis that they were only used when a large number of masons were working on a significant project at the same time, to enable the master mason to distinguish between their work. If this is accepted, it would support the idea that the masons working at Eynsham parish church were also engaged on a constructional programme at the abbey.

Orchard's masons worked on other churches locally as well, notably at South Leigh (nave and tower) and Stanton Harcourt (Harcourt chapel and possibly Pope's tower).

Many of the stones to be found in the village would support the possibility of extensive building, particularly perhaps

Figure 227. Peterborough Abbey/Cathedral. Lavatorium against the north-west wall of the refectory.

of the guest accommodation, the abbot's quarters and indeed the new west window of the abbey church. It may also have been at this time that the circular lavatorium was replaced by one that was erected against the north wall of the refectory such as occurred at Peterborough Abbey/Cathedral (Figure 227), although there is little evidence for the rich blind tracery panelling that can still be seen there.

Figure 228. Three stones found in the collapsed wall of the Co-op in Lombard Street, Eynsham.

Figure 229. Corner fragment from a square-headed window found in a garden in Queen's Street, Eynsham.

Three stones from a collapsed wall in the village (Figure 228)[7] show two mullions with splayed corners and slots for glass, and a moulded mullion base on a large sill. Identical mullions have been found in the garden of a house in the Bitterell, in Twelve Acre farmhouse, and built into a house in Queen's Street. Bainbridge recorded several other examples.

There are in addition, a large number of fragments of square headed doors and windows such as the piece above, found in a garden in Queen's Street (Figure 229). The simple chamfered arch has a slot for glass on its underside and would have been part of a window like that in 'The Elms' in Oxford Road (Figure 230). Similar pieces are built into the 'cairns' around the village and have been found in many gardens and walls.

Figure 230. Re-cycled window in 'The Elms', Eynsham.

Figure 231. Fragment of a window built into an interior wall of a house in Acre End Street, Eynsham.

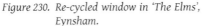

[7] Parrinder S., The Co-op Wall, ER 31, 2014.

Figure 232. Central mullion of a window. W. Bainbridge ©EHG. Now built into St Peter's 'cairn'.

Figure 233. Magdalen College, Oxford. Cloister windows.

Another example, built into a house in Acre End Street (Figure 231) has cusping like that of the windows in the cloister at Magdalen College, Oxford (Figure 233). Again, there are a number of other examples, many photographed by Bainbridge. Two are now built into St Peter's 'cairn'. The piece illustrated (Figure 232) is identical to the top of the central mullion of the Magdalen two light window.

Two squared arch heads are built into the Recreation field 'cairn', one of which has trefoils in the spandrels (Figure 234). Others, some with cusping details, can be found in the market square 'cairn', the 'cairn' next to the football pitch, and in private collections.

A more elaborate arch (Figure 235) belonging to a 15th century doorway or gate has an ogee gothic arch with mythical animals and foliage in the spandrels. It originally had a squared drip mould above (see chapter 12).

A tracery panel, probably a 15th century smokehole from the chimney of one of the abbey's buildings, is now built into the gable wall of a house on the south side of Acre End Street (Figure 236).

A recent find in Holewelle Field consists of a large stone with a cavetto moulding which seems to have been part of a substantial 15th century doorway (Figure 237). No other

Figure 234. Squared arch head built into the Recreation Ground 'cairn', Eynsham.

Figure 235. Ogee arch doorway. Once built into the wall of a cottage in Swan Street (Figure 268), then in the Vicarage garden (Figure 269) and now above the north doorway inside St Leonard's church, Eynsham.

stones were found associated with it but its size, weight and location suggest that it may have come from the gateway to the inner precinct of the abbey.

Evidence for monuments to abbots or distinguished patrons is limited to a single example of part of a delicately carved finial (Figure 238) found in a garden in Newland Street, which probably graced a tomb or a chantry chapel or possibly a screen such as that on the south choir aisle of Lincoln Cathedral (Figure 239). The Eynsham example, still has traces of red pigment and has a hole at its base to attach it to its pinnacle. The fact that it is only three-quarter carved indicates that it was set against a wall.

Figure 236. 'Smokehole' built into the gable of 27, Acre End Street, Eynsham.

Figure 237. Large stone with cavetto moulding. Holewelle field, Eynsham.

Figure 238. Finial from a wall mounted tomb/ monument/shrine or screen. Found in a garden in Newland Street. Dr Bryan Hyde collection.

There are a number of other indications that building activity at Eynsham continued throughout the later medieval period. Nikolaus Pevsner, writing in 1974, made an interesting observation. The entry for Eynsham parish church included a description of the 15th century font (Figure 240) the bowl of which 'is rather too shallow' and 'may be a re-used capital' which suggests that it may originally have come from the abbey after the Dissolution.[8] The 'much repaired'[9] font has a carved mask head with lizard-like animals emerging from its mouth, much like a 'Green Man'. These could be basilisks, legendary animals, half cock and half snake which were said to kill merely by their glance. They were regarded in the Middle Ages as symbols of the Devil who were crushed underfoot by Christ triumphant.[10] The style

[8] Pevsner N. and Sherwood J., *The Buildings of England – Oxfordshire*, Penguin Books 1974.
[9] Crossley A., *Victoria History of the County of Oxford*, Vol. XII: pp. 98-157 OUP 1990. University of London Institute of Historical Research.
[10] Ferguson G., *Signs and Symbols in Christian Art*, Oxford University Press, 1980.

*Figure 239. Lincoln Cathedral. South
choir aisle screen.*

of the carving is not dissimilar to that on the ogee arch above although the latter has been badly weathered.

In 1988, the local historian William Bainbridge made an appeal for the whereabouts of a stone which he had found illustrated in a J.H. Parker's *Glossary of Gothic Architecture* published in 1896. The stone was part of a 15th century cornice with a form of diaper or stylised flower decoration (Figure 241). Unfortunately, his request appears to

*Figure 240. St Leonard's, Eynsham.
Font.*

Figure 241. Illustration from J.H. Parker's Glossary of Gothic Architecture published in 1896.

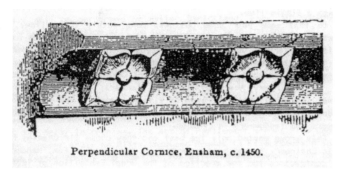

Perpendicular Cornice, Ensham, c. 1450.

Figure 242. St Leonard's, Eynsham. Exterior of the south west corner of the south aisle.

have gone unanswered.[11] Parker's book was first published in 1846 and it is likely that the stone was one of many that were collected and stored in the Vicarage garden in the early 19th century (See Chapter 14).

---

[11] Bainbridge W., *ER* 5, 1988.

All in all, although the evidence is fragmentary and the exact provenance of some of the stones described here is unknown, it is clear that it would be reasonable to suggest that the abbey continued to extensively renovate its facilities in the late 15th century and that the work accorded with the latest Perpendicular style.

In addition to the work at the abbey, most of which has been lost, the abbey would certainly have influenced the architectural updates which are still evident in Eynsham's church, which it had built for the parish. The north aisle and porch, the south door and south west window all date to this period (Figure 242). The high quality of these improvements may well reflect the sort of structural changes undertaken at the abbey itself. Similarly, a number of Eynsham's other churches were re-modelled, repaired or added to at this time.

All these works of course, cost the abbey sums that by this date it probably couldn't afford. The abbey's financial difficulties must have been made worse, at least temporarily, by a disaster in 1454 when its entire flock of 950 sheep, with the exception of one ewe and her lamb, was wiped out by disease. In addition, during the 15th century there were a relatively large number of very poor harvests which reduced the value of the greater tithe.[12] The political instability of the country during the Wars of the Roses also made it more difficult to raise loans. It may be therefore, that the sale by the abbey of some of its property and rights at this time was to make up for the shortfall in income. It is instructive too, that the abbey increasingly gave over its arable land to the less labour intensive and therefore cheaper pasture farming, both of sheep and cattle. The number of permanently employed ploughmen on the demesne, as a result, was reduced from 18 in 1316 to seven in 1467.[13]

Nevertheless, the abbey continued to spend and, as will be seen in the next chapter, seemed oblivious to the Biblical warnings that temporal wealth was subject to corruption and thievery and that it would be better for their spiritual health to 'lay up ... treasures in heaven.'[14]

---

[12] Pounds N.J.G., *A History of the English Parish*, Cambridge University Press, 2000.
[13] Hardy et al., op. cit., p. 511.
[14] Holy Bible, Matthew vi:xx.

Chapter 12

Scandal

A monk ther was, a fair for the maistrie
An out-ridere that lovede venerie;
A manly man, to been an abbot able.

....

The reule of seinte Maure or of seinte Beneit
Bycause that it was old and somdel streit,
This ilke monk leet old thynges pace,
And heeld after the newe world the space.[1]

In the almost complete absence of medical knowledge and expertise, the causes of the plagues that ravaged the country in the 14th century were a total and frightening mystery. They were thus universally seen as God's righteous punishment of a wicked world. It might be expected therefore that people would turn away from decadence, debauchery and trivialities to avoid the dreadful torments of hell. It might be hoped that monks especially, would display greater devotion, and observe the *Rule* of St Benedict more conscientiously than before to appease the wrath of the Lord. It might also be thought that the relatively less favourable economic circumstances of monks would encourage a greater focus on spiritual matters. However, in all respects the reverse was true as many contemporary chroniclers noted. For example, William, a monk of Rochester, commented that the majority of the population had *become even more depraved, more prone to every kind of vice, more ready to indulge in evil and sinfulness, without a thought of death, or of the plague which is just over, or even of their own salvation...So, day by day, the peril in which the souls of the clergy as well as people are to be found has grown more dangerous...*[2]

One possible reason for the declining standards in some monastic institutions was that a number of those able men who might previously have been attracted to the contemplative life as a means of advancement, took advantage of the new opportunities brought about by the fall in the population to better themselves in other ways. As a consequence, the quality of recruits to holy orders seemed to decline and educational levels were lower than those of their predecessors. Some of those that entered monastic houses had little sense of vocation and some, widowed by the plague, were simply seeking for some way to fill the rest of their lives. The shortage of properly trained clerics was recognised and addressed by, for example, the Archbishop of Canterbury Simon Islip who founded Canterbury College at Oxford in 1363 because *those who are truly learned and accomplished...have been largely exterminated in the epidemics.*[3] Likewise, New College Oxford was founded by William of Wykeham, Bishop of

---

[1]   Chaucer G., *Canterbury Tales*, The Prologue, Folio Society, Cambridge University Press.
[2]   Ziegler P., *The Black Death*, p.141, Folio Society, London, 1997.
[3]   Canterbury College was incorporated into Christchurch in the 18th century but is commemorated by Canterbury Quad.

Winchester, in 1379 to remedy the deficiencies in the clerical establishment which were the *result of pestilences...and other miseries of the world.*[4]

Nevertheless, despite the efforts of bishops at Oxford, standards failed to improve. Discipline weakened, rules were relaxed and by the late 14th and early 15th centuries, piety and devotion to Christ had in many religious houses been replaced by worldliness and lip-service to the monastic *Rule*. Eynsham Abbey was perhaps particularly susceptible. Its frequent contacts with the outside world, particularly with the king and nobility, may have had deleterious effects as the worldliness of the court impacted on the spirituality of those who had determined on a claustral existence.

Just one example at Eynsham will suffice for the moment before more serious abuses are detailed. Under the *Rule* of St Benedict, monks were expected to share a dormitory with the rest of the community. However, as the Roll of Eynsham's chamberlain for 1404 informs us, two of the monks in that year, Thomas Kanyng and Richard Oxinforde, had private chambers built within the large dormitory to give themselves more comfort and privacy, costing 13s-4d and 8s-4d respectively. Another, Roger Clere, had an even grander suite built in the infirmary at a cost of 33s-2d.[5] They may all indeed have been following the example of others but the records are not complete enough to be more precise. Surviving examples of what these individual 'cells' may have looked like can be found in the convent of San Marco, Florence, Italy whose simple rooms are decorated with devotional frescos by the 15th century artist Fra Angelico (Figure 243).

Standards of living for Eynsham's monks remained high relative to the majority of the population. John Buckingham, Bishop of Lincoln visited the abbey in 1380 and his subsequent memorandum is instructive. £4-6s-8d per ordinary monk was to be set aside annually to provide them with clothing, meat and wine, supplementary to the regular allowance of bread and beer. In addition, the abbot was also to ensure that each monk received *salt, oatmeal, beans, white peas, butter, cheese, firewood and other necessaries for broth and pottage.*[6] The prior, sub

Figure 243. Monastic cell. Convent of San Marco, Florence, Italy.

---

[4]   Ziegler, op.cit., p. 224.
[5]   Salter H.E., *Eynsham Cartulary,* Vol. 2: p. xcv, Oxford Historical Society, Clarendon Press 1908.
[6]   Salter H.E., *Eynsham Cartulary,* Vol. 1: p. xvii, Oxford Historical Society, Clarendon Press 1907.

prior and of course the abbot, received substantially more. In 1406, the abbot's annual expenses for personal items, excluding food and wine, amounted to £5-10s-6d. This included sums for medicines, boots, hose, caps, gloves, a cowl, an ounce of black silk, spurs and 12s-3d for a *silk belt studded with silver gilt*.

Just a few years earlier, the annual bill for the abbot's kitchen, as detailed in the *Cartulary*, came to £86-6s. It included, amongst other things, salt fish, young pike, red herrings, cows, pigs, white herrings, salmon, rabbits, oatmeal, vinegar, green peas, eggs and part of a 'sea-wolf', probably a cat-fish whose flesh apparently has an excellent flavour and was regarded as a delicacy. By comparison, the total yearly income for most parish priests was about £5 and that of peasant families even less. Monks also lived rent free, in more substantial accommodation than most, and their quarters were maintained by the abbot. They had the services of cooks, a barber, a tailor, a washerman and a cobbler. If any of the monks fell ill, the abbey's infirmary would take care of them and give them preferential treatment whilst they were sick. Few, if any, were now employed in manual labour as recommended by St Benedict. Indeed, during the 15th and 16th centuries the monks increasingly engaged others to cultivate their lands or to collect their tithes. The cellarer's accounts for 1471 for example, indicate that there were at least two shepherds employed on the abbey's demesne or home farm, as well as a cowherd and two men to care for the abbey's pigs. The personal relationship with their land and churches was practically non-existent and subsequently their relationship with the local community waned.

The income of the abbey in 1390 was £772-12s-10½d of which £348-16s-9d was received in rents, a reasonably healthy sum in ordinary circumstances by comparison with some other religious houses. However, as we have noted before, the monastery was frequently expected to entertain visiting dignitaries like bishops, abbots and the king himself. When King Richard II came to Eynsham Abbey in 1390 the bake-house had to be modernised and it was taken over by the royal bakers for the duration of his visit. Extra bread had to be bought in for the monastery and their guests at a cost of 16s-7d and the fishponds had to be restocked with fish bought from the rector of Standlake for 19s. In the same year, for comparison, 7s-5d was spent on clothing for beggars and 11s-2d on distributions to the poor.

Given the levels of hospitality the abbey was expected to provide, Bishop Henry Beaufort had compensated Eynsham by allowing it to appropriate the churches of South Stoke, South Newington and Combe in 1398/9. This might explain the generosity to his successor, Bishop Philip Repyngton and his entourage a few years later in 1406. On the occasion of his visit that year Bishop Repyngton 'received a fee of £10, and his clerks, his nine squires, thirteen valets, three grooms, etc, all had presents', including robes for three men costing 36s. A special trip was made to Oxford to buy a 'pipe' of wine, a cask holding 105 gallons or 477 litres. Other provisions purchased included salt, rabbits, capons, birds, salmon, red herrings, fresh fish, oysters, spice, fruit, oil and mustard. In addition, the abbey bought approximately 25 metres of linen for napkins, two and a half hundredweight of charcoal, two great torches, candles, and wood fuel to provide fires in the great hall, rooms and kitchen. In total, the cost of providing hospitality to the bishop and his entourage was £63, a large percentage of the abbey's annual income.[7] This kind of conspicuous consumption and expenditure does not seem to have been particularly unusual. In 1471, one of the few years for which we have some accounts, the abbot bought two swans which, from bone evidence, probably ended up at his dinner table.

Unsurprisingly perhaps, the public reputation of clerics in general was lower after the Black Death. Some felt embittered and betrayed by a church which had proved impotent in the face of God's anger and some of whose representatives had deserted their parishioners in their hour of need. Being in holy orders had also failed to give any special protection to monasteries whose supposed raison d'etre was to be engaged in spiritual combat with evil. Unquestioning deference to the authority of the church's hierarchy was gradually replaced by a growing cynicism in some quarters. Although there may not have been a decline in religious faith *per se*, there was a sense in some quarters that the church required reform, a feeling that was ultimately given its full expression in the 16th century.

Certainly, resentment at and criticism of the continued opulent lifestyle of some monks grew, as the works of Geoffrey Chaucer and more seriously the scholar and Master of Balliol, John Wycliffe demonstrate. Wycliffe complained about *the appropriation of parish churches by worldly rich bishops and abbots that have more than enough money...yet fail to fulfil their duties as spiritual pastors by teaching, preaching, giving of sacraments or looking after the poor. Instead they appoint an idiot as vicar or parish priest, who cannot or will not carry out properly their curation of souls despite being financially supported by the parish.*[8]

Wycliffe's supporters, popularly known as Lollards, claimed that the church had been corrupted by temporal concerns and denied the special status of the clergy, believing instead in a universal priesthood. Furthermore, they challenged some of the basic tenets of the Catholic faith as un-Biblical, including transubstantiation, the efficacy of prayers for the dead and the 'worship' of images.

In fact, the issue of the Lollards impacted directly on Eynsham Abbey which was at one point expected to act as a prison for those 'heretics' who had recanted their opinions and submitted themselves to the discipline of the Bishop of Lincoln. He commanded the abbey to receive those he had sentenced to *perpetual Penance within your monastery of Ensham there to live as a Penitent, and not otherwise*. The abbey was to give them what they would give paupers, order them to do what work they saw fit and not allow them outside the precincts of the monastery.[9] Nevertheless, the bishops were probably aware that Lollard criticism of the lives of the religious was not entirely unfounded and efforts were made to address the problem. From the evidence of inspections, Eynsham, along with Ramsey Abbey and the convents of nuns at Godstow and Markyate, seems to have been particularly in need of the bishop's care.

---

[7]   Salter, *Cartulary* 2 op. cit. In his book *Medieval Oxford*, Salter states that in the 15th century the abbey was also supplied with wine that was shipped to Bristol from Spain.
[8]   Modern English version by the author of a passage from the works of Wycliffe quoted in Pounds N.J.G., *A History of the English Parish*, Cambridge University Press, 2000.
[9]   Rev Thomas Symonds Collection, *Bodl. MS Top Oxon b 275, p. 191.*

In July 1432, Bishop William Gray made a formal Visitation to Eynsham Abbey and consequently issued a series of Injunctions from which much can be inferred about the state of the house and its inhabitants.[10] It would seem that the monastery was significantly in debt, to the extent that the abbot had pawned the abbey's jewels in order to finance his lavish life style. These he was ordered to redeem and to balance the accounts using the revenues from three of the abbey's most profitable properties: Charlbury, Histon and Mickleton. In addition, the monks' annual allowance for clothing was reduced to two marks (£1-6s-8d), no maintenance allowances (*corrodies*), pensions or gifts of robes (*liveries*) were to be granted or, for five years, *exhibitions* for monks to study at Oxford University. The common seal of the abbey was to be locked away in a chest with three or four keys and was only to be used with the approval of the majority of the house.

However, there were clearly other concerns at this time as the bishop had to spell out that no women, except the mother or sister of a monk, were to be allowed in the abbey. Two small chambers that had been built next to the door of the abbot's lodging were to be demolished, presumably to inhibit his behaviour, and he and all the monks were to sleep silently together in the dormitory with all the doors locked. All monks, excepting the ill or infirm, were expected to attend Matins every night. In addition, no monk was to leave the monastic precinct without permission and then only with an elderly chaperone to monitor their behaviour. Young monks were to be overseen, instructed and corrected by a Master of Novices and the abbot was to investigate whether any monks had private property in contravention of the *Rule.* One monk, Ralf Dadlington, was declared an apostate, i.e. had renounced his religious vows, and was not to be readmitted to the abbey without a written dispensation from the bishop.

In January 1433 Bishop William Gray sent a commission to Eynsham to investigate reports that the monks were ignoring the Injunctions made previously *in order that so great and so renowned a monastery...may not lie a prey to havoc.*[11] Shortly afterwards, the abbey, seemingly contrite, wrote to Gray explaining in some detail how they intended to pay off the debts which the abbey had accrued. The bishop accepted its plans but insisted that all *wandering abroad* expenses and borrowing of further monies should cease and that revenues should be carefully collected, stored and audited. The abbot and his monks were threatened with dismissal if they failed to comply with all the bishop's recommendations.

However, the bishop sent yet another commission to Eynsham the following June, headed by Robert Thorntone, doctor of law and vicar of St Giles, Cripplegate. This was as a result of *rumour and loud whisperings* that the monks had *slackened the bridle of obedience and the reins of chastity, returning as dogs untamed to the lust and vomit of their former life...to the open contempt and vilification of us and of our jurisdiction.* The enquiry reported in the autumn, found the allegations true and revealed that the abbot, since the original Visitation, had openly committed further crimes *such as adulteries, fornications, incest and rapes* with five women. Sir Henry Norwyche, vicar of Eynsham church, was named as his accomplice. The abbot was

---

[10] The preambles and phraseology of these Injunctions can be formulaic but sufficient particular details are included to enable conclusions to be drawn about the condition of Eynsham Abbey.

[11] Thompson A.H. (ed.), Visitations of Religious Houses in the Diocese of Lincoln Vol. 1, 1420-1436, *Lincoln Record Society*, Vol. 7: pp. 54-63, 1913.

Figure 244. Part of the Parliamentary Processional Roll of 1512, © British Library Board, Add MS 5831. W. Bainbridge.

also accused of pimping the women and he and they were summoned to appear before the bishop in person. There is no record of what happened thereafter or if Thomas of Oxinforde was removed from his post.

Another visitation by Bishop Alnwick in June 1445 revealed that whereas in most respects the abbey was well run by John Quenington who had succeeded Thomas as abbot, one of the 14 monks, John Bengeworth, abandoning his vocation, had escaped confinement for bad behaviour and run off with a nun from Godstow. However, he had been brought back to the monastery and was doing penance.[12]

It is surely instructive that none of the last five abbots of Eynsham were appointed from within the community, as was the custom. Perhaps the monks in the abbey lacked the learning, ability and leadership qualities befitting the post of abbot although one, William, was elected Prior of Tickford in 1498.[13] However, appointing monks from outside Eynsham to the abbacy was not necessarily a guarantee of their probity. William Walwayn, who came from Worcester Cathedral in 1469 to lead the Eynsham community, seems to have also instituted himself as vicar of St Leonard's parish church in 1482. It is not possible to determine whether this was a cost-cutting measure or just a way to enhance his income. Whatever the case, it didn't bode well for the commitment to either institution and was theoretically contrary to Canon Law.

Another of the 'imports', Miles Salley (c. 1497-1516) was also a pluralist. He apparently did not reside at Eynsham and for years held the post of abbot as well as being Bishop of Llandaff. Possibly the only known painted image of an abbot of Eynsham is that of Salley on a Parliamentary Processional Roll for 1512 (Figure 244). Salley, as Bishop of Llandaff, is second from the left. To his left is John Fisher, Bishop of Rochester, executed in 1535 for refusing to accept the Royal Supremacy. To his right is James Stanley, Bishop of Ely, younger son of the First Earl of Derby and reputed at the time to be the tallest man in England. The

---

[12] Thompson A.H. (ed.), Visitations of Religious Houses in the Diocese of Lincoln Vol. 2, 1436-1449, *Lincoln Record Society*, Vol. 8, 1919.
[13] Salter, *Cartulary* 2, op. cit., Charter 695, p. 152.

*Figure 245.   St Mark's, Bristol. Chancel north wall. Tomb chest
of Bishop Miles Salley. W. Bainbridge ©EHG.*

Stanleys were to play an important part in the history of Eynsham in the 16th and 17th
centuries.

Salley died in 1516 and his body was buried in the east end of the chancel of St Mark's,
Bristol, which he had financed, and his tomb chest is against its north wall. Again, this has
the only known stone-sculpted image of an Eynsham Abbot although it is difficult to be
certain how accurate a portrayal it was (Figure 245). Salley's heart and bowels are said to be
buried in the chancel of Mathern church, Monmouthshire where the bishop's palace was
located. In his will, dated 29 November 1516, he decreed that *my written bokes in parchment
and my bokes of Hugo de Vienna be delivered to Eynsham.*[14]

Unsurprisingly given Salley's absenteeism, Eynsham felt the lack of a fatherly hand.
Discipline was wanting and in 1503 some monks had so forgotten their calling as to become
embroiled in a violent – some said armed – conflict and public riot with the servants of the
lord of Stanton Harcourt over property and fishing rights.[15]

A year after Salley's death in 1516, and just 20 years before the Dissolution, the Bishop of
Lincoln, William Attwater, sent a Visitation by his Chancellor, to the abbey which revealed
that standards of spirituality and adherence to the *Rule* of St Benedict were lax. Despite
injunctions that except for the sick, monks were to abstain from eating the flesh of four-

---

[14]   Davies E.T., *A History of the Parish of Mathern*, Mathern Parochial Church Council, 1990.
[15]   Townley S., 'Riottes, Extorcions and Inuries' A 16th century affray in Eynsham, *ER* 6, 1989.

footed creatures, the brothers were eating meat in the refectory. In truth, this particular *Rule* of St Benedict had been largely abandoned in Christendom. Meat-eating was anyway allowed on feast days to honour the Saints and the number of these had dramatically increased since the early Middle Ages.

Further criticisms were that the junior monks were not being properly instructed, Matins were sometimes not said and the prior, responsible for the abbey in the absence of the abbot, was frequently inebriated and defamed his fellow brethren. The sub prior was guilty of simony, holding three offices and was presumably remunerated for each. Worse still, the monks were leaving the abbey without licence from the abbot, gambling in Eynsham town and often returning to the monastery somewhat the worse for drink. In addition, certain women, among them the two notoriously debauched daughters of the abbey's gate keeper, were regularly visiting the abbey and causing a great scandal. One monk, Walter Harburgh, was declared an apostate. As a result of the visitation, the monks were forbidden to admit *suspect* women, to leave the abbey without permission, play dice or other *indecent games* and all were to return faithfully and soberly before Vespers at 6.00pm.[16]

Another Visitation in 1520 seemed to show a degree of improvement, possibly under the influence of Abbot Thomas Chaundler (1517-19) who Cardinal Wolsey called *the flower of St Benet's order*. However, the monks were criticised for not sitting two by two together at meals as they should, for not observing silence in the refectory as proscribed by the *Rule*, for failing to get out of bed for Matins at 3.00 a.m. and for mistreating and neglecting the education of novices so that they were not proficient in doctrine. One monk, Thomas Spoforth, was particularly singled out as a habitual liar who was frequently drunk and aggressive. He was a quarrelsome figure, making trouble amongst the monks and between them and the abbot. Furthermore, he showed the bishop's representatives no respect and, an official commented, showed *no self-respect*.

The new abbot himself, Henry Reading (1519-30), was not beyond criticism as not only had he allowed standards to slip but his sister, the monks complained, lived within the precinct and she and several of her relations were a financial burden on the abbey, costing an estimated £140 per annum. In addition, the abbot's 'nephew', Richard, had been put in charge of the monastery's granary and, it was claimed by some, disposed of the grain as he saw fit. Apart from this nepotism, the abbot had failed to submit his accounts and spent large amounts of cash whilst visiting other places which he seemed to do regularly. In addition, the abbot had provided insufficient allowances for the ordinary members of the House including sick monks. Likewise, the precentor Jacob Ashenden, who led and directed the chanting of the monks, had been expected to fully carry out his work and provide the singers with service books and other materials but had been inadequately remunerated. The abbot and the convent were then subjected to a two-hour lecture by the bishop exhorting them to reform.

Although Eynsham probably never had more than 30 to 40 monks and lay brothers, by the 1530s it was reduced to 19 religious, including the abbot and the prior. As the religious houses distanced themselves still further from the district in which they were set, the

---

[16] Salter, *Cartulary* 1, op. cit.

parish church became instead the main focus for a community's religious life. Chaucer had poked fun at the monk's disdain for the constraints of the monastic life in the pursuit of the pleasures of the flesh. In contrast he praised the poor parish priest for his simplicity, his care for his flock, his education, and for setting a good example to his parishioners. Interestingly, few wills now left money to abbeys to pay for prayers for the dead and parish churches rather than monasteries were more likely to receive bequests, although in Eynsham's case the abbey, as rector, would have taken its share. It is noticeable that there was significant re-modelling of St Leonard's parish church in the late medieval period which is also supportive of the idea that it, rather than the abbey, was central to people's devotional practices.[17]

The revelations about Eynsham were mirrored in other places too and provided the basis for Simon Fish's *Supplication of the Beggars* (1529).[18] Fish was a radical Protestant reformer and propagandist and his pamphlet was addressed to *The King our sovereign lord*. It contained a withering attack on many aspects of the ecclesiastical establishment in the country who Fish described as *ravenous wolves*. He claimed these *bloodsuppers* had acquired between a third and a half of the country's landed wealth and in effect created a second kingdom which would, if unchecked, subsume the king's temporal realm. They had fleeced the poor by charging for probate, for tithes, for masses, for burial, for confessions, for pardons, for prayers, for blessings of altars and bells and by accepting gifts from pilgrims. In addition, Fish accused these *holy men* of moral *incontinency*, of stealing other men's wives and of creating *a hundred thousand idle whores* by their excessive wealth. For *who is she that will put her hands to work to get 3d a day when she can earn 20d a day by sleeping an hour with a friar, a monk, or a priest.* Moreover, if anyone criticised the monks, these *hypocrites* would threaten excommunication and brand dissenters with the label of heretic, the enemy within.

The answer to the problem, Fish believed, was to confiscate the land and wealth of the monasteries and to *set these sturdy louts abroad in the world, to get them wives of their own, to get their living by their labour and the sweat of their brows, according to God's commandment.* However, Fish doubted whether King Henry VIII, would be able to *make laws against them* as parliament was dominated by *bishops, abbots and priors* and their *learned* supporters. Further, some of the king's predecessors had tried a *reformation* of the church, *but what availed it?* This was a challenge indeed – and one that, as it transpired, the king was more than up for.

In 1507, when he was still Prince of Wales, Henry had visited Oxford University and afterwards 'repaired to the neighbouring monastery of Eynsham of which Miles Salley, Bishop of Llandaff was abbot'.[19] He may therefore have had more than an inkling of the true state of affairs at the abbey and of the benefits that might accrue if it and other monasteries were subject to *reformation.*

---

[17] Hardy A. and Dodd A. and Keevill G.D. et al, *Aelfric's Abbey – Excavations at Eynsham Abbey, Oxfordshire, 1989-92*, English Heritage. Published by Oxford University School of Archaeology, 2003.

[18] Fish S., *A Supplication for the Beggars*, E. Arber (ed.), The English Scholar's Library, Unwin Brothers 1878. Reprinted by Amazon.co.uk, Ltd, Filiquarian Publishing, 2015.

[19] Walker J. (ed.), *Oxoniana , or Anecdotes Relative to the University and City of Oxford*, Vol. 1: p. 93, Slatter and Munday, 1806.

Chapter 13

Endings

'Idols and images
Have none in usage
(Of what mettel so ever they be)
Graved or carved
My wyle be observed
Or else can ye not love me'[1]

In 1534, the Act of Supremacy acknowledged Henry VIII's claim to be the Supreme Head of the Church of England and in January 1535 the king added the title to his many others. It was the culmination of Henry's campaign to destroy the power of the pope in England which had been embarked upon as a consequence of his desire to divorce Catherine of Aragon and marry Anne Boleyn. It is said that the frustrated Henry read with approval Simon Fish's popular critique of clerics, those *greedy sort of sturdy idle holy thieves* who do *nothing but translate all rule, power, lordship, authority, obedience and dignity from your grace unto them.*[2] In addition, both Henry and his chief minister Thomas Cromwell were aware of the poor state of the Crown's finances and the significant advantages that would accrue from the king taking the place of the papacy in spiritual affairs. The confiscation and sale of monastic property would also be a useful way of ensuring the loyalty to Henry's Reformation of the nobility and gentry, likely to be its chief beneficiaries.[3]

Monasticism as an ideal had diminished by the early 16th century. Eynsham's monks, along with many others, seem to have abandoned even a pretence of adherence to the strict *Rule* of St Benedict and had forfeited much of the respect previously accorded them. A monastery's key role in a district as both secular and spiritual overlord had been undermined. Plans to take over ecclesiastical property were therefore not entirely new. Indeed, Cromwell's predecessor Cardinal Wolsey, had dissolved 29 decayed religious establishments with the acquiescence of the pope. In part this was to provide the monies for his ambitious scheme of a new college in Oxford on the site of the suppressed priory of St Frideswide, later Christchurch. There were clear signs that Eynsham Abbey was an institution in decline too and that it may have had some intimations of what was to come. From the early years of the reign of Henry VIII through to the 1530s, Eynsham was parting with some of its rights like tithes, disposing of property by sale and granting exceptionally long leases on its properties in exchange for a lump sum. As a result, many of the holdings that the abbey had held in the late 14th century were already lost by the time of the Henrician Reformation.[4]

---

[1] The Fantassie of Idolatrie by William Gray, 1538. Controversialist, opportunist and ballad writer, he became MP for Reading in 1547 and accumulated a large share of the estate of the dissolved monastery and building materials from Reading abbey. E.W. Dormer, *Gray of Reading*, Bradley and Son, 1923.
[2] Fish S., *A Supplication for the Beggars*, E. Arber (ed.), The English Scholar's Library, Unwin Brothers, 1878. Reprinted by Filiquarian Publishing, 2015.
[3] Elton G.R., *England Under the Tudors*, The Folio Society, 1997.
[4] Salter H.E., *Eynsham Cartulary*, Vol. 2: pp. vi-vii, Oxford Historical Society, Clarendon Press, 1908.

In 1535 Cromwell, now 'vicar general', ordered a thorough valuation of all church property in England, the *Valor Ecclesiasticus*, a process that was completed in six months. The net income of Eynsham Abbey was put at £421 and the house contained 19 inmates.[5] To provide a justification for a policy that had already been decided, the *Valor* was followed up with a Visitation of religious houses to examine their moral character and gauge their attitude to Henry's declaration of Royal Supremacy. The 'visitors' were under no illusions that they were expected to produce evidence of corruption, vice and decay in the monastic institutions, 'in theory to mend but in practice to end'.[6] Inspector John Tregonwell came to Eynsham and reported that he *found a raw sort of religious persons and all sort of offences among them for which they have been punished by the ordinary. The abbot is chaste in his living, looks well to the reparation of the house: but he is negligent in overseeing his brethren, which he excuses by his daily infirmity.*[7] In Eynsham's case, perhaps Tregonwell was not exaggerating as concerns about behaviour at the abbey were, as we have seen, long standing and he was quite complimentary about other monasteries in Oxfordshire.

In February 1536, a Bill was introduced to do away with the smaller religious houses, those whose annual income was less than £200, but this was only a beginning. The suppression of the lesser institutions in part provoked the so-called Pilgrimage of Grace or Northern Rising, in which many monks, fearful for their future, were involved. The rebellion was ruthlessly put down and, if anything, speeded up the process of dissolving the larger and richer monasteries like Eynsham. Cromwell commissioned another Visitation of the bigger houses in 1538 offering a prepared form of surrender which was usually signed without dissent, particularly as some abbots (of Kirkstead, Whalley and Jervaulx and the ex-abbot of Fountains) had already been executed as traitors for their opposition to the king's will. More were to follow, notably the Abbot of Reading, Hugh of Faringdon who, in 1539, was found guilty of treason on Cromwell's orders and was hung, drawn and quartered.

Eynsham's abbot and monks had already formally acknowledged the king's supremacy in August 1534 and when the request to surrender came, on 4 December, 1538, they readily complied. There were only ten monks left by this point; just over half of what there had been three years earlier and a further indication perhaps that the abbey already understood that its days were numbered. The event merited but a brief reference in the State papers:

No.989 Eynsham Abbey

Surrender to John London, clerk, of the site, etc., of the house, and all its possessions in England, to the King's use. 4 Dec. 30 Hen. VIII. Signed by Anthony the abbot, S.T.P., Edm. Etun, prior, Geo. Brodhurst, sub-prior, and seven others. Enrolled as acknowledged same day before John Williams, Kings Commissioner.[8]

5   Page W. (ed.), Houses of Benedictine Monks: The abbey of Eynsham, *The Victoria County History of Oxfordshire*, Vol 2, London, 1907.
6   Elton, op. cit.
7   Salter H.E., *Eynsham Cartulary*, Vol. 1: p. xxxi, Oxford Historical Society, Clarendon Press 1907
8   Gordon E., *Eynsham Abbey 1005-1228 A Small Window into a Large Room*, Phillimore & Co. Ltd. 1990. The letters S.T.P. stood for Sanctae Theologiae Professor, a degree awarded by Oxford University to a Doctor of Theology.

The remaining inmates of Eynsham Abbey were pensioned off. The seven ordinary monks at Eynsham received an annual pension of £5-6s-8d, about the average wage for a farm labourer. On the other hand, the last abbot, Anthony Dunstone, alias Kitchin, was given an unusually generous stipend of £133-6s-8d and was given the honorary post of Royal chaplain. He became Bishop of Llandaff in 1545 and gave up his pension. He survived into the reign of Elizabeth I despite his 'infirmity' and the vicissitudes of religious policy in the reigns of Edward VI and Mary. He died in 1563 at the Bishop's Palace in Mathern, Monmouthshire, at the age of 92 and is buried in the parish church there. An inventory of his possessions, compiled on 2 November 1563, valued his goods, including cash, at the paltry sum of £109 4s 9d. He is blamed by some for impoverishing the Llandaff diocese by selling off much of its property, an echo perhaps of his time at Eynsham.[9]

It is known that one of the Eynsham monks, Thomas Mill, was a stipendiary of Cirencester parish church in 1540 and vicar of Coaley, Gloucestershire in 1561. Another, Robert Forde, who had been the abbey's cellarer, was vicar of Cassington church between 1545 and 1557.[10] Interestingly, Cassington had been under Eynsham Abbey's jurisdiction from the 12th century. It had made payments to the abbey for burial rights and Eynsham retained the right to appoint Cassington's incumbent until the Dissolution. In that sense therefore, there was more continuity than one might have thought. Cassington and all the rest of Eynsham Abbey's landed assets were passed to the Crown which sold them off.

The Royal Commissioner for Eynsham, John London, has been described as 'a persecutor born'[11] and the few remaining brethren of the abbey were probably right to think that discretion was the better part of valour. Across England the path was now clear for the Crown to exploit its newly acquired assets, to purge the old religion of superstitious and corrupt practices and destroy the symbols of papal authority which had proved so irksome to the king. Those abbeys which also served as cathedrals, a peculiarly English practice, managed to retain their churches whilst losing their conventual buildings. Some abbey churches, like those at Dorchester, Malmesbury and Dunstable were retained for the use of the parish although sometimes in an abbreviated form. Others, like Reading in Berkshire had most of their fine ashlar masonry and sculpted stones removed, leaving much of the inner rubble core of its walls standing precariously until today. Yet others, like England's only Brigettine monastery at Syon in Middlesex, were systematically destroyed so that even the foundation layers were dug out. Eynsham people already had their own parish church, St Leonard's, built for them by the monks, and the abbey church was therefore redundant.

There are no detailed accounts of the dismantling of Eynsham Abbey in the years immediately following 1538 but we may assume it followed a familiar pattern. The first task was to confiscate and send any valuables like money, gold and silver plate, brass, bells, copes, vestments and other ornaments to the Royal Treasurer, Sir John Williams, in London.[12] Williams reported that he had received *soundry Juelles and plate wch came by*

_____

[9] According to Rev. Symonds, antiquary vicar of Eynsham in the early 19th century, this 'occasioned the saying that a bad Kitchen did forever spoil the meat of the Bishops of Llandaff.'

[10] Wright L., *Eynsham Monks at the Dissolution, ER* 9, 1992

[11] Elton, op. cit.

[12] A Tudor inventory containing quite extensive amounts of 'Plate and other Jewelles' is stuck into one of the

Figure 246. Sketch by Hans Holbein the Younger entitled 'A Fool Praying to Superstition.' ©Kuntsmuseum Basel, Kupferstichkabinett. Photo: Kunstmusem Basel, Martin P. Bühler

occasion of the defacing and takinge downe of shrines and uther vayne and fayned thinges called Reliques and uther supfluous plate founde...made for the advydinge thabuse of Idolatrye.[13]

This last phrase serves to remind us that whilst we might bemoan the apparently vandalistic destruction of the greatest repositories of medieval art there was, at least in part, a religious purpose behind it. It was felt that the belief in the efficacy of holy relics and images of Saints and the Virgin Mary had led the weak and credulous to adopt fetishistic ideas and practices, to the detriment of adherence to the truth of written scripture and Biblical injunctions against the worship of idols. One of the leading reformers, John Hooper, who later became Bishop of Gloucester, ridiculed the making of images which were *nothing but the skill and draught of the craftsman, proportioning a shape not like unto Christ whome he never sawe, but (where) his owne fancie leadeth him...and in that case you worshippe not the similitude of our saviour but the conceite of this maker.*[14] A contemporary sketch by Hans Holbein the Younger, showing a peasant before a representation of St Christopher and entitled 'A Fool Praying to Superstition', makes the point even more succinctly (Figure 246). It gives pause for thought that fundamentalist Islamic groups have used similar arguments to justify their spoliation of historically important sites and artefacts in the 21st century.

In England, the initial focus fell particularly on images and references to St Thomas Becket, that 12th century challenger of royal authority who had by his martyrdom unwittingly humiliated the king's namesake Henry II. Later however, and particularly in the reigns of the more clearly Protestant Edward VI and Elizabeth I, there were systematic culls of religious imagery. Another wave of iconoclastic fervour took place during the Civil War and Commonwealth period in the mid-17th century. Parliamentary troops were based in

---

versions of the *Visio* in the Bodleian (*MS Selden Supra 66*) but there is no indication that it came from Eynsham.
[13] Harrison S., *Art Under Attack – Histories of British Iconoclasm*, Barber T. and Boldrick S. (eds), Tate Publishing, 2013.
[14] Rosewell R., *Medieval Wall Paintings*, Boydell Press, 2008.

Eynsham for a while and the parish accounts for 1649 record the cost of *sending a hue and cry for the church goods lost* and the repair of windows.[15]

The archaeological evidence suggests that the abbey church and its associated buildings were systematically cleared of fixtures and fittings before dismantling of the main structures began. Those which were not considered reusable or saleable were dumped in the abbey's latrines.[16] The roof of the abbey church with its precious lead lining would have been quickly removed and along with the lead from the plumbing, smelted into ingots for ease of transportation. This could take quite a while – at Jervaulx Abbey in North Yorkshire it took four months – and may have taken place in the nave of the church. It seems that even the windows were deliberately smashed to wrench the glass from the lead came. The fuel used to smelt the lead may have included timber from the roof, wooden furnishings like misericords, even books from the library. Some of the abbey stone found in the village shows clear signs of burning that may have been the result of this process. Fragments of medieval glass that may have come from the abbey can be seen in the windows of the south aisle of St Leonard's church. A few other pieces were found in the excavation of 1989-92.

With the roof removed the whole building would also have become subject to the natural ravages of the weather. The usual practice was then to pull down the central crossing tower to ruin the church and it seems that the western part of the cloister garth was used as a storage area for parts of the abbey fabric that were recovered as a result. There was certainly considerable movement of materials around the precinct after the Dissolution. The stone, floor and roof tiles, timber and furnishings would have been sold to, or looted by locals to build houses and walls and repair roads. It is known that one of the richer Eynsham villagers, just seven years after the Dissolution, was a certain Master Pynnocke who was noted as 'bailiff and collector for monasteries' and was possibly the local official charged by the Crown with supervising the process.[17]

John London, the commissioner for Eynsham, had boasted to Cromwell in 1538 that he had demolished and defaced a friary so thoroughly as to make it extremely difficult for it ever to be re-established. In order to forestall any possible local opposition, Royal commissioners often supervised the process of destruction in person and/or brought in labourers from a different area who were not connected to the abbey in any way and thus less likely to be inhibited by any local sympathies for an old familiar building. It is known, for example, that a local man, 'Willouby of Einsham' was involved in the demolition of nearby Osney Abbey and was paid 20 shillings for taking its bell 'Great Tom' to St Frideswide's in Oxford.[18] Perhaps though, in Eynsham this caution was unnecessary as villagers may have been anxious not to miss out on the obvious benefits that would accrue to them. It may be that they would have justified their actions like one of those who participated in the destruction

---

[15] Richards P., *Eynsham: A Chronicle*, Eynsham History Group, Robert Boyd Publications 2005.

[16] Hardy A. and Dodd A. and Keevill G.D. et al., *Aelfric's Abbey – Excavations at Eynsham Abbey, Oxfordshire, 1989-92*, English Heritage. Published by Oxford University School of Archaeology, 2003.

[17] Atkins B., *Eynsham's Muster Roll of 1542, ER 17*, 2000. Interestingly, his will made in 1557 demonstrated his continuing Catholic sympathies as he bequeathed his *sowl to all mighty god, to our blessed ladie saynt Marie and to all the holye companie of heaven.*

[18] Gordon, op. cit., p. 148.

Figure 247. Part of the Corpus Christi Map of its Eynsham property, drawn by Henry Wilcocke, April 1615. CCC Oxford MS 533/1 f.9. By permission of the President and Fellows of Corpus Christi College, Oxford.

of Roche Abbey in Yorkshire. He famously protested: *Might I not as well as others have some profit of the spoil of the abbey? For I did see all would away; and therefore I did as others did.*[19]

A number of the 16th century properties in the village, including 'The Shrubbery', 'The Elms', 'Twelve Acre Farm' and 'Lord's Farm' incorporate re-used ashlar, fireplaces, fragments of carved stone and probably structural timbers from the abbey site.[20] Both 'Lord's Farm' and 'The Elms' appear on a map of Eynsham drawn for Corpus Christi College in 1615 (Figure 247).[21]

'The Elms' in particular has a number of re-cycled stone windows with four-centred heads which may have come from one of the abbey's domestic ranges (Figure 248).

Some carved stones are embedded in the fabric of 'The Elms' and there are numerous fragments of worked stone in the grounds.

By the 16th century, good quality large beams were becoming increasingly scarce in part because of the large-scale clearance of old forests and inadequate management of surviving woodland resulting in the premature felling of trees. In addition, much of the best timber

[19] Scarisbrick J.J., *The Reformation and the English People*, p. 70, Blackwell, 1984.
[20] A fireplace in 'Twelve Acre' Farm has some incised graffiti. According to W.H. Kelliher, curator of manuscripts at the British Library in 1996, it is part of a jingle often found in pen-trials in the flyleaves of 16th century manuscripts. It usually runs '[someone someone] is my name, and with my pen I wrote the same.' In this instance the word 'nife' is supplied in place of 'pen'. Kelliher's opinion was that the inscription could be as early as the 16th century.
[21] The map shows 'The Parke' as belonging to Sir Edward Standlake but this is a cartographer's error for Sir Edward Stanley (1562-1632) Lord of the Manor and probably the last resident of the site of Eynsham Abbey.

*Figure 248. Windows at 'The Elms',
Eynsham.*

was reserved for ship building. Whereas it is impossible to know exactly where re-cycled timber came from, many houses in the village have re-used oak beams and one house in Acre End Street contains a beam with unusually elaborate mouldings and an apotropaic motif that must originally have graced a high-status building (Figure 249). The same house

*Figure 249. Beam with apotropaic motif in a house in
Acre End Street, Eynsham.*

Figure 250. 'The Shrubbery', Eynsham. 15th century door frame.

Figure 251. 16th century cartouche built into the east wall of 'Abbey Stones', Abbey Street, Eynsham.

has fragments of columns and gothic tracery built into its inside walls which would support the idea of the beam's abbey provenance.

'The Shrubbery' in Oxford Road also has two large oak-planked doors, one with a late 15th/ early 16th century hood-moulding in wood which may have come from one of the abbey's buildings (Figure 250). A significant number of abbey stones from all periods of the abbey's history have recently (2019) been discovered in the garden of 'The Shrubbery' which would support the idea that the house was built from re-cycled materials.

On the corner of Abbey Street and Swan Street, lay the 'Old Farm', sometimes known, appropriately, as 'Abbey Stones'. Built into the east wall of what was the farmhouse is a stone carved with a small cartouche, within which is the date 1561 and the initials T.P. (Figure 251). Although it has been suggested that this was a later insertion in a much-altered fabric, it could well represent the date at which the building was originally constructed. Lying just opposite the inner precinct of the abbey, there are some fine ashlar blocks and a few barely visible decorated stones in its construction which almost certainly came from the demolished monastery. It has reasonably been suggested that the initials stand for Thomas Perkins of Eynsham who appears as one of the better off residents in the Muster Roll of 1542 and who left a will when he died in 1582.[22]

---

[22] Richards, op. cit. Alternatively, they could be the initials of Thomas Pynnock who, ironically, was the sole executor of the will of William Pinnock 'bailiff and collector for monasteries' referred to above.

Figure 252.   Black Friars Priory, Gloucester. Scriptorium.

In addition to jewels and plate and coin the king was also interested in books and John Leland, the first antiquarian of 'modern' times, was charged by Henry VIII with the task of finding old manuscripts in monastic libraries. He apparently discovered three at Eynsham[23] and four others have been identified as having belonged to Eynsham although not necessarily written or illuminated there. There must have been many in addition and it has been suggested that there were at least 240 books on the abbey's library shelves[24] although only one survives that clearly bears the mark of *St Mary of Eynsham*.[25] The position of the library and scriptorium at Eynsham is unknown but the latter may have been a separate building like that at Black Friars Priory in Gloucester (Figure 252) or had carrels built into the cloister as at the Cathedral in the same city (Figure 253).

Leland also made his 'Itinerary' of England between 1535 and 1543 and presented it to Henry VIII in 1546. Unfortunately, he does not describe Eynsham and the only reference to the abbey is a note that Robert D'Oyley, the founder of Osney Abbey, was buried there and that Eynsham was exchanged for Swillington, Yorkshire, by Sir George Darcy who passed it to

[23] John Leland (*De Rebus Britannicis Collectanea*, T. Hearne [ed.] Vol. 4: p. 161) describes them as: *Prosper de vita contemplativa et activa; Historia Huntingdunensis;* and *Gulielmus Meldunensis super trenos Hieremiae*. Gordon interprets these as: Prosper of Aquitaine, *Concerning the contemplative and the active life*, a popular monastic theme; Henry of Huntingdon, *History of the English*; William of Malmesbury, *Concerning the Lamentations of Jeremiah*.

[24] Hardy et al., op. cit., p. 12. A fragment of what may have been an Anglo-Saxon ivory book cover was found in the course of the excavation.

[25] *Bodl. MS Laud Lat 31*. 'liber sancte Marie de Eynesham'

Figure 253. Gloucester Cathedral. South walk of the cloister with carrels facing the garth. The late 14th/early 15th century fan vaulting is exceptional. The roof of Eynsham's cloister would have been much plainer

Figure 254. Conduit House, North Hinksey, (Oxon).

Sir Edward North in 1543.[26] North surrendered it to the Crown in 1545 and in the same year it was granted to Edward Stanley, Third Earl of Derby. He was distantly related to Henry VIII and had helped the king to put down the Pilgrimage of Grace. Another early antiquarian, William Camden (1551-1623), wrote in his book *Britannia* in 1586 that the *Abby...now is turned into a private dwelling house and acknowledgeth the Earle of Derby thereof*.[27]

Clearly, although much of the monastery may have been demolished, substantial parts of the abbey buildings and particularly the abbot's lodgings, kitchen and private chapel probably remained. The archaeology showed that the monk's kitchen was substantially remodelled to suit the more modest demands on its use and that part of the domestic range was probably retained too. Other buildings and cellars appear to have been used for the disposal of rubbish. The Corpus Christi map of 1615 shows the Conduit House still standing and presumably supplying water to the kitchen and other parts of the abbey site. Situated at the junction of Conduit Lane and Back Lane the well house was probably stone built and may have looked something like that at North Hinksey which dates to the early 17th century (Figure 254). The field to the west of central Eynsham was still described as Conduit Field in Thomas Pride's map of 1769.

[26] Leland J., *Itinerary*, Lucy Toulmin Smith (ed.), Centaur Press Ltd, 1964.
[27] Wright L., The Stanleys in Eynsham, *ER* 2, 1985.

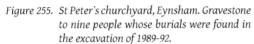

Figure 255. St Peter's churchyard, Eynsham. Gravestone to nine people whose burials were found in the excavation of 1989-92.

The Stanley family appear to have used the abbey on and off for about a century and, as 'papists', may have been responsible for preserving more of the buildings than would otherwise have been the case. They may also have allowed the secret burial of three recusants, Catholics who refused to attend the Church of England, within the half-demolished abbey. Their remains were found by archaeologists in the late 20th century and in June 2012, appropriately reburied in St Peter's Roman Catholic churchyard with the remains of six others, presumed to be monks of the abbey (Figure255).[28]

The wreckage of the great abbey church, increasingly overgrown, must have made a sorry sight and brings to mind the reference in one of Shakespeare's sonnets to *Bare ruin'd choirs, where late the sweet birds sang.* Indeed, it is just possible that the bard could have visited Eynsham on his journeys between Stratford and London via Oxford and interestingly, one of the printers of Shakespeare's early work was the Eynsham born John Danter.[29]

What may be an early illustration of the post-Reformation abbey was made in the 1590s as part of the Ralph Sheldon Tapestry Map of Oxfordshire (Figure 256). Such representations were often little more than symbolic and rarely based on actual observation. However, the image does appear to show the surviving western towers of the abbey church, the parish church, some ruinous structures and a large domestic structure with outbuildings which may be the residence of the Stanleys converted from the abbot's house and some of the other parts of the monastery.

---

[28] Father Martin Flatman arranged the service and was also responsible for setting out the abbey trail in the churchyards of St Peter's and St Leonard's in 2011.

[29] Rogers J.K., 'Enisham...was my birthplace' The Life and Career of a Sixteenth Century London Printer, ER 12, 1995.

Figure 256. Part of the Ralph Sheldon Tapestry Map of Oxfordshire. Bodleian Library, University of Oxford. ©V&A Images. Printed in Turner H.L., No Mean Prospect: Ralph Sheldon's Tapestry Maps, Plotwood Press, 2010.

Later, in 1647, John Aubrey, antiquary, natural philosopher and would-be scholar wrote that some of the locals told him that the abbey had contained *a worlde of painted Glasse, Stones, Coates of Armes etc. There were curious buildings, excellent carved wainscot and wainscot ceilings guilded: a curious Chapelle.*[30] In a narrative of his own life he rather wistfully remarked that he *wished monasteries had not been put down.* In his account of the career of the famous beauty Venetia Stanley, who lived at Eynsham Abbey in the early 17th century, Aubrey notes that *At the west end of the church here were two towers as at Wells or Westminster Abbey, which were standing till about 1656. The rooms of the abbey were richly wainscoted, both sides and roof.*[31] He later wrote, in 1684, that the two towers were on the ground.

The wood panelling he refers to may well have been taken to decorate the walls of a nearby residence in the same way that the linenfold panelling from Notley Abbey (Bucks) was acquired by Weston Manor, north of Oxford. Likewise, the carved panelling in the hall of Magdalen College, Oxford, is said to have come from Reading Abbey after the Dissolution. A house in Mill Street, Eynsham, which probably dates to the 17th century, has some quite elaborate panels of similar form which could indeed have come from the abbey as a result of the second stage of demolition (Figure 257).

Aubrey's erstwhile friend and fellow antiquary Anthony Wood actually visited Eynsham and his 'kinsman' Thomas Barncote on 16th September 1657.[32] Whilst there he made a rough sketch of what remained of the abbey church at the time (see chapter 3). Wood was *wonderfully strucken with a veneration of the stately, yet much lamented, ruins of the abbey there, built before the Norman Conquest. He saw then there two high towers at the west end of the church, and some of the north walls of the church standing. He spent some time with a melancholy delight in taking a prospect of the ruins of that place. All which, together with the entrance or the lodg, were soon after pul'd downe, and the stones sold to build houses in that towne and neare it. The place hath yet some ruins to shew, and to instruct the pensive beholder with an exemplary frailty.*[33] In a note of 1658 he adds that *about 20 yeares agoe was a pardon of the pope found in digging in some of the*

---

[30] The word curious here means skilfully wrought, fine or noteworthy.
[31] Aubrey J., *Brief Lives*, Folio Society, London 1975.
[32] Atkins B., John Whiting's Survey of Eynsham, 1650, *ER* 6, 1989. Barncote or Barncott seems to have lived in Mill Street and had been prosecuted and excommunicated for burying one of the recusants referred to above in 1630.
[33] *Bodl. MS Rawl. D 97*, 'The Diarie of the Life of Anthony á Wood Historiographer of the most famous Universitie of Oxford.'

ruins of Ensham Abby Oxon, and was sent to the earl of Derby, lord of that mannor.

It would seem that by the late 1630s the Stanleys had abandoned the site although it remained formally in their hands until 1649 when James, Earl of Derby was deprived of the manor as *a delinquent in armes against the Parliament.* It was given by Cromwell to Henry Marten MP of Beckett in Berkshire, one of the regicides, who in turn sold it on in 1651. The

Figure 257. Detail of linenfold panelling in a house in Mill Street, Eynsham.

archaeology points to some further demolition occurring at this time. The abbey passed through several hands until 1657 when the manor of Eynsham and site of the monastery was bought by a wool merchant, Thomas Jordan of Witney, for £4950. The Jordan family held the estate until 1718 and seem to have been responsible for the abbey's final demise shortly after Wood's visit.[34]

Wood's reference to the second phase of the demolition of the abbey is supported by some fragmentary accounts (Figure 258) bound into the Court books for Eynsham, which obviously relate to the sale of building materials from the abbey and were probably made by the manor's bailiff in the late 1650s.[35]

The accounts include large quantities of walling stones at 1s a load or 1d a foot, joists, rafters and boards. Some of the latter may have included the panelling referred to above. There were also windows, doors and doorposts, timber and a table from *the greate hall* which sold for 10s-6d. A Charlbury carpenter paid £14 for six bays of the stables, the remainder of which were removed in 1802 by the Duke of Marlborough demonstrating that they must have been quite extensive.[36] Interestingly, there were in addition a large number of bricks sold for 2s per 100, indicating the construction of possible outbuildings in the late 15th or early 16th centuries. Although the materials could have been sold to anybody in the area, a number of purchasers were clearly locals including Richard Wastie who paid 6s for *100 boards,* John Paty, the smith, who paid £2-8s for a *parcel of timber,* James Quaterman who paid 14s-8d for two *transoms* and Mr Wood who paid the huge sum of £4-19s for *18 loads of*

---

[34] 'Notes on the History of Eynsham or Some Account of the History of Eynsham,' Unpublished, undated typescripts c. 1930, possibly by the wife of the local doctor, Mrs Cruikshank.
[35] Oxfordshire History Centre, Oxford. Palm 1/i ff 1-3.
[36] Crossley A., *Victoria History of the County of Oxford*, Vol. XII: pp. 98-157 OUP 1990. University of London Institute of Historical Research.

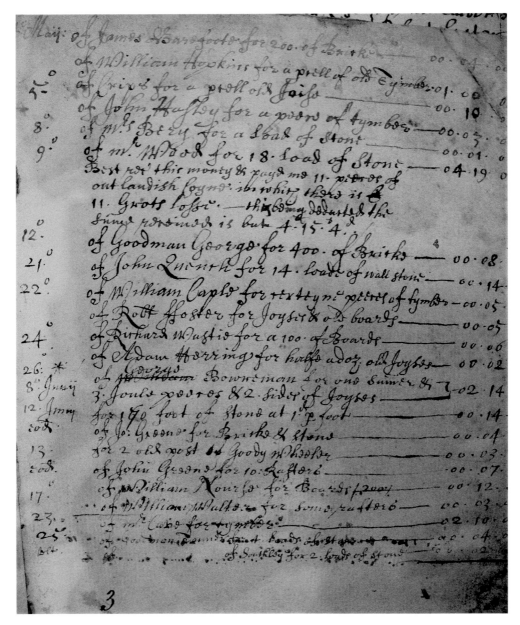

Figure 258. Page 3 of the manorial accounts of the sale of abbey materials.
Courtesy of The Oxfordshire History Centre Palm 1/i ff. 1-3.

stone. Many of those mentioned were also noted in Whiting's Survey of Eynsham,[37] 1650, and in the parish Registers which survive from 1653.

---

[37] Oxfordshire History Centre, Oxford, *Palm IV.*

Figure 259. Hardwick Mill, Hardwick (Oxon). Part of an abbot's tomb slab in the mill race.

The accounts are written in cursive script on three sides of vellum and are clearly part of a larger sequence as there are references to previous purchases which are not included. There are also some faint sub totals which may be amounts to be carried forward and there are the hands of several different persons. All of which would seem to indicate that the sale of the remaining abbey fabric was a piecemeal affair, spread over several months or even years, presumably reflecting the gradual demolition of the abbey structures and the preparation of saleable materials.[38]

The west front of the abbey church, the inner gatehouse, the remains of the cloister and the abbot's house and kitchen were the main targets. Even the tomb slabs of medieval Eynsham abbots were not immune as a number have been found locally: a fragmentary one at Hardwick Mill (Figure 259), possibly that of Thomas de Wells, abbot from 1281 to 1307,[39] and another of John of Cheltenham, abbot from 1317 to 1330, in the vestry of Elsfield church (Figure 260), reused by a certain Michael Pudsey in 1645.[40] Yet another was used to patch the floor of St Leonard's Parish church until it was taken up in the 1820s (Figure 122).

[38] Parrinder S., Eynsham Abbey – The Final Accounts, *ER* 32, 2015.
[39] Gordon E., Adventure at Hardwick Mill, *ER* 1, 1984.
[40] Bainbridge W., Looking for Abbots, *ER* 1, 1984. The stone, with its inscription complete and without the later dedication, was drawn by J.C. Buckler in 1820 when it was in the chancel at Elsfield. *Bodl. MS Top Oxon f. 232.* Sometime after, the stone was moved to the vestry and badly hacked at one end to fit the floor. The inscription reads HIC: IACET: FRATER: IOHANNES: DE: CHILTENHAM: QUONDAM: ABBAS: HUIUS: LOCI: CUIUS: ANIME: PROPITIETUR: DEUS: which translates as 'Here lies John of Cheltenham sometime Abbot of this place. May God have mercy on his soul'.

Figure 260. St Thomas of Canterbury, Elsfield (Oxon). Tomb slab of Abbot John of Cheltenham in the vestry. W. Bainbridge ©EHG.

All three would have come from what had been the floor of the abbey chancel, near the high altar and there must have been many others.

The Abbey Farm site seems to have been used as a breaking yard during this phase of the demolition of the remaining abbey buildings and it is possible that at least some of the farm buildings were subjected to the same process or partially rebuilt with better quality stone obtained from the abbey.[41] Some of the worked stone found in the vicinity of Abbey Farm Barns show clear signs of being roughly hacked to provide a more usable construction material.

Many villagers in the late 17th and early 18th centuries seem to have again seized the opportunity created by this ready supply of accessible building materials to rebuild or extend their properties. One house in Acre End Street has a wooden beam over the inglenook fireplace with the date 1659 and the letters AMI contained within a roughly carved shield (Figure 261). The beam may well have come from one of the surviving abbey buildings and the date is surely instructive.

Even foundation layers of stone were removed from the abbey site at this time as the later excavations make clear. This process was given added impetus by the outbreak of fires in Eynsham in 1681, 1696 and 1710.[42] The first, according to Anthony Wood, resulted in *about 20 houses burnt*.[43] That of 1696 destroyed a substantial part of Newland Street which has

---

[41] Moore J. Heritage Services, *An Archaeological Watching Brief at Abbey Farm Barns, Station Road, Eynsham, Oxfordshire, February 2013*.

[42] Richards D., An Eynsham Fire in 1696, ER 3, 1986.

[43] Anthony Wood, *Life and Times*, quoted in Cruikshank Mrs, Notes on the History of Eynsham or Some Account of the History of Eynsham Unpublished, undated typescripts c. 1930.

Figure 261. Fireplace beam in a house in Acre End Street, Eynsham.

yielded many of the abbey stones discussed above and that of 1710 was estimated to have resulted in the loss of property worth the enormous sum of £1474-11s-6d.[44] Quite a number of houses in the village date to the period during or just after the abbey's final destruction and, like the owner of the lintel above, some were sufficiently proud of their achievements to insert stones with their initials and dates into their walls. For example, in Queen's Lane there is a house with the date 1658 or 1668 and the initials RC, possibly Richard Castle who bought a quantity of material from the demolished abbey. Similarly, the thatched cottage in Church Street where a number of abbey stones have been found, has the date 1725 and the initials K I S.

The houses and barns on the south-westerly part of Mill Street were mostly built in the late 17th and early 18th centuries and unsurprisingly perhaps, the area was re-named Abbey Street. Both the 'Swan Hotel' and the 'Jolly Sportsman' date to the same period. The former became the venue for Eynsham manor courts whilst the latter was converted into a pub in the late 19th century.[45] The so-called 'Old Manor House' on the north eastern corner of Lombard Street and Acre End Street is another example of this re-building activity. According to John Whiting's Survey of Eynsham of 1650 the site was occupied by Mr Green who ran a pub there called 'The Green Dragon'. In the accounts of the sale of construction materials referred to above, John Greene paid four shillings for several loads of brick and

[44] Kebell G., A Very Late Afterthought on an Eynsham Fire, *ER* 4, 1987.
[45] Crossley, op. cit., p. 108.

stone and seven shillings for ten rafters.[46] The building he constructed contained many abbey stones in the walls, fireplaces and stone windows (See chapter 15). 'The Gables', 'Home Farm' and 'New Wintles' also date to this time. It wasn't just Eynsham villagers who used the abbey as a quarry. Others came from South Leigh and, as already mentioned, from as far away as Charlbury to pick at the remains of Eynsham's once famous abbey.

A contemporary and acquaintance of Wood was the antiquary William Dugdale (1605-1686). Dugdale evidently saw Wood's drawing and in his most famous work *Monasticon Anglicanum,* written between 1655 and 1673, notes that all that survived of the abbey were *some old foundations and a gatehouse.* The memory of this once important building rapidly faded thereafter, so much so that some locals apparently believed that the site was that of a former castle.[47] It would be another 300 years before serious attempts were made to rescue it from obscurity.

---

[46] In his *Parochial Collections*, Anthony Wood describes a monument in the churchyard to a John Greene who died in 1652. If this is the same man referred to above, it would date the accounts and the start of the final destruction of the abbey buildings to an earlier period than first thought.

[47] Hardy et al., op. cit., p. 520. Rev. Symonds for example described how 'In 1824 in digging for gravel in the meadows south of the churchyard, we found in every direction the remains of old buildings and foundations which I at first imagined to have been offices belonging to the Abbey but which I have now every reason to suppose to have been the site of the castle.' We now know of course that his first thoughts were correct. There never was a castle at Eynsham.

Chapter 14

Rediscovery

'There's a fascination frantic
In a ruin that's romantic'[1]

To modern eyes, the destruction of over 800 monastic houses like that at Eynsham can stir feelings of desolation for what seems like the wanton and mindless spoliation of beautiful buildings and their artistic treasures. Moreover, despite the fact that the Dissolution amounted to the greatest redistribution of land since the Norman Conquest, there seemed to be minimal resistance to the process at the time. Instead, individuals took the chance to enrich themselves and use the abbey sites as convenient quarries. In part, this careless attitude might have reflected the fact that monasticism was on its last legs; that it no longer played a useful part in the community and that its supposed spiritual role lacked credibility.[2] The growth of nationalism and Protestantism also contributed to this indifference. Monasticism was associated with Catholicism, the old 'superstitious' faith which owed allegiance to a foreign power based in Rome. In many people's minds, Roman Catholicism became identified with treason and, after the reigns of Charles I and James II, with tyranny as well.

Furthermore, with the exception of a few of the educated elite like Wood and Aubrey, most people were not 'past-centred' as many in England tend to be today. Old buildings were often viewed as 'mean' and contemporary architectural achievements such as the re-birth of Classicism more worthy of focus. It is perhaps not surprising that the very word used to describe much medieval architecture, 'gothic', was, initially at least, a derogatory term used to describe the works of a barbarous culture that had destroyed Roman civilization and ushered in the 'Dark Ages'. These prejudices were slow to fade and interest in historical ruins remained the preserve of a small number.

One of the exceptions, and a frequent visitor to Eynsham in the early 18th century, was the historian and diarist Thomas Hearne (1678-1735). He was based at Oxford University and for 16 years was assistant librarian at the Bodleian. He edited many of the medieval English chroniclers and his extensive diary was entitled *Remarks and Collections*. On a visit to the village in 1706 he noted that Eynsham Abbey was supposed to have had 52 fishponds, one for every week in the year, a fact that he mistakenly believed to be true because of the various *Holes near to ye Place where the Monastery stood...Now nothing is left but an outer gate on the West side which however in some measure shews it to have been a stately place.*[3]

---

[1] W.S. Gilbert, The Mikado, Glinert E. (ed.), *The Savoy Operas: The Complete Gilbert and Sullivan*, Penguin Classics, 2008. The section in this chapter on Thomas Hearne was largely printed in the *Eynsham Record* 33, 2016.
[2] Elton G.R., *England Under the Tudors*, The Folio Society, 1997.
[3] Hearne T., Diaries published as Remarks and Collections, Oxford Historical Society. Quoted by P. Richards in *Eynsham: A Chronicle*, Eynsham History Group, Robert Boyd Publications, 2005.

Figure 262. Sketch by Thomas Hearne 8 November 1713 of the outer, west gate, of the abbey precinct. The Bodleian Library, University of Oxford, MS Hearne's Diaries Vol. 50, 1714 p. 221.

This last comment would seem to confirm that the *entrance or the lodg* which Wood stated had been torn down shortly after his visit, was the gateway to the abbey's inner precinct which would have stood on the east side of the present Abbey Street close to the junction with Abbey Place. The *outer gate* Hearne refers to must have stood on Station Road, at the junction with Abbey Farm Barns, built after the extension of the original precinct by Abbot Adam in the 13th century and the closure of the old road to Stanton Harcourt by making Abbey Street a cul-de-sac. At the end of his Diaries for 1714, Hearne made a very scrappy doodle with the title *'1713 Nov. 8th at Eynsham. The Abbey Gate as I stood about a Furlong from It, on ye East Side.'* (Figure 262). He would therefore have been standing roughly in Abbey Street and would not have been able to make out much detail.[4]

Nevertheless, the scale of the gateway was sufficient to cause Hearne to believe the abbey itself was *stately* and although crude, the drawing does appear to show a roofed, pinnacled building. It had a large gothic arch of several orders and a tunnel passageway for horses and carts which had been filled with *modern stone* to create a wall. A lower arch for pedestrians on the north side was also gothic and may originally have had a twin arch on the south side as Hearne notes that the wall that abutted it was modern. In basic shape it may have looked something like the late 15th century western gateway of Abingdon Abbey although Eynsham's gate, with its pinnacles, seems more elaborate and more akin to the 14th century gateway to the Vicar's Close in Wells (Figure 263). A famous local resident, Hercules Humphries who died in September 1800 in his 102nd year, claimed that he could remember the gatehouse Hearne described but gave no further details.[5]

---

[4]   *Bodl. MS Hearne's Diaries Vol. 50, 1714.*
[5]   *Bodl. MS Top Oxon b 275*, Rev Thomas Symonds Collection.

Figure 263. *14th century gateway to the Vicar's Close in Wells (Somerset).*

Hearne also noted that *About a Furlong from the Gate Eastwards some Remains of an Out Housething. 'Tis now a barn and they commonly call it the Abbey-Barn, and the Ground between this House and the Gate (as I was informed by a Country Man whom I met) is now to this Day called the Abbey* (Figure 264). The barn must be the large stone-roofed building running east to west on the corner of Abbey Street and Abbey Farm Barns, No.3 of the 2012 development. Parts of this structure are believed to be medieval, possibly 13th century, and the remains of early buttresses, such as are found on larger barns, exist on its south side. It may have formed part of the abbey tithe barn like that at Great Coxwell (Figure 265).

However, after the Dissolution much of Eynsham Abbey's barn was demolished and Hearne's sketch may show just the remaining part of what was originally a much larger building. Indeed, the enclosure map of 1802 seems to show that even at that date the barn extended further to the west than it does now. Later still, after Hearne, a large extension running north to south was added to the barn at its south-west end. A rather childish representation of the earlier building was included by Hearne which shows a large rectangular structure with a projecting gabled porch on one side, presumably for carts, and a window or hay loft. The sketch must have been taken from the north, from the current driveway of Abbey Farm. The large opening has been preserved as a full height window but the hay loft has disappeared,

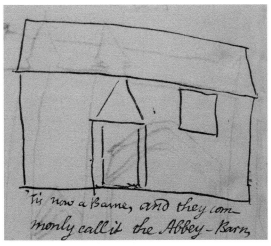

Figure 264. *Sketch by Thomas Hearne in 1713 of the Abbey Barn. The Bodleian Library, University of Oxford, MS Hearne's Diaries Vol. 50, 1714 p.222.*

Figure 265. Great Coxwell (Berks).
Tithe barn.

presumably when the extension was added later in the 18th century. The existing small window is a recent addition.

Abbey Farm and its associated lands was acquired by the Dukes of Marlborough after 1718 and remained as part of their estates until 1922. According to Hearne, he was told in 1727 that one of their tenants at Eynsham, a certain Richard Goddard, *hath over the door of his House an old Stone, supposed to have come from the Abbey of Eynsham, upon which is an Angel, holding an escutcheon, on which escutcheon are four Saxon letters.*[6] Some 143 years later, in 1870, the artist Alfred F. Cobb drew the figure, which had been incorporated into a gateway in the garden of Eynsham's Vicarage in Mill Street in the early 19th century.[7] The stone (Figure 206) was donated by the vicar to the Oxfordshire Museum in 1974 and is currently stored at the Museum Resources Centre at Standlake. Despite Hearne's belief, there are no *Saxon letters* visible but some plant forms, possibly fleur-de-lys or thistles, with intertwined rings below. Cobb attributed the coat of arms to Miles Salley, Abbot of Eynsham *c.* 1497-1516 and from 1500 also Bishop of Llandaff, and there are resemblances to a coat of arms in Standlake church which has also been described as those of Salley.[8]

At the same time that he drew the abbey gate, Hearne made a rough sketch of St Leonard's parish church (Figure 266). Although it is clear that Hearne was no artist, the body of the church, with the different heights for the roof of the nave and chancel, the corner buttresses, and the number and disposition of the doors and windows, is basically accurate.

---

[6] Richards P., op.cit.
[7] *Bodl. MS Top Oxon d 514.*
[8] Cooper H.C.D., Eynsham Armorial, *Oxoniensia* XXXVII, 1972. If indeed the upper register of the coat of arms contains thistles it may well be related to the coat of arms on 'Twelve Acre' farmhouse - see chapter 15. This raises the possibility that the date of the 'Eynsham Angel' is later than thought, although it may be that Salley's Arms were carved on the existing shield at a later date.

Figure 266. Sketch by Thomas Hearne in 1713 of St Leonards Church, Eynsham. The Bodleian Library, University of Oxford, MS Hearne's Diaries Vol. 50, 1714 p.220.

The fact that he only drew the door and the eastern window of the chancel is explained by his statement that the view was taken *from ye South West*. The two westernmost windows of the chancel would have been obscured by the body of the nave and were only visible when *standing exactly South*. He clearly chose his viewpoint in order to show the full extent of the tower and as a result he reveals an intriguing detail.

On the outside of the west end of the church he shows a large multi-arched tunnel structure with steps which seems to either abut the tower or be part of its lower storey. Could this be the remains of the northern gateway to the abbey precinct which has since disappeared or incorporated into the west end of the church as has been suggested? [9]

The surviving records for St Leonard's are not particularly helpful in this regard. The churchwarden's accounts for the period 1775 to 1864 still exist but are often rather vague about what monies were spent on. Clearly there were regular payments for repairs to the structure of the church and expenditure per year on these and other things usually amounted to about £10. However, in 1786 the exceptional sum of £59-17s-2½d was spent on building works to the church. Three years later, another substantial bill for £49-5s-6½d was paid, again for repairing the roof of the church and tower and a new door to the latter was inserted in 1790. Could these works be related to a westward extension to the church

---

[9]   Chambers R.A., Eynsham Abbey Excavations, *ER* 7, 1990.

which resulted in the tower arches being incorporated into the main body?[10] The existing west wall of the nave is certainly of a different construction from the rest of St Leonard's. Built of extremely rough un-coursed rubble, it looks very much like a later cheap addition.

Unlike most of the church, the tower is built of ashlar masonry and is unusually placed for a medieval church, being attached to the north-west corner of the north aisle. The majority of churches with western towers have them on the same axis as the nave. On the other hand, it was not uncommon practice for abbeys to construct chapels for their servants, guests and parishioners adjoining one of the gateways to the abbey precinct. Such was the case at Reading (St Lawrence), at Abingdon (St Nicholas), and at Osney, (St Nicholas). Interestingly, in his discussion of a bird's eye view painting of Eynsham 'ca 1780', the local historian Brian Atkins commented that St Leonard's church tower 'appears to be a separate edifice to the north!'[11] This adds credence to the idea that the tower may originally have served a different purpose. The extensive medieval graffiti on the tower arch would also support the proposition.[12]

Lastly, when the church was restored in 1892, 'some proposed alterations, notably the reopening of the tower archways, were not carried out.'[13] All of which seems to substantiate the suggestion that at least the base of the tower might have formed the original northern gateway from the town into the abbey precinct. It might also be that it served a dual purpose from the beginning, being both a gateway to the abbey and the belfry of the parish church, much like the Norman tower of St Edmund's Abbey at Bury in Suffolk. In which case, Eynsham's tower gatehouse would be the only significant survival of the abbey *in situ*, unwittingly drawn by Hearne in 1713.[14]

Another traveller to Eynsham, later in the 18th century, was John Byng, Viscount Torrington. On 5 July 1785, he noted that he *walk'd down Eynsham Hill, wonder'd at the new steep bridge and enquired in the village concerning the old abbey of an intelligent barber...a man of reading and remark. He bade me observe the town house, and the cross behind it, on which are monastic figures; and then guided me to where the abbey stood and, till within these few years, a fine old gateway of approach, which the Duke of Marlborough pull'd down for some business at Blenheim: I should like him to read this page, to feel ashamed and to know that such pieces of antiquity are as enviable gems as any he possesses.*[15] This would seem to be indicative of the growing curiosity about the visible remains of our history amongst people who were not academics and antiquaries. However, Byng's righteous indignation at the vandalising of our heritage rings a little hollow when it is realised that just a few days later, whilst in Stratford, he bought a slice of *Shakespeare's old chair* and stole a tessellated tile *from the Roman pavement at the head of Shakespeare's gravestone* in the church.

---

[10] Oxfordshire History Centre, *PAR 100/3/F1/2*.
[11] Atkins B., 'A View of Ensham ca. 1780', *ER* 16, 1999.
[12] Parrinder S., Graffiti in St Leonard's Church, *ER* 32, 2015.
[13] Crossley A., *Victoria History of the County of Oxford* Vol. XII: p. 150, OUP 1990. University of London Institute of Historical Research.
[14] Parrinder S., Thomas Hearne's Eynsham, *ER* 33, 2016.
[15] Byng J., *Rides Round Britain*, Adamson D. (ed.), Folio Society, London, 1996.

The gate Byng was referring to must be the one described by Dugdale in the late 17th century and by Hearne in the early 18th century. What happened to it thereafter is a mystery as there is no sign of it at Blenheim and, despite 'a fairly detailed search', the archivist there was unable to find a reference to it in the papers that remain at Blenheim.[16] Recent (2013) excavations of service trenches at the junction of Station Road and Abbey Farm Barns showed no evidence of footings for the gate. Rather ominously, the architect Sir William Chambers wrote to the Fourth Duke recommending that for the sake of economy he could use old stone for building a gate at Blenheim.[17] What could be simpler than to use the old gate that stood on his property in Eynsham as a core for a new one?

Despite the Duke of Marlborough's apparently cavalier attitude, there were signs in the 18th century of a change in approach to the remains of medieval buildings. The so-called 'Gothick Revival' became fashionable in certain circles. This resulted in the rather dilettante gothicisation of houses and the construction of sham ruins or follies as picturesque eye-catchers in the landscape. Indeed, Eynsham's western gate may have been taken by 'Capability' Brown for his plans to build a number of gothicised buildings in the park at Blenheim, although none actually materialised. Gothic architecture seemed to have lost some of its previous connotations and medieval decoration, particularly battlements and pointed arches, was increasingly seen as more romantic and interesting by comparison with the severity and symmetry of Classical architecture.

The art historian Nikolaus Pevsner dismissed much of this gothicisation as 'incorrect ornament incorrectly applied'[18] but it represented the beginning of a widening admiration for the artefacts of the past and a belief that they should not just be visited but preserved and recorded. This process was facilitated by the steadily improving transport links which enabled an increasing number of people to experience the surviving glories of medieval architecture around the country. In the next century the Gothic Revival became more accurate and serious and imbued by some with a high moral purpose. Knowledge of medieval architectural detail was also more archaeologically based.

A new class of wealth creators and accumulators emerged as a consequence of the industrial revolution that needed an architectural aesthetic to distinguish themselves from the old classically educated aristocracy. The fashion for medievalism continued throughout the 19th and early 20th centuries, in part perhaps as a reaction to the devastation and squalor inflicted on the country by uncontrolled industrialisation and urbanisation. Medieval rural England came to be regarded as some kind of golden age, to be valued and conserved as part of our inalienable heritage.[19] Moreover, the narrow identification of medievalism with popery and sedition disappeared and there was a developing interest and respect for our 'catholic' inheritance in the broader sense.

One indication of this growing interest was the production of prints of abbeys and castles sometimes bound into books such as the following hand coloured version of S. and N. Bucks

[16] John Forster letter to the author, 26/8/14.
[17] *British Library Add Mss 41, 133 f.5.*
[18] Pevsner N. and Sherwood J., *The Buildings of England - Oxfordshire*, Introduction. Penguin Books, 1974.
[19] Strong R., *Lost Treasures of Britain*, Guild Publishing, 1990.

Figure 267. Mid-19th century hand coloured print of S. and N. Bucks tidied up copy of Anthony Wood's original sketch of the Abbey ruins in 1657. A gift to the author.

tidied up copy of Anthony Wood's sketch which probably dates to the mid-19th century (Figure 267). This romanticised version has managed to gothicise some of the tower arches, transform blind arcades into open windows, install the bases of the nave walls and move the north aisle of the abbey church 90° to the west. For aesthetic effect, a large hill has appeared in the Witney region to the west which bears an uncanny resemblance to Wytham woods in the east. Nevertheless, this rendering of Wood's original misled Pevsner, and others, about the nature of Eynsham Abbey's architecture.[20]

Likewise, an increasing number of pictorial records of old buildings were made by painters and illustrators. In the early 19th century, perhaps the most prolific and famous of these was the artist and sometime architect John Buckler (1770-1851). He visited Eynsham several times and one of his drawings, made in 1813 is particularly interesting. This was of a doorway, 'conceivably from a vestry door of the abbey church',[21] although equally it could have come from any of the abbey buildings, built into a cottage that stood on the south-west corner of Swan Street at its junction with Station Road (Figure 268). The gateway was sometime afterwards reconstructed at the entrance to the back garden of the Vicarage in Mill Street, possibly in the 1840s.[22]

Indeed, one of the 19th century incumbents of St Leonard's, the Reverend Thomas Symonds (1773-1845), polymath antiquarian, curate and then vicar of Eynsham between 1796 and 1845, clearly had a passion for collecting medieval stone as the Vicarage garden became

---

[20]   Nairn I. and Pevsner N., *The Buildings of England – Surrey, Introduction*, Penguin Books, 1971.

[21]   Eynsham Conservation Area Advisory Committee, *Eynsham, A Mediaeval Town by the Thames* CAAC, 1984.

[22]   Bainbridge believed that the gateway came from the north wall of the house known as 'Abbey Stones' at the junction of Swan Street and Abbey Street but Buckler's attribution is accepted.

Figure 268. John Buckler's drawing, made in 1813, of a doorway built into a cottage that stood on the south-west corner of Swan Street at its junction with Station Road. The Bodleian Library, University of Oxford, MS Top Oxon a 66 f. 250.

littered with worked and carved pieces from all periods.[23] The provenance of most of it is unknown although given the size and weight of some of the pieces the chances are that they were either found on the abbey site, possibly as a result of grave digging, or in other parts of Eynsham.

The origin of one slab was described by Symonds for, *about the year 1826 a stone in the aisle of Ensham Church, being of a soft material was nearly worn thro, and was taken up to make the Pavement even, when it proved to be a Grave Stone of one of the Abbots without Doubt. The Cross Fleury on Top is of Norman workmanship. It is now in the Front Court of the Vicarage* (Figure 122).

In his extensive scrapbook/notebook Symonds included a passage from Watson's *History of Kidlington* (1815) in which he noted the *elegant shaft of the cross at Ensham. I know of no other of this once magnificent monastery except the rude capital of a pillar with a date in the stone work 1484 surmounted by a stone escutcheon with supporters preserved in the Vicar's Garden.* It is not known what this stone actually looked like or its current whereabouts but the gravestone referred to by Symonds was donated in 1974, with a number of other stones, to the County Museum in Woodstock by the vicar of St Leonard's, Rev. J.W.G. Westwood.[24] These have now mostly been transferred to the Museum Resources Centre at Standlake.

In 1890, the Vicarage garden was pictured by Henry Taunt (1842-1922), the famous Oxford photographer (Figure 269). Taunt's photo shows 'Buckler's' gate surmounted by a coat of arms which has been attributed to the Chandos family, explained by the fact that Anne, daughter of William Stanley, Earl of Derby, married Grey Bridges, Lord Chandos.[25] Corbels and gargoyles were built into the piers on either side of the arch with what looks like a small Romanesque capital resting next to the coat of arms. In the foreground are fragments

[23] Parrinder S., Thomas Symonds – Antiquary Vicar of Eynsham, ER 36, 2019
[24] Hockedy D., 'The Mystery of Eynsham Cross', ER 23, 2006.
[25] Crossley A., *Victoria History of the County of Oxford* Vol. XII: pp. 98-157 OUP 1990. University of London Institute of Historical Research.

Figure 269. Henry Taunt's 1890 photo of the garden of Eynsham Vicarage. © English Heritage Archive, Swindon. CC56/00796

of stonework including sections of quatrefoil pillars, springers for a vault, column pieces, octagonal capitals, a small cinquefoil headed window, column bases, at least one large decorated Norman capital and a roughly pyramidical stone with a rosette and two 'nail-head' motifs.

There are two other gateways to the right and left of the ogee arch, overgrown with ivy but of similar character and possibly removed from the abbey site in the 19th century. Above the left hand gate is the Anglo-Saxon panel referred to in Chapter 2. The right-hand gate, cobbled together with other disparate bits of stone, appears to be the one drawn in *Eynsham Old Rectory* by Alfred F. Cobb in *c.* 1870 (Figure 270).[26] It shows a stone doorway with cusped tracery in the spandrels surrounded by a squared drip mould. Above the door and cutting into the drip mould is the figure of an angel holding a coat of arms which must be the same figure noted by Hearne some 143 years earlier.[27] Above the doorway is a pediment with a large cusped oval (Figure 161) and, either side, two heraldic beasts. Surmounting the whole is a fragmentary finial similar to the pyramidical stone shown on the ground in Taunt's photo.

---

[26] *Bodl. MS Top Oxon d 514 f27b.*
[27] The editors of Dugdale's *Monasticon Anglicanum* noted that by 1819 'a small doorway and a shield, with the date 1504 (had been) placed in the vicarage garden.'

Figure 270. Drawing made at 'Eynsham Old Rectory' by Alfred F. Cobb in c. 1870. The Bodleian Library, University of Oxford, MS Top Oxon d 514 f. 27b.

In the 19th century more of the material remains of Eynsham Abbey began to be revealed. In the 1850s, a certain Mr Joseph Day was planting trees in the area east of St Leonard's Church cemetery known as Nursery Field. He came across a large number of decorated floor tiles, human bones and steps leading to a stone lined cistern, fed from a spring by a shallow stone-lined drain. According to his own account he also discovered a very large iron key and *a figure, the head and arms of which were gold and weighed seventeen guineas.*[28] The remainder of the figure was made of leather but no more details are known and its whereabouts is a mystery.

Some abbey tiles survive and one, noted by Mr Day, shows a mounted knight charging into battle and is on display in the Ashmolean Museum (Figure 271). Another, of the same design, was built into the hall floor of a house in Acre End Street. Some fragmentary tiles are stored in the parish church (Figure 272) and others remain in the possession of villagers such as the one displayed below (Figure 273). Unfortunately, cart loads of tiles were sold in the 19th century for use as hardcore.[29] Similar tiles of the charging knight can be found at Romsey Abbey

Figure 271. Eynsham Abbey tile on display in the Ashmolean.

---

[28] Gray M. and Clayton N., Excavations on the site of Eynsham Abbey, 1971, *Oxoniensia*, Vol. XLIII, 1978.
[29] Crossley, op. cit.

Figure 272. Fragmentary Eynsham Abbey tiles kept
at St Leonard's Church, Eynsham.

Figure 273. Eynsham Abbey tile, originally from the
graveyard. Privately owned.

(Hants) and Dunstable Priory (Beds) attributed to the 13th century.[30] Another was found in St Martin's church, Carfax, and donated to the Ashmolean, probably by Percy Manning.[31] Seven of the other designs, including that of the eagle have been found in the church of St Peter in the East in Oxford and elsewhere in the county. It is thought that these latter tiles were the product of a local workshop which was active in the first half of the 14th century.[32]

A number of tiles, and fragments of tiles, were decorated with a double-headed eagle and probably date to the late 13th century (Figure 274). These are counter-relief tiles made with wooden stamps, the resulting indents being filled with white slip. The double-headed eagle design tends to be associated with empire and their use at Eynsham could be a reference to Richard Earl of Cornwall who was elected Holy Roman Emperor and crowned at Aachen in 1257. It may have been thought that Richard was a descendant of Aethelmaer Earl of Cornwall, one of the founders of the abbey in 1005. On the other hand, Leofric, the Saxon Earl of Mercia, indirectly a benefactor of the abbey, also used a double headed eagle

[30] Van Lemmen H., *Medieval Tiles*, Shire Publications, 2016.

[31] Heaney M. (ed.), *Percy Manning, The man who collected Oxfordshire*, Archaeopress, 2017.

[32] Emden A.B., Medieval Floor-tiles in the Church of St. Peter in the East, Oxford, *Oxoniensia*, Vol. XXXIV, 1970: pp. 29-45 For further illustrations of Eynsham Abbey tiles see Foster C., Medieval floor tiles, with reference to Eynsham Abbey, *ER* 34, 2017.

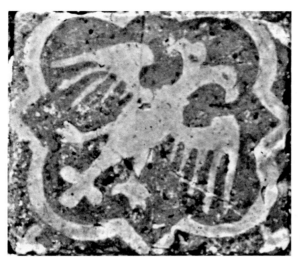

Figure 274. Eynsham Abbey tile. W. Bainbridge
©EHG. Whereabouts unknown.

as his personal emblem. However, the same design graced the floor of the Latin Chapel of St Frideswide's Priory in Oxford, now Christchurch Cathedral, and can also be found at Cleeve Abbey in Somerset so it is not an exclusively Eynsham motif by any means.

Day's discoveries were noted by a Mr Shurlock, a local resident, in a letter to Professor J.O. Westwood in Oxford, dated 15 April, 1851. In his letter he also enclosed *an outline of part of a shaft of a pillar, or rather respond, which came to light a few months ago, when a very old cottage fell down close to the so-called Abbey barn. One portion I have in my garden, two feet in height; nine others were found, but Mr Druce intends building with them again. It is certainly part of the Abbey.*[33] The respond was quite substantial, being 0.91m at the back and 50.80cm deep from its fillet moulded roll. Alan Crossley suggests that it may have been part of the west side of a gateway which straddled the south end of Abbey Street.[34] The comment about Mr Druce is interesting and suggests that the remaining responds may be built into the Abbey Farm barns or one of the surrounding walls which were constructed in the mid-19th century.

Another indication of the growing interest in the lost abbey of Eynsham was the publication in 1907 and 1908 of H.E. Salter's monumental transcription from medieval Latin of the *Eynsham Cartulary*. This collection of the monastery's records, in roughly chronological order was, as we have seen, begun in about 1196 by Adam, a monk who later became Abbot of Eynsham. Volume 1 of Salter's transcription contains a lengthy introduction with details of Eynsham's Abbots through to the Dissolution, extensive footnotes, and transcriptions of Visitations to Eynsham by the Bishop of Lincoln or his representatives in 1445, 1517 and 1520.

Volume 2 has a long preface with a list of the more than 150 Harleian Rolls or accounts belonging to Eynsham Abbey at the British Library. Four of the most extensive and interesting of these are also transcribed. The information in all the Rolls is incorporated in a detailed account of the properties that belonged to the abbey at one time or another. In addition to the second part of the *Cartulary* which dates from the mid-14th century onwards, Salter includes 100 charters from various sources ending with the receipts from the dissolved abbey for the year ending 29 September, 1539. He concludes this volume with

---

[33] *Bodl. G.A. Oxon c 317 ([20])* Letter from M. Shurlock Esq to Professor J.O. Westwood, 15 April, 1851. Shurlock donated a tile with the charging knight to the Ashmolean as did Percy Manning.
[34] Crossley, op. cit.

a transcription of a Latin version of the *Vision of the Monk of Eynsham*. A transcription of the printed, 15th century Middle English *Revelation to the Monk of Evesham* (*sic)* had been made by Edward Arber in 1869.

Salter's work and scholarly commentary proved invaluable to later historians, most notably to a local resident, Sir Edmund Chambers whose short volume *Eynsham Under the Monks* was published in 1936. Chambers places greater emphasis on the 'bottom up' perspective and on local history, characteristic of the methodology of the 20th century. His more personal account of Eynsham's history is in some ways more accessible than Salter, particularly as he translates some of the Charters and Rolls into English. Salter very much belonged to the old school and would probably have been bemused by the fact that it is no longer axiomatic for historians to be fluent in medieval Latin.

Chapter 15

Rescue

As regards Eynsham I can confirm that poor
old town is the most Godforsaken hole in England[1]

In the second half of the 20th century, a combination of factors resulted in a growing interest in the lost Abbey of Eynsham and a greater determination to rescue it from the shadows. From a sleepy agricultural backwater of a mere 1757 souls in 1901, with little apparently to recommend it, the village of Eynsham became a more obviously thriving community, a desirable place to live, within easy reach of the glittering spires of Oxford on the one hand and the beauties of the Cotswold countryside on the other. The process was encouraged by significant changes in communication, especially road transport, and a major programme of house building in the period after 1945. The establishment of industrial estates provided much needed employment and many of those who worked in Oxford found it relatively easy to commute from the village where property prices were then a little more realistic. By the turn of the millennium, Eynsham's population exceeded 5000 and is due to rise still further. Modern Primary and Secondary Schools were built in the village and History became an important element in the curriculum.

Although many failed to recognise it, the Second World War and de-colonization thereafter put an end to the reality of Britain as a world power. Partly as a reaction to this imperial decline there was a growing interest in what had made Britain great in the past, including the distant roots of its one-time dominance of the global stage. History as an academic subject also developed in different ways. The emphasis on those who ruled Britain from the top began to be augmented by a study of history from the perspective of ordinary people and a greater importance attributed to examining local and indeed, family history. Individual communities became more interested in their own roots and how they fitted into the wider regional and national picture.

Archaeology too underwent significant changes in the 20th century, becoming more professional and scientific. The amateurish and sometimes highly speculative approach of antiquarians was replaced with a more systematic and thorough examination of the material culture of previous eras. However, these changes were not immediate or widespread as evidenced by the building of the Roman Catholic church of St Peter's on the abbey site. This was commenced in 1939 but, due to the Second World War and the period of austerity after it, was not completed until the 1960s. In the course of its construction some remains and architectural fragments were discovered and stored in the church car park. Unlike today however, when such developments are generally subject to at least a watching brief, no evaluation was carried out and it was not until 1992 that the finds were recorded.

---

[1] A wandering churchman. Oxford Times, 28 October 1876. Quoted in *ER* 2, 1985.

In 1954, the building that stood on the south-east side of the junction between Mill Street and Acre End Street where the Co-op now stands, was largely demolished. Only the western gable wall facing the 'Jolly Sportsman' was retained. There is a tradition that the building had been the old court house of the manor and the *Victoria County History* suggests that in the 16th century it was occupied by the Blackman family, key figures in the community from the late medieval period to about 1600, often operating as manorial officials.[2] In the 17th century the building appears to have been an inn, in a later incarnation it became a shop and in the 20th century a branch of Barclay's bank before its current status as a supermarket.

In the course of the demolition it was inspected and evaluated by the architect and local historian H.C.D. Cooper who wrote up his findings in *Oxoniensia*.[3] According to his report, the L-shaped building was put up in two phases. The first was a rectangular two-storey structure, 14.02m x 5.18m, which ran north to south on the same axis as the eastern side of Mill Street but set back from Acre End Street to its north. Its orientation suggests that it was on the line of the original approach to the abbey which would have made a more impressive entrance than that currently afforded by the much narrower Lombard Street. Cooper dated this building, rather vaguely, to the period after the Dissolution of the monasteries partly on the basis of the discovery of a coin from the reign of Elizabeth I, and the fact that the walls contained some carved stones from the abbey. These included a 15th century door moulding, a springer for a vault and a column drum. All of these were stored in the parish church and, much later, some were incorporated in the Heritage Trail 'cairns' in the village. A late 12th century Anglo-Norman chevron voussoir was also found but subsequently disappeared.

The house had a grand, four-centred stone fireplace on the ground floor and two further fireplaces with moulded arches on the ground and first floors, all of which dated from the late 15th or early 16th centuries. Two large stones, here roughly 'stitched' together, may have formed one of these fireplaces or the four-centred door moulding referred to above (Figure 275). They were possibly re-cycled from the abbot's lodging and/or guest accommodation and further supports the conclusions arrived at in Chapter 13. The ground floor contained a square-headed stone-mullioned and transomed window which again may have come from the abbey site.

Cooper implies that this structure was built in the 16th century but if he is correct in assuming that the fireplaces came from the abbot's house and/or accommodation for visitors to the abbey this may not be so. After the Henrician Reformation, as we have seen, Eynsham manor, including the abbey site was granted to the Earls of Derby in 1545. The family turned part of it, probably the abbot's lodging, kitchen and guest wing, into a country retreat and seem to have lived there on and off for nearly 100 years. After the Civil War the site passed through a number of hands until 1657 when it was bought by a clothier, Thomas Jordan of Witney who seems to have been responsible for the destruction of the remaining abbey buildings. It would therefore seem more likely that the 'Manor House'

---

[2]   Crossley A., *The Victoria History of the County of Oxford* Vol. XII: pp. 98-157, OUP 1990. University of London Institute of Historical Research.
[3]   Cooper H.C.D., The Old Manor House, Eynsham, Oxon, *Oxoniensia*, Vol. XIX, 1954.

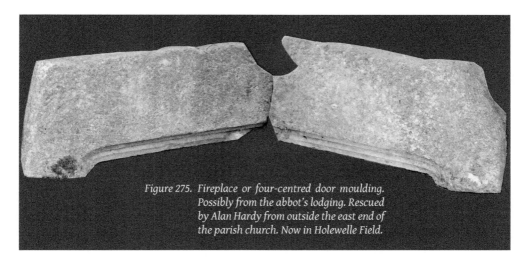

Figure 275. Fireplace or four-centred door moulding. Possibly from the abbot's lodging. Rescued by Alan Hardy from outside the east end of the parish church. Now in Holewelle Field.

Figure 276. Medieval padlock key found in the foundation layers of the collapsed wall in Lombard Street in 2014. Curated by the author.

building dated to the third quarter of the 17th century, replacing an earlier structure that had stood on the site. This suggestion is supported by the piecemeal accounts of the sale of construction materials from the second stage of the demolition of the abbey in the late 1650s and early 1660s. In addition, in the trench excavated by the contractors for the new concrete foundations of the wall in Lombard Street in 2014, a 17th century copper alloy annular buckle was found. Furthermore, there was a medieval iron padlock key similar to those excavated on the abbey site in 1989-92, probably part of the sweepings of the monastery when it was dismantled (Figure 276).[4]

Sometime in the 18th century, a new wing was added to the 'Manor', running east to west at right angles to the north of the original building. It fronted onto Acre End Street and impinged onto what had been Mill Street, now Lombard Street, substantially reducing its width. A drawing of the building was made before its demolition (Figure 277).

In the 1960s, substantial new development west of Mill Street was authorised and a barn that stood on the site of the present parade of shops, including the Post Office, and the

---

[4]   Another medieval key, a door key, was unearthed in Abbey Place in 1984. See Atkins B., The Key to Eynsham Abbey? *ER* 9, 1992.

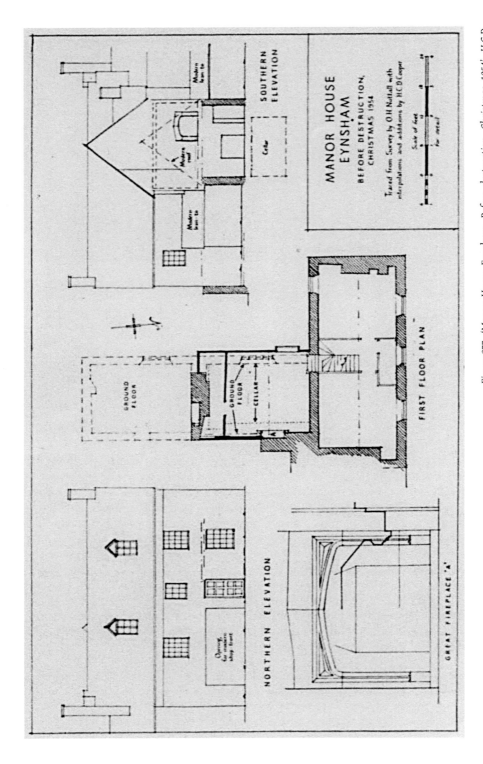

Figure 277. 'Manor House Eynsham. Before destruction, Christmas 1954'. H.C.D. Cooper, The Old Manor House, Eynsham, Oxon. Oxoniensia, XIX, 1954. Courtesy of Oxfordshire Architectural and Historical Society.

Figure 278. Detail of a barn in Mill Street, Eynsham, demolished in 1962. W. Bainbridge ©EHG.

Figure 279. Coat of Arms once in Coates Barn in Back lane, Eynsham, demolished in 1963. Now re-set in the Market House in the Square, Eynsham.

new John Lopes Road, was demolished in 1962. In the process, a piece of window tracery believed to be from the Abbey was removed. The photo above shows the stone in its position in the barn (Figure 278). A clearer picture of the stone can be found in Chapter 6 (Figure 171).

In 1963, Coate's barn in Back Lane was demolished and some 13th century voussoirs 'with very fresh colour wash' came to light, along with 'a stone from a Norman arcade' and a coat of arms which was later re-set in the east wall of Eynsham's Market House in the Square (Figure 279).[5] The arms show a stringed hunting horn on the left and a lion rampant on the right and are said to refer to Aethelmaer 'the Fat', Duke of Cornwall, who was charged by King Aethelred with the foundation of Eynsham Abbey in 1005. Although heraldry did not exist in the early 11th century, later medieval heralds were quite happy to award coats of arms to all sorts of historical figures and some

---

[5]   Bainbridge W., Eynsham's Market House, *ER* 2, 1985.

*Figure 280. Coat of Arms under the eaves of No. 6 Abbey
Street, Eynsham.*

mythical ones. A very similar coat of arms, wrongly set on its side, was built into the east
wall of 6 Abbey Street, just under the eaves (Figure 280).[6]

It has reasonably been suggested that these arms may originally have been positioned on
the abbey gatehouse leading to the inner precinct. In Standlake church nearby, there are
a couple of nave corbels which also relate to the abbey and which may have been taken
there after the Dissolution. One contains the same coat of arms as above but with the lion
and the hunting horn reversed (Figure281). The other has small fleur-de-lys and two pairs
of interlaced rings similar to those on the 'Eynsham Angel' (Figure 282). Fleur-de-lys have
apparently been called 'sallies' and it is thought that this is a play on the name of Miles
Salley, Abbot of Eynsham in the 1490s, whose coat of arms this is said to be although it bears
no relation to other coats of arms associated with Salley.[7] The corbels seem to have been
inserted when Standlake's nave clerestory was added and the roof lowered in the early 16th
century, which would add weight to the idea that they were either inspired by Eynsham or
removed from the abbey site at the time of its destruction.

Another coat of arms, built into the wall of 'Twelve Acre' farmhouse in Eynsham, may also
have associations with Miles Salley (Figure 283). It consists of two separate pieces with

---

[6]   Cooper H.C.D., *Eynsham Armorial*, *Oxoniensia*, Vol. XXXVII , 1972. The heraldic terminology is 'per pale, dexter
an hunting horn stringed sinister a lion rampant crowned'.
[7]   Bainbridge W., Looking for Abbots, *ER* 1, 1984.

Figure 281. St Giles, Standlake (Oxon). Corbel with coat of arms in the nave.

Figure 282. St Giles, Standlake. Corbel with coat of arms.

Figure 283. Twelve Acre farmhouse. Reconstructed coat of arms from stones built into the north wall.

thistle decoration put together with three other stones. The thistle in the medieval period was an emblem of the Virgin Mary, to whom the abbey was dedicated, and also one of the symbols of the Passion of Christ. However, there is also a coat of arms ascribed to Miles Salley as Bishop of Llandaff on a Parliamentary Roll of 1515 (Figure 284).[8] Miles Salley, as a bishop, was entitled to sit in the House of Lords despite remaining Abbot of Eynsham. If the two pieces of stone are put together as here, they are similar to the heraldry of the Parliamentary Roll. Such coats of arms of course, would originally have been brightly painted like that on the Roll.[9]

---

[8]   Bainbridge describes the blazon as 'Or between three thistles slipped proper a fess Azure'. *ER* 1, 1984.
[9]   In his *Parochial Collections*, Anthony Wood refers to other coats of arms which were *in one of the houses at 'Einsham'* and also in windows of the church. The former are described as: *Arg. a cross fleury between 4 martlets sab., arg., lyon ramp. gules. Within a bord. charged with bezants (Edm. E. of Cornwall) arg., a fess blew between 2 birds and a rose gules, stalked and leaved vert.* It is assumed these were abbey glass but all, including those described in the church have since disappeared. Some fragments of medieval stained glass have been randomly put together in a south aisle window in St Leonard's.

Figure 284. The Arms of Miles Salley, Bishop of Llandaff and Abbot of Eynsham from a Processional Roll of 1515. © British Library Board, Add. MS 40078. W. Bainbridge.

Also in Standlake church, in the north aisle, are two headless stone torsos which Pevsner dates to the 15th century and suggests an association with Simon of Evesham's chantry.[10] One of these has been identified as that of St Thomas Becket (Figure 285) and the other of St John the Evangelist (Figure 286). The Becket figure, which retains some of its original red

Figure 285. St Giles, Standlake. Headless torso of Thomas Becket in the north aisle.

Figure 286. St Giles, Standlake. Headless torso of St John the Evangelist in the north aisle.

[10] Pevsner N. and Sherwood J., *The Buildings of England - Oxfordshire*, Penguin Books 1974. Simon of Evesham was rector of the church in the 14th century.

Figure 287. Bracket for a statue found in Church Street, Eynsham.

paint, is wearing an archbishop's pallium. Given the other apparent associations with Eynsham Abbey and the size of the figures is it too fanciful to conclude that these two fragmentary figures may once have graced a somewhat grander building than Standlake parish church? Brackets for such statuary, or others, have been found around Eynsham. A couple are built into the 'cairns' and another (Figure 287), found within the abbey precinct, is very similar to those in the nave of Waterperry church and the south porch of Northleach Church (Gloucs) although without the angel supporters (Figure 288).

As we have seen, Eynsham Abbey stones were distributed far and wide after the demolition of the monastery's buildings in the 16th and 17th centuries and re-cycled for different purposes or incorporated in different buildings. On the other hand, it would perhaps be wise to be somewhat circumspect about suggestions that any random local stone of obviously ecclesiastical origins necessarily derived from the abbey. Such is the case for

Figure 288. Bracket for a statue in the porch of St Peter and St Paul, Northleach (Gloucs).

example, of two 13th or 14th century label stops of a king and bishop, built into a house in a neighbouring village. (Figures 289 and 290). Local tradition has it that they came from Eynsham Abbey but as yet there is means of being certain.

Similarly, a recent find in Holewelle Field, within the enlarged abbey precinct, would seem to provide evidence for the roofing of some of the abbey structures. It is an unusual, green-glazed cresting tile to decorate the ridge of a building (Figure 291). Dating to about AD 1400, this Brill/Boarstall ware from kilns in Buckinghamshire may indeed have graced a part of the abbey complex and similar examples were found in the excavations of 1989-92.

Figure 289. Head of a king label stop built into the wall of a house in a neighbouring village.

Figure 290. Head of a bishop label stop. As 289.

Figure 291. Medieval cresting tile, dating to c. 1400. Found in the excavation of the spring in Holewelle Field.

However, it is known that the field was used as a dump by the adjoining farm and some of the village in the late 19th and early 20th century and therefore may have originated elsewhere.

The first archaeological excavation in the abbey precinct took place in 1962 when two trial trenches were dug by Mr J. Hanson in the modern extension to St Leonard's churchyard. The results were briefly reported in *Oxoniensia* and consisted of rubble and floor tiles from medieval structures. In addition, cobbled surfaces and possible robber trenches were revealed.[11] It was noted that grave-diggers had unearthed two burials, one in a stone coffin and another in a lead coffin. Dr E.L. Jones also reported finds of Romano-British wares and some 11th and 12th century pottery from a small excavation in the field south of the abbey site in what is now known to be the abbey fishponds. In 1963/4 a 30 metre trench and four test pits were dug in the western part of Nursery Field, to the

---

[11] Hardy A. and Dodd A. and Keevill G.D. et al., *Aelfric's Abbey - Excavations at Eynsham Abbey, Oxfordshire, 1989-92*, p. 15, English Heritage. Published by Oxford University School of Archaeology, 2003.

Figure 292. Photo, provenance unknown but in possession of Alan Hardy, of 'a part of Eynsham Abbey uncovered about 20 years ago on land then belonging to Mr Hunt, in or near Nursery Field. A skeleton found close by was photographed but later the photo discarded.' The description has a date, 11-4-90, and it is assumed that the photo dates to the 1971 excavation. Possibly therefore, part of the abbey's infirmary complex.

east of the churchyard, by the Oxford University Archaeological Society. Walls and graves were located but the results were not published.

A more extensive excavation of the same area, including a magnetometer survey, took place in 1971 and discovered fragmentary floor and roof tiles, pottery ranging from prehistoric to late medieval, window glass, animal and human bone, demolition debris and a few substantial foundations (Figure 292). The skeletal remains were interpreted as belonging to the cemetery of the Saxon abbey. Pieces of worked abbey stone were also found and some of the main finds were deposited with the Museum Resources Centre at Standlake. A report on the excavation appeared later although unfortunately the archaeologists were, like Pevsner and Sherwood, misled by a copy of Wood's original drawing.[12] However, as a result of the excavation, the Nursery field and gardens to the south of Oxford Road were incorporated into a Scheduled Ancient Monument in 1973.

In the early 1970s, the vicar of St Leonard's, Rev. J.W.G. Westwood, became aware of the fragility and importance of some of the loose stones in the Vicarage garden. He therefore donated them to the County Museum in Woodstock. They were later transferred to the

---

[12] Gray M. and Clayton N., Excavations on the site of Eynsham Abbey, 1971, *Oxoniensia* Vol. XLIII, 1978.

Museum Resources Centre in Standlake and included the Saxon 'Trinity' (Figure 10), the 'Eynsham Angel' (Figure 206), two gargoyles (Figure 222), three roof bosses, (Figures 209-211), a tomb slab (Figure 122), a piece of tracery, a vaulting springer, a piece of an arch moulding and the tapered pyramid-shaped stone with fluted edges and panels of egg and dart decoration which can be seen in Taunt's photo (Figure 269).

A key event in the recovery of Eynsham's history came with the publication of the first edition of the *Eynsham Record* by the Eynsham History Group. The group had formally come into existence in 1959 but the *Eynsham Record*, which has been produced annually ever since 1984, is probably its most significant achievement. Many articles relating to the abbey have been written over the years and it is an invaluable source for anyone with an interest in Eynsham's lost monastic foundation. The Eynsham History Group has also supported a number of other publications, notably *Eynsham: A Chronicle* by Pamela Richards.

One of the *Eynsham Record's* contributors and an assiduous pursuer and recorder of Eynsham Abbey's surviving remains was local resident and stalwart of the Eynsham History Group, William Bainbridge, whose photographic archive of 178 negatives relating to the abbey and its stones was later deposited with the National Monuments Record (English Heritage Archive) in Swindon. His collection of slides, left to the Eynsham History Group, has recently been digitised and is a valuable record. In 1980, Bainbridge put together a pamphlet listing those Abbey stones around the village which were then visible to the public.[13] This is now out of date as many pieces have found new homes and others have been discovered and displayed in the last few years. Unfortunately, it is also true that a number of the stones that Bainbridge recorded photographically have left the village as people have moved. Others, including some important pieces have completely disappeared.

Figure 293. *Abbey stones built into the south wall of 'Lord's Farm', Oxford Road, Eynsham.*

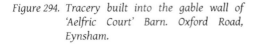

Figure 294. *Tracery built into the gable wall of 'Aelfric Court' Barn. Oxford Road, Eynsham.*

---
[13] Bainbridge W., *Visible Remains of Eynsham Abbey*, Information Printing Ltd, Eynsham, 1980.

Figure 295. Two abbey tiles from the Margaret Foote bequest to the Oxfordshire Museum, Woodstock, OCMS.

Another local resident with an interest in Eynsham Abbey was Margaret Foote, who lived at 'Lord's Farm'. After she bought the property in 1952 she began to renovate both the main house and the adjoining cottages known as 'Lord's Row'. In the process, Tudor fireplaces were revealed which were thought to be built from materials from the abbey. Some carved stones from the abbey, including a fragment of the Norman fret/crenellation motif and roll mouldings, were found in the walls and these were built into the wall over the new porch facing Oxford Road in 1959/60 (Figure 293). Across the road, pieces of 14th/15th century tracery were set upside down (not by Margaret Foote) in the gable walls of a reconstructed barn in Aelfric Court in 1978 (Figure 294). A similar piece of cusped tracery is built into the interior of a house in Thames Street (Figure 218).

When Miss Foote died in 1983, she left her abbey relics to the County Museum at Woodstock and there were a couple of medieval floor tiles on display there that almost certainly came from her bequest (Figure 294). However, the majority of her collection was transferred to the Museum Resources Centre (MRC) at Standlake. Unfortunately, the MRC lacks adequate funds and although there are two Open Days annually, the Eynsham Abbey stones are mostly held in 'deep storage' and are not readily available to members of the public. More disturbing is the fact that a number of pieces once there can no longer be traced.

In 1985 the old Vicarage in Mill Street was sold and Brian Atkins of the Eynsham History Group arranged for the removal of the abbey stones which had been kept there since the 19th century. Most of the stones were stored temporarily in the church or churchyard and were later (2003) randomly built into the six 'cairns' which mark out the Eynsham Abbey Heritage trail. One exception was the arch illustrated by Buckler in 1813, which is now inside St Leonard's Church, above the north door. Four stones, a Romanesque capital and three corbels were given to St Peter's church and are built into the western wall of the lobby between the church and the Tolkein Room. Other carved pieces from the Vicarage and

Figure 296. The Abbey Street 'cairn'.

elsewhere are still stored privately, awaiting the establishment of an Eynsham Museum.[14] The 'cairns' contain useful illustrations of the Abbey site from different perspectives drawn by the famous freelance artist Harry Lange.[15] One downside of this solution to the problem of storing the stones is that they are exposed to the weather, particularly frost, and some of the stones are showing signs of wear such as those in the Abbey Street 'cairn' (Figure 296). In addition, one of the best stones from the recreation ground cairn has disappeared and it and other cairns have been subject to vandalism.

In 1990, Bishop Eric Gordon's book *Eynsham Abbey* was published. In the main, this was a scholarly examination of the early history of the abbey, and the great figures associated with it, based largely on manuscripts, especially the *Cartulary*. Gordon translated 27 Eynsham Charters in his book, adding to those that he had used for fascinating articles in the *Eynsham Record*. There was a short chapter on buildings, reproductions of the Anthony Wood sketch and its subsequent copies, and eight photos of Romanesque stone fragments

[14] Parrinder S., Eynsham Abbey Stones – The Brian Atkins Collection, *ER* 31, 2014.
[15] Atkins B., Rescuing Eynsham Abbey Stones, *ER* 20, 2003. Harry Lange was the award winning Artistic Director of Stanley Kubrik's *2001, A Space Odyssey*.

taken by William Bainbridge. A couple of these stones are now at the MRC at Standlake. Bishop Gordon concluded that 'Eynsham Abbey never grew outstandingly rich. Had it done so, it might have done more to replace the Norman aspects of its church...it was brought up to date, here and there, in sundry centuries, but never totally replaced.' This view contrasts with that of Alan Crossley who wrote the Eynsham entry for the *Victoria History of the County of Oxford*, also published in 1990. Crossley believed that although Eynsham itself was a small village 'by the end of the Middle Ages (the abbey) was one of the richest religious houses in Oxfordshire.' Crossley's view was echoed by R.A. Chambers of the Oxfordshire Archaeological Unit who described Eynsham as 'a top-ranking monastic establishment.'[16]

Perhaps the most important developments in the rescue of Eynsham Abbey took place between 1989 and 1992 as a result of a major investigation on part of the site of the abbey cloister, its associated buildings and domestic ranges, by the Oxford Archaeological Unit. The incentive for the excavation was the planned extension by St Peter's Catholic Church and St Leonard's Anglican Church of their respective cemeteries. It was followed by a geophysical survey of Nursery Field, to the east of the main abbey complex but within its precinct. This revealed the foundations of substantial buildings, possibly an infirmary complex, which await excavation sometime in the future. A further small-scale excavation took place in 1993 on the site of a new parish room for St Peter's church. In addition, an excavation and earthwork survey had taken place on part of the site of the abbey fishponds in 1991/2.

The archaeology resulted in the publication of a short report in 1995,[17] an extensive and very detailed report by Hardy and others in 2003, and a more 'popular' summary booklet at the same time.[18] As we have seen, significant evidence was found for the Saxon, Norman and post-Norman phases of the abbey complex and the continued occupation of parts of the site after the Dissolution in 1538. Although the Museum Resources Centre at Standlake stores some of the best examples of worked stone found in the course of the excavation,

[16] Chambers R.A., Eynsham Abbey Excavations, *ER* 7, 1990.
[17] Keevill G.D., *In Harvey's house and in God's house: excavations at Eynsham Abbey 1991-3*, Thames Valley Landscapes Monograph No. 6, Oxford Archaeological Unit, 1995.
[18] Hardy A. and Smith R., *Eynsham: A village and its Abbey*, English Heritage, The Holywell Press, 2003.

Figure 298. St Peter's church 'cairn' and display board.

many of the stones were, like those from the Vicarage garden, built into the heritage trail 'cairns' around the village.

Another barn in a yard off Thames Street was demolished in the 1990s and a gothic style 'smokehole' was rescued and later given to the Museum Resources Centre at Standlake (Figure 141). The photo above (p 231), taken by Bainbridge (Figure 297), shows the stone in its original position.

Many more stones from the abbey have been found in recent years as property has been renovated, new houses built or walls collapsed. One notable example of the latter was the fall of part of a wall in Church Street/Lombard Street in January 2014 after a long period of rain. Subsequently, for health and safety reasons, the whole of the wall was taken down prior to the re-building of most of the structure with its original materials. Conscious of the proximity of the site to the old abbey, the contractors were approached and asked to put to one side any worked and carved stones to enable them to be recorded. In the event, over 40 abbey stones came to light. Some of the larger pieces of stone were taken to St Peter's carpark where they now border a flowerbed next to the existing 'cairn' of abbey stones (Figure 298). Smaller pieces were put on one side and collected by the author.[19]

Although most worked or carved stones like these have been discovered within or in the immediate vicinity of the old abbey precinct, a number have turned up on the outskirts of the village and in one instance across the Thames to the east. All these finds have further stimulated the study of Eynsham's medieval history and, in contrast to the calumny at the beginning of the chapter, the words of Peter Ridley, Vicar of Eynsham, written in 1981 now seem more appropriate. 'The historic and beautiful village of Eynsham is singularly fortunate in the number of people who take a serious interest in its past and who care deeply for its future.'[20]

---

[19] Parrinder S., The Co-op Wall, *ER* 31, 2014.
[20] Wright L., *St Leonard's, Eynsham*, Parchments of Oxford, 1981.

Ironically perhaps, the vicar was distantly related to Nicholas Ridley, the Bishop of London in the reign of Edward VI. A leading Protestant reformer, he would doubtless have approved Henry VIII's sweeping away of the monastic houses, including that at Eynsham. Some of its former monks in turn may have been gratified by Ridley's 'martyrdom' at Oxford in the reign of Henry's daughter, 'Bloody' Mary.

Appendix 1

Eynsham's abbots[1]

Aelfric *c.* 1005–*c.* 1010. See chapter 1. An amateur local historian claimed that he was witness to a will of 1020 but failed to give details.[2] The online *Encyclopaedia Britannica* (2007) puts his death at 1025 but again does not provide evidence. 'Aelfric' was not a particularly uncommon name at the time.

About 1051, *the abbot and all the community of Eynsham* were witnesses to an agreement concerning the lease of Great Tew by St Albans Abbey but the abbot is unnamed.

Columbanus Mentioned in Domesday, 1086, and in 1094 in writs of William II. He is also referred to in notes taken by Nicholas Bishop about 1430 from Eynsham's lost Cartulary of its Oxford properties.[3] According to the *Eynsham Customary* he appears in the monks' daily prayers, before Abbot Walter.[4]

Nigel 1109? –9 May 1128.[5]

Walter I 1128? Previously prior, second in command of St Albans Abbey (Herts) and present there as Abbot of Eynsham when the remains of St Alban were inspected on 2 August 1129. A 'Walter, Abbot of Eynsham' was a witness in December 1136 to three grants made by Queen Adeliza to Reading Abbey in honour of her late husband Henry I.[6] However, the reference may be to his successor. Likewise, at the dedication of Godstow Abbey in 1139 Walter is named but may also be Walter II.

Walter II *c.* 1150.

William *c.* 1150–*c.* 1151/2 He appears in the Godstow *Cartulary* as witness to a deed, midsummer 1151.

Godfrey *c.* 1151/2–*c.* May 1195. Previously prior of Eynsham[7] His possible tomb slab is now in the Museum Resources Centre, Standlake (Figure 122). See chapter 5.

---

[1] Based largely on Salter H.E., *Eynsham Cartulary* Vols. 1 and 2, Oxford Historical Society, Clarendon Press 1907/8. Extra notes added by the author.

[2] ? Cruikshank Mrs, *Notes on the History of Eynsham or Some Account of the History of Eynsham* Unpublished, undated typescripts c. 1930, possibly by the wife of the local doctor.

[3] Carpenter D.X., *The Charters of William II and Henry I - Eynsham Abbey*, https://actswilliam2henry1.wordpress.com, 2016.

[4] Gordon E., *Eynsham Abbey 1005-1228 A Small Window into a Large Room*, p. 106, Phillimore & Co. Ltd. 1990.

[5] Not mentioned by Salter but see Gordon, p. 169. Based on a chronicle by John of Worcester who, correctly, states that Nigel was succeeded by Walter. Dugdale, using Willis, states that Nicholas was abbot in 1115 and was succeeded by William in 1138 and then Richard, Godfrey, Robert and Eustachius. From Abbot Adam, Dugdale's list is largely accurate.

[6] Kemp B.R. (ed.), *Reading Abbey Cartularies* Vol. I: pp. 301, 353, 404, Royal Historical Society, 1986.

[7] His dates are debatable but I have deferred to recent scholarship. Easting R. (ed.), *The Revelation of the Monk of Eynsham*, Oxford University Press, 2002.

Vacancy *c.* May 1195–November 1197. The vacancy was due to Bishop Hugh's dispute with King Richard I about who had the right to appoint the Abbot of Eynsham. The case was won by Hugh, aided by the work of Adam, then prior of Eynsham.

Robert November 1197–1208. Previously prior of Dover Priory (Kent). Initiated an unsuccessful legal case to try to re-gain the manor of Yarnton which was lost in the late 11th century but which the abbey continued to lay claim to. In 1200 Robert initiated but then withdrew a lawsuit respecting the tithes of Langney, an island in the Thames between Eynsham and Bablockhythe.

Vacancy 1208–1213 England was under a papal interdict due to a quarrel with King John who became the patron of Eynsham until the dispute with the pope was resolved. In 1212 the custody of the abbey was granted to Roger de Nevil by the king.

Adam *c.* July 1213–*c.* November 1228. Previously prior of Eynsham. Deposed. He was granted the manor of Rollright for his maintenance. He died after 1233. He wrote the *Vision of the monk of Eynsham,* the first part of the *Eynsham Cartulary* and the *Life of Hugh*, Bishop of Lincoln, later Saint Hugh. See chapter 5.

Nicholas December 1228–1238/9. Previously prior of Frieston Priory (Lincs), a monastic cell of Crowland Abbey. During his abbacy, or possibly that of his successor, Henry III came to Eynsham and on 18 April 1238, gave his assent to the election of Richard of Chichester as Abbot of Reading.[8] Nicholas resigned as abbot but continued to live at Eynsham Abbey until he died in February 1242. He seems to have occupied a house, with outbuildings, which was not within the inner precinct of the abbey. See John of Oxford.

John de Douor (Dover) 1238/9–*c.* April 1241. Previously prior of Eynsham. The relic of St Andrew was acquired during his abbacy. Not clear if he resigned or died.

Gilbert of Gloucester April 1241–January 1264. Onetime cellarer at Eynsham. The cellarer took charge of the goods and property of the monastery, like a modern-day bursar. He procured provisions for the monks and their guests.

Alexander of Brackley May 1264–March 1268. A monk at Eynsham appointed by the bishop, possibly because the monks were unable to agree a candidate.

John of Oxford April 1268–July 1281. Formerly cellarer, again appointed by the bishop. Involved in a lengthy boundary dispute with Adam of Hanborough.[9] Resigned but continued to live at the abbey with a generous allowance including the house and outbuildings previously occupied by Abbot Nicholas. His lavish lifestyle and failure to abide by the *Rule* created some dissension in the abbey and, following a report by the Archbishop of Canterbury John Peckham, his allowances were reduced and his obligations to the religious life more clearly spelled out. He died after 1284.

---

[8] Kemp, op. cit., p. 28.
[9] Gordon E., Adam of Hanbrough: Much Ado about a Ditch, *ER* 7, 1990.

Thomas of Wells January 1282–1307. During his abbacy, a long-standing dispute with Abingdon Abbey about the use of Swinford ferry was resolved in April 1299 (see Appendix 2 under 'Eynsham'). Thomas' tomb slab was taken after the Dissolution and re-used in the mill race of Hardwick Mill. The brass effigy of the abbot was ripped from its surface.[10]

Adam of Lambourne June 1307–1316.

John de Cheltenham January 1317–March 1330. Prior of Eynsham. Resigned due to ill health. Tomb slab taken to Elsfield church after the Dissolution and apparently re-used by Michael Pudsey who died in 1645.[11] In his *Parochial Collections*, Anthony Wood implies that in his time the tomb slab and the brass plate for Michael Pudsey were separate, as does the drawing by Buckler in the early 19th century.

John de Broughton 1330–1338. Appointed by the bishop at the request of the abbey's officers.

Nicholas de Upton October 1338–May 1344. Had been cellarer and prior of the abbey. A controversial figure. Deposed. See chapter 8.

William Staunford May–July 1344. Forcibly deposed by Nicholas de Upton.

Nicholas de Upton 1344–1351/2. Resigned but continued to live at the abbey until at least 1366.

Galfridus (Geoffrey) de Lambourn 1351/2–July 1388. The *Cartulary* reveals him to have been a somewhat obsessive-compulsive measurer and calculator of land, notably in his survey of Newland in 1366 which is accurate to one third of an inch. He was criticised by a Bishop's Visitation of the abbey between 1363 and 1366 for letting valuable books go missing from the abbey's library but blamed everybody but himself.

Thomas Bradingstock October 1388–1413. A monk of Eynsham. In 1406 he was attended on by a physician called John Merston who was paid 13s-4d for his services and 29s-4d for preparing medicines.[12] Bradingstock and the abbey won a dispute with the bishop about who should have the profits of the House during a vacancy.

James of Ramsden 1413–1431 During his tenure, a long-standing dispute with Lincoln over the sale of Eynsham Abbey materials was finally settled and the Bishop's Visitor was able to report that *all points had been settled*. 'An Abbot with many skills.'[13]

Thomas Oxinford February 1432–1440/1. Possibly deposed for bringing the abbey into disrepute. A Richard Oxinford was a monk of Eynsham in 1404 and may have been Thomas' elder brother. See chapter 12.

---

[10] Gordon E., *Adventure at Hardwick Mill, ER* 1, 1984.
[11] Bainbridge W., *Looking for Abbots, ER* 1, 1984.
[12] Harris M.J., *Medical Care in Eynsham, ER* 14, 1997.
[13] Deans H., *Abbot James, ER* 18, 2001.

John Quenington 1440/1–1457. Formerly a monk at the abbey. Said to have reformed the abbey which contained just 14 religious. He also secured a change of day for Eynsham's market, from Sundays to Mondays.[14]

Robert Faryndone 1457–1469. Enthroned at Eynsham by Bishop John Chadworth. Resigned but remained at Eynsham. Still alive in 1470.

William Walwayn October 1469–*c.* 1497. A monk of Worcester Cathedral. He had obtained the Sanctae Theologiae Professor (S.T.P.) a degree awarded by Oxford University to a Doctor of Theology. Possibly the same 'Brother William Walwen' who was instituted as vicar of St Leonard's in 1482.[15]

Miles Salley *c.* 1497/8–December 1516. Also, Bishop of Llandaff from 1500 and largely absent from Eynsham thereafter. It has been claimed that he was Abbot of Abingdon before coming to Eynsham but there is no evidence of this.[16] However, Rev. Thomas Symonds claimed he was once almoner of that abbey.[17] Mieneke Cox says that he was the kitchener, i.e. cellarer, and that he was implicated in a plot with John Sant, the Yorkist Abbot of Abingdon, against Henry VII.[18] This would seem supported by the Parliamentary Rolls for 1489 (*Rot. Parl. VI p. 436/7*) in which he is named as the monk who delivered money to a certain Christopher Swanne *to execute and perform (his) false and traitorous purpose.*

Coats of arms attributed to Salley are on the 'Eynsham Angel', a corbel in Standlake church and built into the north wall of 'Twelve Acre' farmhouse. See chapters 12 and 15.

Thomas Chaundler 1517–*c.* 1519. Originally from Christ Church Canterbury, warden of Canterbury College, Oxford (S.T.P.) and then Abbot of Wyndham in the Norwich Diocese.

Cardinal Wolsey called him 'the flower of St Benet's order' and recommended him to the Bishop of Lincoln for the abbacy of Eynsham.

Henry Reading *c.* 1519–1530 A William Redyng, possibly Henry's brother, was a monk at Eynsham in the 1530s. See chapter 13.

Anthony Dunstone (alias Anthony Kitchin) May 1530–December 1538. Previously a monk at Westminster Abbey which he joined in 1511 at the late age of 34. Later, prior of Gloucester Hall, Oxford, now Worcester College. S.T.P. Briefly suspected of involvement in the Pilgrimage of Grace in 1537 for speaking *obtractuouse words.* Bishop of Llandaff from May 1545 until his death in 1563, by which point he was in debt to the Crown for the clerical taxes of his diocese. He is a controversial figure and has frequently been accused of being

---

[14] Crossley A., *Victoria History of the County of Oxford* Vol. XII: pp. 98-157, Oxford University Press, 1990. University of London Institute of Historical Research.

[15] Wright L., *St Leonard's Eynsham. The story of an English Parish Church*, Parchments of Oxford, 2009.

[16] *Wikipedia.*

[17] *Bodl. MS Top Oxon b 275.* Rev Thomas Symonds Collection. The early part of Symonds' 'Catalogue of the Abbots of Eynsham from the Registers of Lincoln and Dean Kennett's collection' is significantly different from Salter's list but is not to be trusted.

[18] Cox M., *The Story of Abingdon*, Vol.2: p.106. Privately published, 1989.

unprincipled, wily, greedy and incompetent. However, for a spirited defence see Professor Madeleine Gray's lecture "The Disaster of our Estate: Anthony Kitchin and the diocese of Llandaff", based on her article 'The Cloister and the Hearth: Anthony Kitchin and Hugh Jones, two Reformation bishops of Llandaff'. *Journal of Welsh Religious History*, Vol.3, 1995. See also chapter 13.

Appendix 2

Eynsham Abbey's Property[1]

Appleton (Berks): Tithes to the value of £1-6s-8d in 1291. Disposed of between 1531 and 1535. A tithe was a tax of a tenth of an individual's yearly income from all forms of agricultural production and was an old practice prescribed by the Old Testament (Leviticus: 27:30), enjoined by King Edgar (959-975) and sanctioned by Canon Law. Originally paid in kind but sometimes commuted to a money payment. A landowner was free to give the tithe of any part of his land or produce to whatever religious institution he wished, whether in his own parish or another. A large part of a monastery's income, as much as 25%, came from tithes.[2]

Ashley (Northants): Before 1109, Ralph Basset, Justice of all England, granted his tithe from one hide, approximately 120 acres, and the tithe from all his wool.

Baldon: 1. Tithes of the demesne, the personal estate of the lord of Marsh Baldon. Sometime before 1239 they were granted by Eynsham to Dorchester Abbey in exchange for an annual sum of 12s which was still paid in 1535.

2. A virgate, roughly 30 acres, of land in Marsh Baldon was given by Robert de la Mare in the early 13th century. Rented out for 6s-8d. Possibly lost by 1535 or included in the return for Wood Eaton.

Banbury: 1. Property worth 24s in 1254 and later 30s. In 1535 Eynsham granted a 90-year lease of its properties in Banbury, Hardwick and Bodicote to Maurice Wogan.

2. Tithes in Banbury and Cropredy given in 1094 by Bishop Robert Bloet on his demesne or home farm. Together with the rents of property it was worth £10-6s-8d annually.

Barton Hartshorne (Bucks): A meadow in the manor was given to Eynsham between 1160 and 1180. No records of it thereafter.

Bloxham: In 1235, King Henry III granted a clearing of two and a half acres in a wood next to the chapel of St John.

Bodicote: Tithes of six virgates, about 180 acres, given by William Clement before 1239. Worth 6s-8d in 1269.

---

[1] Based largely on Salter H.E., *Eynsham Cartulary* Vol. 2, Oxford Historical Society, Clarendon Press 1908.
[2] Pounds N.J.G., *A History of the English Parish*, p. 60, Cambridge University Press, 2000.

Brize Norton: 1. About 1175, two virgates were granted to the abbey by Walkelin Hareng but by 1269 just one virgate remained, worth 13s-4d. Walkelin was regarded as one of Eynsham's main benefactors and was remembered in the prayers of the monks.[3]
2. St Britius' church was given to Eynsham in about 1180 and paid it 4s per annum. It was appropriated about 1268. The rectorial tithes were worth £10 to Eynsham in 1535.

Broughton Poggs: In 1192, Ralf Murdac gave Eynsham a cart-load of wheat annually for making bread for the Eucharist. In 1390, the amount was described as a quarter of corn, being a rent from Broughton Mill. Ralph Murdac III was the son of Ralph Murdac II, Lord of Broughton, and Beatrice née De Chesney. He became Sheriff of Nottingham. Ralph was also remembered in the prayers of Eynsham's monks.

Carswell, Witney: Sometimes taxed with Curbridge. Between 1223 and 1228 William de Elmel gave Eynsham two virgates of land, worth 13s-4d in 1279, and services from four other virgates, worth 8s-10½d. The value of rent from Carswell in 1535 was only 13s-4d.

Cassington: 1. St Peter's church was given to Eynsham before 1123 by Geoffrey de Clinton who built it. It was consecrated by Bishop Robert Bloet. Geoffrey de Clinton was the Chamberlain and treasurer to Henry I. The church was endowed with a virgate of land – its glebe – and the tithe of both crops and beasts.[4] About 1198 the abbey appropriated it. Value to Eynsham in 1535 was £12-1s-8d. 'Geoffrey the Chamberlain' was remembered in the prayers of Eynsham's monks. Geoffrey de Clinton also gave the abbey his serf, Hugh de Sumerford in restitution for a cope which he had borrowed and lost! In the 19th century the church was said to have had a stone cross like that at Eynsham.
2. Some rents but diminished in value and in 1467 worth only 2s.

Caversham: From this manor, the abbey received a quitrent of two lbs of wax from the canons of Notley Abbey for common pasture in South Stoke wood which stretched east from the village to the Thames. Notley owned the church here and leased some land from the manor. The quitrent was worth one shilling in 1530. A quitrent was a small sum paid in lieu of services that might be owed by them to Eynsham.

Chadlington: See Charlbury.

Charlbury: Extensive property in a parish that included nine hamlets: Charlbury, Chadlington, Childeston, Thurne, Shorthampton, Walecote, Finstock, Fawler and Cote, and two dependent chapels at Chadlington and Shorthampton.
1. St Mary's church Charlbury was given to Eynsham by Robert Bloet, Bishop of Lincoln in 1094 for the loss of Stowe. It made a payment of five marks to the abbey annually. A mark was equivalent to 13s-4d. The church was appropriated by the abbey in 1293 and took all the Great Tithe. The value of the property was increased in 1353 when King Edward III granted it the tithes of the wild beasts and other animals in Cornbury Park in Charlbury.
2. St Nicholas chapel, Chadlington, paid the abbey 14s annually. From All Saints chapel, Shorthampton, Eynsham received annually the crop of two acres.

---

³ Gordon E., *Eynsham Abbey 1005-1228 A Small Window into a Large Room*, p. 106, Phillimore & Co. Ltd., 1990.
⁴ Pounds, op. cit., p. 31.

3. The manor of Charlbury was also given to the abbey in 1094 by the bishop and, like South Stoke, had probably been part of the land of the Bishopric of Dorchester before the See was moved to Lincoln. In 1256 King Henry III granted a weekly market and annual fair to the town. The woods of Charlbury, enclosed in 1332, amounted to 321 acres and were worth £15-6s-8d per year in 1363. In 1448, the tenants of Charlbury paid a rent of three barbed arrows to the abbey for an acre of land called the 'Pleyying place'.

4. Donations of land in Fawler began in the first half of the 13th century and the abbey's holdings grew steadily. By 1528 the rent from Fawler amounted to £11-8s-4d.

5. Radulfus Basset gave the land of Finstock to Eynsham before 1154, amounting to 43 acres and a virgate of assart, i.e. land converted to arable from forest. Peter Thalesmasche quitclaimed to Eynsham half a knight's fee of four virgates in 1205. A third holding, known as Tapwell or Topples and consisting of ten acres, was given to the abbey by the Grant family between 1241 and 1264. It had eight tenants in the early 14th century. The value of the property increased with enclosure in the 14th and 15th centuries. A Deserted Medieval Village (DMV) but the name survives in Topples Lane and Wood.[5]

6. About 1173, Matilda de Clara gave the abbey half a virgate of land in Chadlington. John Heynon gave about 100 acres in Chadlington before 1264. Rents in 1447 amounted to £1-7s-5d.

7. Cote/Coat had 12 tenants of the abbey in the early 14th century and ten in 1447/8. DMV. The total value for Eynsham's properties in Charlbury and its constituent parts, including tithes, rents and profits from courts, was £47-8s in 1535 making it one of the abbey's most profitable properties. At the Dissolution, the manor of Charlbury was granted to Sir Edward North, the same man who took possession of Eynsham in 1543. He sold it in 1555 to Sir Thomas White, the founder of St John's College, Oxford.

Chastleton: About 1152-4, Henry d'Oilly gave four hides of land in Chastleton (Brookend), in memory of his father who was buried in Eynsham Abbey. It had 13 tenants in 1363 but by 1441 only three remained. The manor was let to John Hacher in early 16th century. Worth £6-6s-8d in 1535.

Cirencester: In 1158 Eynsham Abbey was given Wigewald mill by Manasserus Biset, Baron of the Exchequer and a royal justice. It was rented at 30s annually, and the abbey received 10s a year from another mill. In 1535 one mill was valued at 10s but the other is not included and may have been sold.

Claydon: Before 1109, Richard de Newark gave two thirds of his tithe.

Claywell in Ducklington: Formerly called East Weld. In 1360 six tenants paid £5-1s-3d in rent to Eynsham Abbey.

Cogges: Before 1191, Manasser Arsic, Sheriff of Oxfordshire, gave Eynsham five acres of meadow in Cogges. It was worth 3s annually in 1270 but was not referred to thereafter. The monks also had ancient rights to the crop of four acres of arable from the demesne of Cogges. According to the VCH this was for burial rights.[6] It was worth 6s-8d in 1270 but lost sometime after 1390.

[5] Finberg H.P.R. (ed.), *The Deserted Villages of Oxfordshire*, Leicester University Press, 1965.

[6] Crossley A., *Victoria History of the County of Oxford*, Vol. XII: pp. 98-157, OUP 1990. University of London Institute

Colesbourne (Gloucs): Tithes in Colesbourne, Duntisbourne Rouse and Elkstone were given to Eynsham before 1110 by William son of Bernard. Not mentioned in 1535 but possibly granted to Bruerne Abbey for a payment of 40s p.a.

Colston Basset (Notts): In 1120 Ralph Basset and his wife gave the abbey a carucate of land i.e. land equivalent to the area that could be ploughed in a year by one plough and eight oxen, and a rent of 20s with a monk they sent to the abbey. Abbot Geoffrey (1351/2–1388) later gave the estate to Laune Priory (Leics). See Ashley (Northants).

Combe: St Laurence church was given to Eynsham by the Empress Matilda in 1141 and paid 10s p.a. to the abbey. It was appropriated in 1399. Appropriated by the bishop in 1478 and given to Lincoln College, Oxford which paid Eynsham £3 p.a. Eynsham surrendered the £3 in return for a lump sum of £60 in 1534. The church was re-built by Eynsham Abbey in 1395 and hardly altered since.[7] Lincoln College still holds the patronage of Combe.

Cornwell: Great and small tithes granted by Richard de Gray before 1109 but lost by 1320. Briefly held the church, St Peter's, in the 12th century receiving from it 1lb of wax annually. Supposedly given by Stephen de Punsold and Alice his wife.[8] Eynsham still had the tithes of the demesne in 1239 but seems to have lost them by 1320.

Cropredy: Tithes of the bishop's demesne. Two thirds of the tithe of Geoffrey de Cropredy given in 1109. In 1539 it was worth £5-13s-4d.

Croxton (Leics): Tithes granted before 1167 worth 3s-4d per annum. Worth 3s in 1539.

Dallington (Northants): Mill granted to Eynsham by Roger de Chesney on his deathbed in 1165 but not mentioned thereafter.

Deddington: About 1180, Matilda de Chesney, the Bishop of Lincoln's niece, gave Eynsham a third of Clifton Mill in Deddington. Her cousin, Ralf Murdac, gave another third in 1192. The prior of Bicester who held the other third, paid rent to Eynsham, worth £2 in 1390. In 1535 the amount was £1 per annum, half of its previous value. 'Lady Matilda de Chesney' was also remembered in the monks' prayers.

Dornford and Woodlays in Wootton: Tithes given to Eynsham by Richard de Gray before 1109. Worth 20s per annum in 1454. In 1535 the value was 6s-8d. DMV.

Dotard's Mill: About 1160, William de Chesney gave Eynsham a mill in Deddington worth 20s p.a., the same in 1535. William held the town and castle of Deddington and was possibly Sheriff of Oxfordshire. His brother Robert, was Bishop of Lincoln (1148-66).

of Historical Research.
[7] Pevsner N. and Sherwood J., *The Buildings of England - Oxfordshire*, Penguin Books, 1974.
[8] Rev. Symonds quoting Anthony Wood. Cruikshank Mrs, *Notes on the History of Eynsham or Some Account of the History of Eynsham* Unpublished, undated typescripts c. 1930, Oxfordshire History Centre.

Duntisbourne and Elkstone (Gloucs): According to the *Taxatio* of Pope Nicholas, Eynsham had a small portion of the tithe, possibly granted by the De Gardino family.

Eynsham: 1. 'Nova Terra' or Newland borough: created by Abbot Adam in 1215. Approximately 20 acres of land let at four shillings an acre. Tenants were not liable for feudal service or dues and could will or sell their property for a fee. In 1390 rents amounted to £3-6s-9d. It had its own court to settle disputes and elect officers, probably held at what is now the White Hart, the oldest domestic building in the village. Fines were paid to the abbot but in 1442 these amounted to only 6s. The borough remained within Eynsham parish.

2. The Old Borough: Also had a court, producing £2-0s-10d in 1442. Rents amounted to £45-16s-0d in 1390. Sales of wool and hay contributed significant amounts to the abbey's income.

3. Eynsham Manor: Tenants subject to all feudal dues and services although it was possible to buy your freedom. The manorial court was profitable and in 1442, for example, produced £9-11s-4d.

4. Powkebridge Court: Its business was to supervise pannage i.e. the privilege of pasturage for pigs in the abbey's woods and fines for over grazing.

5. Tilgarsley: A hamlet comprising 24 virgates and tenanted by villeins. Wiped out by the Black Death. The land then became part of the abbot's demesne. By the early 15th century the land had been enclosed and let to tenants. See chapter 8.

6. Hampstall/Armstalls: A hamlet adjoining Eynsham. Usually taxed with South Leigh. In 1306 it had nine tenants but only three in 1369. In 1467 the single remaining tenant paid the abbey over £23 in rent. Still one cottage there in 1930 but now a DMV, remains of which lie south of the lane leading to the 'Nunnery'.

7. St Leonard's 'chapel': first referred to in 1197. Built by the abbey for the use of the parish and probably on the footprint of a Saxon chapel. The abbey appointed its vicar and took a proportion of his income. In 1291 for example, the living was valued at £21-6s-8d but the abbey paid the vicar £5.[9]

8. Fishery in the Thames: yielded a significant 450 eels in Domesday (1086). Worth £4-6s-8d in 1390. In the 1450s, a William Aylewyn was the 'farmer' of the fishery for which he paid £4-13s-4d rent.

9. Swinford Ferry: Although Abingdon Abbey owned the ferry, from 1299 they paid Eynsham a shilling annually for the right to use the Eynsham bank of the river. In addition, the monks were granted the use of the ferry, free of all tolls. Token payments of bread and beer were nevertheless to be levied on the persons of the abbot, cellarer and steward and on carts. N.B. The ford itself was part of the king's highway and available to all who wished to wade through the river but could be treacherous as John Wesley later discovered.

10. Eynsham Wharf: Built by the early 13th century at the junction of the Chilbrook and Limbrook, where the Talbot Inn now stands. Salt from Droitwich was brought here to send to Oxford and beyond. By the 14th century it is known that stone from Taynton quarries near Burford was transported by wagon to Eynsham and then by river to Merton College, Oxford and also to Windsor Castle.[10]

---

[9] Crossley, op. cit.
[10] McCreadie M., A History of the River Thames at Eynsham, *ER* 21, 2004. See also Atkins B., History of the Wharf and Wharf Stream, *ER* 30, 2013.

11. Eynsham Mill on the Hanborough Road: The miller paid the abbey an annual rent of ten shillings and 450 eels, an important supplement to the monk's diet.[11]

12. A weekly market in Eynsham was granted to the abbey by King Stephen and a twice yearly fair by King Henry II.

13. Tannery: An entry in the *Cartulary* for 1389-90 refers to the sale of leather, parchment and skins and implies the existence of a tannery. This was let for between £2 and £3 yearly in the later medieval period.[12] A 14th century whetstone for sharpening needles has been found in Tanners Lane, Eynsham and may relate to glove making on the site. See MacGregor J., Finds at Hythe Croft, *ER* 10 1993.

14. Relics: The abbey acquired the arm of St Andrew about 1240. Donor unknown but said to be a crusader returning from Jerusalem. In common with other abbeys, Eynsham certainly had others, a significant source of income from pilgrims.

Filkins: The abbey was given half a hide by Ralph Murdac in 1174. It was worth 6s in 1390. By 1535 it had disappeared – possibly included in the properties leased to Bruerne Abbey

Fulbrook (Bucks) Two hides given to the abbey about 1155 by Wigan of Wallingford, valued at 60s p.a. Granted to the Purcell family between 1180 and 1190 for a rent of two marks p.a.

The abbey bought further land in Fulbrook in 1252 and leased it at a rent of six marks. In 1535 it was valued at £3-8s-4d.

Gloucester: The abbey owned several tenements here from the mid-13th century, worth 18s in rent in 1390. By 1535 the amount was only 4s from one property.

Graffam (Sussex): Eynsham had property here, possibly granted by the De Chesney family in the late 12th century, but there are no details thereafter.

Great Rollright: Tithes of one hide, worth 6s-8d in 1291. Given to the tenant of Little Rollright in 1435. About 1189, Juliana Tirel gifted seven acres to the abbey worth 3s p.a. in 1275 but not referred to thereafter.

Goring: About 1150 one hide and 27 acres was given by William Druval. Included under South Stoke in the monastic accounts. The land is adjacent to the South Stoke border and was apparently called 'Childeslande'. Some woodland and an eyot in the Thames were donated by Thomas Druval sometime later.

Hanborough: Rents worth about 15s p.a. partly paid by Osney Abbey until 1441. Not mentioned in 1535.

Hempton: About 1213, Wido de Diva and his wife Lucy de Chesney, granddaughter of William de Chesney, gave a virgate of land in the parish of Deddington, worth 10s p.a. Not mentioned in 1535 but probably included in the rent from the lordship of Milcombe.

---

[11] Harris M., *From Acre End, Portrait of a Village*, p. 13, Chatto & Windus Ltd, 1986.

[12] Crossley, op. cit., p. 138

Heyford ad Pontem or Lower Heyford: About 1173, half of the value of the church was given to Eynsham and in 1197 Bishop Hugh granted a pension from it of 20s p.a. – the same in 1535. The Rev. Symonds claimed that the gift was made by the De la Mare family in about 1060.[13]

Heyford Warren or Upper Heyford: A hide of land worth 8s p.a. in rent – the same in 1535.

Histon or Histon Abbats (Cambs): The demesne of the manor was given to the abbey by Bishop Robert Bloet in 1094 for the loss of Stow. 15 hides and three virgates. Valued at £58-3s-4d in 1291 but only £32 in 1535. From 1191, the church paid Eynsham four marks p.a. (£2-13s-4d). St Etheldreda's church was appropriated in 1268 and was valued at £20 net in 1291 and £20 gross in 1535. The rectory and manor produced £81-10s-1d in 1390, making it one of Eynsham's most valuable properties. At the Dissolution, the church and manor were granted to Thomas Elliot. The church was demolished in the 1590s by Sir Francis Hinde to provide building materials for Madingley Hall. The site of St Etheldreda's is still adjoined by Abbey Farm. The existing church at Histon, St Andrew's, was part of a nearby manor owned by Denny Abbey.

Langley: About 1180, the abbey was granted one third of the tithes of the demesne, worth 5s in 1270. Lost by 1535.

Letcombe Basset (Berks): Before 1110 Gilbert Basset granted the abbey the tithe of the cheese and wool of all his land. Worth 26s-8d in 1291 but by 1535 only 13s-4d.

Lemhill: A mill in Lemhill near Broughton given by Ralf Murdac in 1192, worth 8s in 1390 but lost by 1535. Possibly sold or gifted in the late 15th century.

Little Rollright: In Domesday, Eynsham possessed five hides of land in Little Rollright, held by *the monk Columban*. The manor was granted to the abbey at its re-foundation in 1109 and was valued at £13-1s-10d in 1279 but only £8 in 1535.
St Philip's church also belonged to the abbey and paid Eynsham 10s annually until the Dissolution.

Merton: David, King of Scotland and the Empress Matilda's maternal uncle, gave Eynsham St Swithun's church here between 1123 and 1148 which paid the abbey 30s p.a. It was appropriated in 1357. In 1390 the tithes were sold for £24. In 1535 the gross value was £12-9s. The early 14th century church is, according to Pevsner, 'one of the grandest and most ornate in this part of the county'. The tithe barn, built by the abbey, still stands to the west of the church but was barbarously treated in the late 20th century when it was converted into several residences, and is now barely recognisable.

Mickleton (Gloucs): The manor, consisting of 14 hides, was granted to Eynsham in the foundation charter of 1005 and was still one of Eynsham's properties in 1086 when it was valued at £10. Domesday lists 5 ploughs, 20 villeins, 7 borders with 10 ploughs, 8 slaves and 2 servants.

---

[13] *Bodl. MS Top Oxon b 275*, Rev Thomas Symonds Collection.

It also entitled Eynsham to 24 measures of salt from Droitwich. The ancient Saltway from Droitwich to Oxford passed close to Mickelton and probably transported Eynsham's salt and that of its manor at Little Rollright.[14] Profits of the manor in 1390 were £22-1s-8d. The Abbot of Eynsham had a rabbit warren here, an important supplement to the abbey's diet. St Lawrence church belonged to Eynsham from early times. Its first known rector in 1180 was Bartholemew De Eynsham, the 'nephew' of Abbot Godfrey who appointed a vicar, Magister Ricardus, to be the incumbent priest. The church was appropriated in 1351 and in 1390 the abbey received £35 from its tithes and £4-14s-10d from other dues. In 1535 the total value of Mickleton was £80. Sir Henry Spelman claimed that there was effectively a curse on those who appropriated the lands of Eynsham Abbey here, citing the example of the Greville family, one of whom was shot by his brother who in turn was pressed to death for failing to plead in a case of false imprisonment.[15]

Milcombe: Nigel d'Oilly gave three and a half hides to Eynsham before 1109, valued at 40s annually. About 1256, Eynsham was given one virgate in Milcombe by Edwin de Blockesham, worth £3-10s in 1291 and £5 in 1535. Eynsham had a manorial court here which, between 1451 and 1457 yielded more than £14 in fines and heriots, a payment made to a lord on the death of a tenant.

Milton, near Thame: About 1094, Robert Bloet gave Eynsham the tithes of his demesne here, worth 50s in 1254, which were surrendered to the bishop before 1290. Before 1169, Roger de Cundi gave four acres of land here to the abbey. Rents were paid at Wood Eaton and were probably included in the sums returned from there in 1535.

Milton-under-Wychwood: Tithes of two hides given to Eynsham before 1167 by Richard son of William. Roger son of Salomon gave 12 acres before 1180. Both the tithe and the land were given to the Abbey of Bruerne in the 14th century for a rent of 26s-8d annually. Bruerne Abbey, like Eynsham, has completely disappeared. Two fragments of Norman arcading are built into the gateposts of the large 18th century house that replaced it.

Minster Lovell or **Little Minster:** Before 1109, Roger de Chesney, father of the future Bishop of Lincoln, gave the tithe of his land there, worth 10s in 1270. Also, the tithe of all his wool throughout Oxfordshire. Lost sometime after 1390.[16]

Moulsford (Berks): Robert de Oilly gave his one hide of land there to Eynsham before 1135. Granted away before 1350 but the abbey retained a quitrent of 4s until the Dissolution.

Naunton (Gloucs): Ralph D'Oilly gave the tithes of his demesne in the mid-12th century. There was a dispute at the time about these tithes between the Abbot of Eynsham and the priest, Alan Slaughter. In 1253 the tithe was granted to Little Malvern Priory for 25s p.a. but no longer held by 1291. Half a hide of land given about 1180 by Hugo D'Oilly, worth 9s in rent in 1390 and paid up to 1465. Probably included in the rents from Wyck Rissington in 1535.

---

[14] Gordon, op.cit., p.155.
[15] *Bodl. MS Top Oxon b 275.*
[16] Carpenter D.X., *The Charters of William II and Henry I – Eynsham Abbey*, p.14 https://actswilliam2henry1.wordpress.com, 2016.

Nether Worton: About 1255, Eynsham was given a virgate of land by Henry de Blockesham worth 4s in rent. Included in the return for Milcombe in 1390 and 1535.

North Leigh: St Mary's church was given to Eynsham about 1150 by John de St John but seems to have been lost by 1200.

Oxford: Eynsham had about 50 properties both inside and outside the walls of the city, including mills (Blackfriars and one other), shops, houses and tenements. The location of some has been suggested by Salter e.g. Stapell Hall in School Street and Plummer Hall adjoining the city's north wall.[17] In total worth over £15 p.a. in 1279. Most of these seem to have been disposed of by 1535 as their value had decreased to £2 p.a. In 1534 the abbey granted Richard Gunter a lease of all their rents in Oxford for 99 years for £10 p.a. In the same year, it surrendered a fee of £3 from Lincoln College for a lump sum of £60 (See Combe). The Eynsham Cartulary detailing the Oxford properties has been lost. The church of St Ebbe's was given to the abbey before 1086 and paid it annually 1 mark, the same in 1390.
See also Walton, in St Martin's parish.

Pentecostals: the gift by Bishop Alexander in 1138 of ancient offerings known as 'smoke-farthings' or Pentecostals. These were donations of a farthing from every house due to Lincoln cathedral at Pentecost but thereafter, so far as Oxfordshire was concerned, payable to Eynsham. They were worth £7-5s-½d in 1535. Great processions to deliver the sums would be made to the abbey yearly from every parish and it was expected that some of those in attendance would make extra offerings. The *Cartulary* indeed, refers to gifts of gold, silver and silk. At the Dissolution, the monies were paid to the king by the churchwardens of St Leonard's and is mentioned in their accounts of 1695.

Peter's Pence: An annual tax of 1d from each householder having land of a certain value paid to the pope. The abbey had the right to pay no more than 8s for the churches of Eynsham, Cassington, Yarnton, Charlbury, South Stoke, Little Rollright and Shifford. However, the abbey seems to have collected a larger amount from their tenants, thereby making a small profit.

Pheleleie: A small community of Benedictines at Stonesfield headed by a prior. The monks and their endowments were transferred to Eynsham in the reign of King Stephen.

Pudlicot: A chapel here was given to Eynsham before 1167 but seems to have closed by the end of the 12th century. Tithes were worth 20s but after 1448 there is no mention of them. It is assumed that they were merged with the rectory of Charlbury. The abbey also owned a meadow in Pudlicot given by Alexander de Rumeli between 1180 and 1197 and rented for 4s.

Quinton (Gloucs): Two hides of land worth about 10s but given to Winchcombe Abbey in the late 13th century for a sum of 10 marks. Tithes to the value of £4-18s in 1325 but no trace subsequently and possibly included in the tithes from Mickelton.

---

[17] Salter H.E., *Medieval Oxford*, Clarendon Press for the Oxford Historical Society, 1936.

Sarsden: St James' church given to Eynsham in the late 12th century and paid the abbey 13s-4d annually until the Dissolution.

Saxey (Berks): In the late 14th and 15th centuries Eynsham received a rent of 10s for a 'close' here. Not mentioned in 1535 and may have been disposed of.

Shifford: The manor, with its court, was granted to Eynsham Abbey at its foundation in 1005 and amounted to approximately 620 acres. Worth £5 in 1086. To it the abbey attached its property in the neighbouring hamlets of East Weld in Ducklington, Cote and Bampton Aston. About 1179, Ralph de Chesney gave one hide in Weld. In 1269 it was worth a total of £7-3s-8d. Ralph was regularly remembered in Eynsham's prayers.
In Aston the D'Oyley family gave half a hide in the 1130s and another virgate between 1160 and 1180. Ralf de Chesney gave one and a half hides at the same time. Gunnora de la Mare gave half a virgate of Alvescot to Aston in the 1240s.
In Cote, the abbey had four half virgates.

Shipton: In 1390 the abbey received 13s-4d in rent from Shipton Mill but there are no other references to it and, like quite a few of the abbey's properties, must have been disposed of in the 15th century to meet the abbey's debts.

Shorthampton: See Charlbury.

Showell (near Swerford): Henry d'Oilly gave Eynsham half a hide of land between 1154 and 1163, worth 9s in rent. By 1535 the land had been transferred to Bruerne Abbey which paid Eynsham 40s p.a. for it and other properties.

Somerton: Three virgates granted to Eynsham in 1148 but before 1200 two of them were given up in perpetuity for a rent of 10s p.a. In 1291 the remaining land was worth 15s, reduced to 10s by 1390. No records of this property thereafter.

Souldern: St Mary's church given to the abbey by Jordan de Sai before 1161 to commemorate the burial of his son William in the abbey. It paid Eynsham 100s annually. One of its 12th century rectors was Ralph, the 'nephew' of Abbot Godfrey. By 1535 the sum paid to the abbey had been reduced to 53s-4d.

South Newington: Before 1166, Hugh de Chesney, brother of Robert de Chesney, bishop of Lincoln, and his wife Dionisia de Bereford (Barford St Michael) gave the church of St Peter Ad Vincula of South Newington to the abbey. Bishop Hugh of Lincoln granted a payment from it of 4s p.a. in 1197. The church was appropriated in 1399 and the tithes were leased. In 1537 Eynsham granted George Gifford an exceptional lease of the rectory for 90 years for £8 annually.

South Stoke: The manor, of 17 hides and one virgate, and St Andrew's church was given to Eynsham by Bishop Bloet in the 1090s as part of the compensation for the loss of Stow, Lincolnshire. South Stoke, sometimes known as Bishopstoke probably belonged to Dorchester before the See was moved to Lincoln in 1072. Worth £6 in 1086. After its

acquisition by Eynsham it was sometimes referred to as Stoke Abbas or Abbotstoke. From the church the abbey received 1lb of pepper per annum. Pepper was sourced from southern India via Italy and could cost 4s per pound, the equivalent to two week's wages for a master mason in the 13th century. It also received a portion of the tithe, worth £5-6s-8d p.a. in 1291. The church was appropriated in 1399. The manor, including the land in Goring was worth £42-6s-11d in 1291. It was leased in the 15th century and, exceptionally, a lease of 80 years was granted in 1536 to Walter Barton, with the exception of the 'Abbots wood', for the sum of £53-6s-8d. In 1546, after the Dissolution, South Stoke was granted by King Henry VIII to Christchurch Cathedral, Oxford, the seat of his newly created diocese.
See also Caversham, Goring, Woodcote and 'Peter's Pence.'

Stanton Harcourt: About 1136, Adeliza, Henry I's widow, gave Eynsham a hide of land at Stanton Harcourt. The land was lost by the end of the 12th century, seized by the king after 1176. Adeliza also granted land at Stanton Harcourt to Reading Abbey.[18]

Stanton St. John: St John the Baptist church given to Eynsham by John de St John between 1135 and 1150. It paid the abbey 20s p.a., the same in 1535. Sold to the Bishop of Lincoln in 1537/8 for £44-3s-2½d.

Stoke Talmage: Service due from a virgate here given to Eynsham about 1222 by Peter Thalemasche. Worth 11s and paid by Thame Abbey until the Dissolution.

Stow (Lincs): Tithe of altar wax granted by Bishop Bloet in the 1090s. 'A token of spiritual affinity' according to Eric Gordon.

Stratton: Gilbert Basset gave Eynsham two thirds of his tithe here before 1110. It was given to Bicester Priory in 1188 for the sum of 12s p.a., the same in 1535. He also gave all the tithe from his wool and cheeses from all his land.

Tackley: Between 1170 and 1195 Robert fitz-Nigel and Robert de Neofuilla gave two mills in Tackley, the tithes of a mill, and a fishpond. The tithe was worth 5s in 1291. After 1320 there is mention of only one mill, Cattesham, and Eynsham granted a lease on it for 60s p.a. By 1535 the rent was only 10s.

Tetbury (Gloucs): St Mary's church given to Eynsham by Reginald of St Walery between 1154 and 1161 and paid the abbey £2 p.a. In 1291 the rectory was valued at £24. The church was appropriated about 1361 and in 1390 the tithe was worth £16. At the Dissolution the church was granted to Christchurch College.

Thame: Tithes *in corn, beasts, wool and cheeses, as also one smallholder, together with two acres.* Granted by Bishop Bloet.

Turweston: A portion of the tithes given to Eynsham at an early date. Worth 4s in 1390 but not mentioned in 1535.

---

[18] Kemp B.R. (ed.), *Reading Abbey Cartularies*, Vol. I: p. 406, Royal Historical Society, 1986.

Walton (Oxford): A hide granted by Henry of Oxford shortly after 1156. Eynsham monks regularly included him in their prayers for benefactors of the abbey.[19] This is probably the land referred to in the Hundred Rolls as lying in St Martin's parish.[20]

Westcot Barton: St Edward the Confessor church given to Eynsham about 1190. It paid a half a mark to the abbey from the time of Bishop Hugh until the Dissolution.

Whitfield (Northants): St John Evangelist church given to Eynsham about 1178 by Gilbert de Monte. The abbey received 30 quarters of wheat and two marks annually. It was appropriated in 1240 and its value in 1390 was £5. Eynsham resigned its profits from the church in 1441.

Wickham: Robert son of Walchelin gave all his tithe from this part of Banbury before 1109. The tithe was resigned in 1293.

Witham (Berks): The abbey was granted half a virgate in this manor but leased it in the mid-13th century for a rent of 6s-8d. Not mentioned in 1535 but probably included in the rents of Eynsham.

Woodcote: The manor with its valuable woodland was given by Bishop Bloet in the 1090s. St Leonard's chapel here also seems to have belonged to the abbey. During the time of Abbot Robert (1197-1208), land that was *held of our church in Woodcote* was granted to William de Frith and his wife Sabine for a rent of 22s a year to be paid in four instalments of 5s 6d on the feast of St Michael, the feast of St Thomas the Apostle, at Easter and on the birthday of St John the Baptist.[21]

Wood Eaton: The manor was granted to Eynsham by Walkelin Hareng between 1170 and 1190. Estimated to be worth £20 p.a. in 1366 but only £14-15s-5d in 1535.

Wyck Rissington (Gloucs): Between 1241 and 1264 five virgates were given to Eynsham by Henry de Teyden who held the advowson. In the same period two further virgates were added by John Longe and William Bastard. A further carucate, about 100 acres, was given by Robert le Lung in 1311. The land was initially farmed by the abbey via a bailiff but in 1390 it was leased for £6-13s-4d. In 1535 the rent was £7. Pevsner credits the monks of Eynsham with the building of the 'remarkable' chancel and tower of St Laurence's church in the 13th century.

Yarnton: The manor, consisting of 10 hides, was apparently given to Eynsham at the time of its foundation in 1005 but by Domesday was held of the abbey by one of the Bishop of Lincoln's knights and never recovered despite attempts by, for example, Abbot Robert (1197–1208).

---

[19] Keats-Rohan K.S.B., The Making of Henry of Oxford: Englishmen in a Norman World, *Oxoniensia* Vol. LIV: p. 294, 1989.
[20] Salter H.E., *Eynsham Cartulary*, Vol. 1: p. xxxiv, Oxford Historical Society, Clarendon Press 1907.
[21] Hearne T., *Remarks and Collections*, printed for the Oxford Historical Society at the Clarendon Press. Vol VII (1719-22) reprinted by BiblioLife.

St Bartholomew's church always belonged to the abbey. The vicarage was worth £8-5s-4d in 1535 and the rectorial tithes £7. South of the church door, in the graveyard, is the lower half of a stone cross carved with figures under canopies. Possibly 14th century it is similar to Eynsham's original market cross and was probably erected by the abbey.

N.B. The references to 1291 concern a valuation of ecclesiastical property in England and Wales for taxation purposes, the *Taxatio,* ordered by Pope Nicholas IV to raise money for a Crusade. Those to 1535 are Thomas Cromwell's record of the assets of monastic properties, the *Valor Ecclesiasticus* of that year. References to 1539 refer to the receipts from the dissolved abbey for the year ending 29 September 1539. The revenues of the abbey by this time amounted to £441-16s-1d.

It should be remembered that the documentary evidence for Eynsham is far from complete. Several royal acts are omitted from the *Cartulary* and Salter believes that there must have been at least one other Cartulary dealing with the abbey's properties in Oxford, now lost. It was described about 1430 by a certain Nicholas Bishop, a citizen of Oxford, but may have been destroyed at the Dissolution.

The abbey's accounts are fragmentary and there is no complete record of income for any year except 1390 which also gives part of its expenditure. All valuations are given in pre-decimal currency.

Appendix 3

Some notes on the William Bainbridge collection of slides relating to Eynsham Abbey

The photos were acquired or taken in the 1970s and 1980s (dates, where known, in brackets) and some slides have brief notes of provenance. Many of the loose stones illustrated are now built into the six Heritage Trail 'cairns' around the village. Some are in the Museum Resources Centre (MRC), Standlake, but not all have been fully indexed. Others are held privately. A few have disappeared as their original owners died or moved away. Bainbridge's attributions have been included as well as his dating. Minimal extra notes added by the author. The collection has recently been digitised by Eynsham History Group to whom they were left, although the Index of the earlier slides is not complete and in its early parts out of order. The negatives were deposited with the English Heritage Archive in Swindon and these notes are based on the order of that archive.

1. Drawing by the Oxford antiquarian Anthony Wood of the ruins of the west end of Eynsham Abbey church, looking west from the nave, 16 September 1657. (*Bodl. MS Wood E1*, f 45) (18.8.78)
2. Photo of the inside of the ruins of Castle Acre Priory, Norfolk.
3. Detail from the Sheldon Tapestry Map of Oxfordshire and Berkshire, the Queen's Room, Oxburgh Hall, Norfolk. Woven in 1647 it is a copy of one of Ralph Sheldon's tapestry maps made in the 1590s and now in the Bodleian Library. (10.7.92)
4. A 'tidied up' version of the Anthony Wood drawing, engraved by S. and N. Buck in 1729.
5. The west front of Southwell Minster, Nottinghamshire (1106-1150) West window 1450, spires restored 1880. (20.4.69) Eynsham Abbey could have looked something like this.
6. Castle Acre Cluniac Priory – a reconstruction by Alan Sorrell, 1958. 'Possible appearance of Eynsham Abbey.'
7. 12th/13th century male corbel head. Found in Conduit Lane, Eynsham. W.E. Beauchamp, 50 Clover Place, previously 58 Acre End Street. (21.5.75)
8. Male corbel head, W.E. Beauchamp. 58 Acre End St, Eynsham. Side view of 7. (21.5.75)
9. Stone corbel head. Part of the Museum Resources Centre (MRC) collection. 'Head, with suggestion of hair or hood on each side carved on a block of oolite limestone with flat base' (MRC Index) Previously collection of Miss M.B. Foote, Lords Farm. (1.8.75)
10. Stone corbel head 12th /14th century? Found in wall and now re-set over back door of 100 Acre End Street. Dr T.W. Tinsley. (26.4.75)
11. Small grotesque head built into a gable wall of a garage at 3 Bitterell, Eynsham. Romanesque. Removed from St Leonard's in 1983. K.J.W. Sheffield. (26.6.88)
12. Illustration from an exhibition at the Ashmolean of an 'Anglo-Saxon' rectangular slab with one large and two smaller heads above a possible arch. The actual stone

appears in a Henry Taunt photo of Eynsham Vicarage garden taken in the late 19th century. The carving is currently on long-term loan to the Vale and Downland Museum in Wantage from The Museums Resource Centre (MRC) at Standlake. 'Central head, staring eyes, heavy furrowed brow, grotesque mouth, flanked by smaller heads either side on ¾ relief on flat rectangular base' (MRC Index).

13. Illustration of two stone corbels from Eynsham abbey from an exhibition catalogue, Ashmolean Museum. Slide 11 may be the upper part of the lower illustration.

14. Stone corbel head, 'female funeral effigy', late 14th century. Dr Bolsover. (2.6.77)

15. Stone corbel head/label stop. Possibly the original of 19.

16. Stone label stop. Head of a woman, 13th century? Originally Dame Helen Gardner, Myrtle House.

17. Stone corbel head. Crowned female head, second half of 14th century. Dowel hole at the back. Miss M.B. Foote, Lords Farm. (1.8.75) Supposedly at the MRC but 'not found'.

18. Label stop. Small male head, 13th century? Originally Dame Helen Gardner, Myrtle House. (4.3.77)

19. Stone corbel, male head. Early 16th century. From Nursery Site. 'recently flaked'. In 1980s at F. Hunt, 107 Banbury Road, Kidlington. (28.9.77)

20. Stone corbel head. 15th century. In the 19th century it was part of a large collection of abbey stones in the Vicarage garden, Mill Street, Eynsham. Photographed there by Henry Taunt in 1890 when it was part of a garden arch. After the sale of the Vicarage in 1985 it was stored in the churchyard and suffered serious weathering. This was one of four stones given to St Peter's RC church and subsequently built into the wall of the lobby between the church and the Tolkein Room. Likewise, Nos. 21, 22 and 24.

21. Small corbel head. 12th century? Eynsham Vicarage.

22. Respond capital with stylised volutes. Romanesque, 12th century.

23. Dogs head gargoyle. Once in the Vicarage garden. (7.9.78) Now in the MRC, Standlake. 'Heavy brow, gaping jaw, staring eyes, sculpted wavy fur head and neck. Square sectioned channel back of neck to throat and mouth.' (MRC Index)

24. Double headed corbel. Male and female. Romanesque. Now in lobby of St Peter's RC church.

25. Romanesque 'Agnus Dei' capital (c. 1170). Once at 3 Bitterell. Mrs M. Street. (15.10.82) Whereabouts unknown

26. Other side of 25. Beast or bird with foliate tail.

27. Fluted capital 12th century. Garden wall in Newland Street. A. Burden. (28.9.75)

28. Norman Capital in Murray House greenhouse. H.C.D. Cooper. 29 Acre End St. (26.4.75) No longer in the village.

29. Small engaged capital with scalloping from Nursery site. Hunt, 107 Banbury Rd Kidlington. (28.9.77) Now in a garden in Acre End Street.

30. Plain Romanesque capital. Provenance unknown.

31. Clustered and engaged capital c. 1250, eight inches high. W. Bainbridge. (15.8.74)

32. As 31. (9.5.75)

33. Norman scalloped twin respond capital 'newly excavated' at 45 Acre End St. (14.5.84) Now built upside down into Abbey Street 'cairn'.

34. Small foliated engaged capital *c.* 1300. 'Buchanan gift from The Holt', 47 Mill St. (5.9.87) Now built into the 'cairn' in St Peter's carpark.
35. 13th century capital of nook shaft. 10 Newland St. Formerly Buchanan. (31.10.80)
36. 'Small double capital *c.* 1300. Churchyard.' (23.10.87) Probably from the Vicarage garden. Brian Atkins collection.
37. Like 36 but found in Newland Street, possibly after the closure and demolition of Sawyer's store in 1971. Some of the other stones in Newland Street were probably derived from the same source.
38. 'Small E.E. capital/base *c.* 1320'. Vicarage garden/churchyard. (23.10.87) Brian Atkins collection.
39. 'Early English column base – 'water holding' moulds.' Nursery site. Hunt. 107 Banbury Rd Kidlington. (28.9.77) Now in a garden in Acre End Street.
40. Stone fragment. 'Base with ivy carving *c.* 1300. Churchyard/Vicarage'. (23.10.87)
41. Pillar base and inverted capital. E.E. Dame Helen Gardner. Myrtle House, Eynsham. Corbel head on top (See 18)
42. Base of clustered columns. 13th century? Dr B. Hyde. Newland Street.
43. Bases of recessed shaft *c.* 1240. Found in demolished wall of Sawyers shop in Newland St.
44. Twin engaged shaft base. 14th century? In garden wall of 9 Queen's Lane. A.E. Faulkner.
45. Base of nook shaft. Found in interior wall of 43 Acre End St.
46. Section of clustered columns. 1450? 65 Newland St, Dr B.J. Hyde. Actually, vaulting fragment.
47. Roll moulding. Dec. In wall of a garden in Newland St, A. Burden. Probably vaulting fragment.
48. Section of roll moulding found in walls of Sawyers store in 1980, Newland St.
49. Roll moulding in garden wall in Newland St.
50. Triple nook shafting moulding found in interior wall of 43 Acre End St.
51. Two mouldings. Mrs M. Streat, 3 Bitterell.
52. Roll moulding. Peter Hayes collection. Keeled shaft?
53. Section of roll moulding from the garden of Maltshovel House, formerly a pub in the High Street. William Bainbridge, 10 Newland St.
54. Reverse of 53. Simulated masonry joint in red paint.
55. Missing.
56. Corner moulding. Peter Hayes collection.
57. As 56
58. Fragment with carving of a leaf (or bird) 14th century? and a piece of moulding. 58 Acre End Street. W.E. Beauchamp.
59. 3 Abbey stones supporting a slab. Witney Road. Mrs J.A. Underwood.
60. Abbey fragment. St Leonard's churchyard.
61. Vaulting. From churchyard. Now in Recreation ground 'cairn'.
62. Section of a large respond column 12th century. Vicarage garden. Now part of the 'cairn' in Abbey Street. Possibly part of the gatehouse to the inner precinct to the abbey.
63. Section of moulding from Nursery site. Hunt, 107 Banbury Rd, Kidlington.
64. Sill. Desmond Pimm garden. Park House, Eynsham.

65. Part of an arch with chamfered edge. Pimm collection. Mill Street.

66. As 65

67. Fragment of 'nailhead' decoration. Late 12th early 13th century. Inserted in barn wall at Lord's farm. M.B. Foote.

68. Another section of 'nailhead' built into a wall. 13 Newland Street.

69. 'Ballflower' decoration. *c.* 1300 Originally S.M. Evans until 1944. W.B. Now in garden in Newland Street.

70. 'Ballflower' in a hollow moulding. Garden wall in Newland St, A. Burden

71. Moulding with rosette. 65 Newland St, Dr B. Hyde.

72. Illustration from *A Concise Glossary of Terms Used in Gothic Architecture* by John Henry Parker, published in 1896. Reprinted in *The Eynsham Record* No 5, 1988. The stone was part of a 15th century cornice with a form of diaper or stylised flower decoration (rosettes?) and supposed to come from Eynsham. Now unknown.

73. Fragment of 14th century gothic tracery. Churchyard. Now built into the St Peter's 'cairn'.

74. Fragment of Perpendicular tracery. 15th century. Found in wall of 100 Acre End St. In garden of Acre End House. Dr T.W. Tinsley.

75. Small arcading late Dec., *c.* 1360. Peter Hayes collection. Probably part of a two-light window.

76. Fragment of Perp. tracery. 15th century. Dr T.W. Tinsley's garden.

77. Small cusped spandrel *c.* 1430, slot for glass. Dr B.J. Hyde. 65 Newland St.

78. 14th century miniature arcade fragment. Eynsham Vicarage. Removed 15/5/1986 Current location unknown.

79. Small cusped arch. Churchyard. Drawn by Alfred Cobb in 1870 when it was part of an arch in the Vicarage garden. Now in the MRC, Standlake.

80. 'Beakhead' voussoir, *c.* 1160-70. Vicarage garden, later churchyard. Brian Atkins collection.

81. Rudimentary 'beakhead' voussoir. From Nursery site. Hunt. 107 Banbury Rd, Kidlington.

82. Gothic tracery and another view of 80.

83. Modern (1992) arch on the east side of Mill Street in Eynsham with many examples of simple chevron voussoirs on large roll mouldings. The stones were found in the garden of 'The White House'. Another voussoir from the same source is now in the Queen's Head pub in Queen's Street.

84. Spandrels of cusped ogee doorway 15th century. From the garden of Maltshovel House.

85. Reverse of 84

86. Fragment of Perp. Tracery. 15th century. Dr T.W. Tinsley.

87. Fragment of 15th century Perp. tracery. In garden of Acre End House. Found in wall of 100 Acre End St, Dr T.W. Tinsley.

88. 16th century spandrel. Vicarage.

89. Sections of arch lately at Vicarage. 'Now at east end of church'. See 98

90. Two pieces of tracery. 58 Acre End St. W.E. Beauchamp.

91. Fragments of EE mouldings. Peter Hayes collection.

92. 15th century tracery inserted (upside down) into the gable wall of a barn in Aelfric Court, Oxford Road/High St south side, Eynsham.

93. Ribbed vaulting keystone built into a wall in the Bitterell. (H.S.W. Sheffield)
94. Rib vaulting Y junction. W.E. Beauchamp. 58 Acre End St. Possibly a springer for an arch.
95. Vaulting springer. Eynsham Vicarage. Now built into Market Square 'cairn'.
96. Vault springer and tracery fragments removed from the Vicarage and stored at the east end of the church. Also the two responds built into the Abbey St 'cairn'.
97. Vault springer built into a wall of what was the Catholic Apostolic church, John Lopes Road.
98. Ogee gothic arch with mythical animals and foliage in the spandrels and a squared drip mould above 14th century? Photographed in the back garden of the Vicarage in Mill Street. Removed 16/5/1986. The arch is now above the north doorway inside St Leonard's parish church, Eynsham.
99. The same arch drawn by the artist and sometime architect John Buckler in 1813 when it was in a cottage on the south-west corner of Swan Street. (*Bodl. MS Top Oxon a 66 f250*). Bainbridge says 'side of 2 Abbey St' and that the arch was removed in 1843.
100. Gothic tracery for a circular window. Formerly at the Vicarage.
101. Formerly at the Vicarage. Removed 15.5.86. Small 16th century window. (20.10.84)
102. Drawing by Alfred Cobb in 1870 of one of the gateways in the vicarage garden (*Bodl. MS Top Oxon d 514* A.) 'Angel at Woodstock – rest still at Vicarage re-arranged.' (20.10.84). Surmounting the whole is a fragmentary finial similar to the pyramidical stone shown on the ground in Taunt's photo (See 142). This latter stone is now in the MRC. 'Pinnacle. Tapered tall pyramid in shape; fluted edges bordering panels of egg and dart decoration.' (MRC Index) The gateway was removed with other stones in 1986.
103. 16th century angel corbel, Oxon Mus. Woodstock. (7.9.78) Now in the MRC. 'Standing figure, winged, robed, hair bunched at either side of face. Coat of arms over skirt at waist, At back, extension base for setting in, or for arch spring.' (MRC Index)
104. 15th century tracery panel rescued from the gable of a barn in Mill Street behind the Post Office which was demolished in 1962. (7.9.78) Now at the MRC.
105. As 104 but in situ. Barn on site of what is now John Lopes Rd. Copy of a photo taken by M.B. Foote in 1962. The photo was taken from the garden of 'The Holt.'
106. 15th century tracery in the western gable of 27 Acre End Street. (29.8.77)
107. Gothic chimney vent in gable of Seeney's barn at the rear of 7 Thames Street. (27.11.74) The barn was demolished in the 1990s and the 'smokehole', rescued by Sue Chapman, is now at the MRC.
108. Chimneystack, The Chequer, Abingdon Abbey, late 13th century. (11.10.77)
109. Chevron voussoir, 12th century. Found in the walls of Sawyer's store in 1980. (31.10.80) Now set above side door of the pottery.
110. Chevron voussoir. Previously belonged to Dame Helen Gardner, Myrtle House. (4.3.77)
111. Two chevron voussoirs from the Nursery site. Hunt, Banbury Road, Kidlington. (28.9.77) The larger one is now in a garden in Acre End Street.
112. Point to point chevron. Vicarage garden. (20.10.84) Brian Atkins collection.
113. Part of a door jamb? Chevron forming a lozenge shape. Murray House greenhouse, H.C.D. Cooper. (26.4.75)
114. Chevron built into garden wall in Newland St. A. Burden. (28.9.75)

115. Romanesque decorated column, 3-stranded interlace forming lozenges with flowers. 65 Newland Street, Dr B.J. Hyde. (25.7.84)

116. Units of diaper pattern built into a fireplace at Lords Farm. Formerly Miss M.B. Foote. (1.8.75) Now Oxford Preservation Trust.

117. Romanesque stone fragments built into the east wall of 'The Elms.' (30.6.84)

118. 13th century flooring tile, imperial eagle. Originally 146 mm square. From the Vicarage. (20.4.76) Now at St Leonard's.

119. 13th century tiles from the Nursery site. Now Hunt, 107 Banbury Rd. Kidlington. (28.9.77)

120. 3 fragments of tile with eagles. L. Pimm. (14.2.83)

121. Encaustic tiles, one with glaze. Wings of Imperial eagles. Largest 13.5 cm square. Vicarage collection. (20.4.76)

122. Tile fragments from grave diggings in St Peter's churchyard. (25.1.86)

123. 14th century flooring tile in the Ashmolean No 1967-637. Drawn by W.B. (22.2.80)

124. Two 14th century flooring tiles, passage floor, 37 Acre End Street. Mrs E. Morley. (19.8.82)

125. Detail of 124. Knight.

126. 1 tile and 2 fragments with diagonal gothic inscription. L. Pimm collection. (14.2.83). See *ER* 34, 2017

127. 13th/14th century fragment of encaustic tile 4 inches wide. Found by S.M. Evans. Passed to W.B. (15.8.74)

128. Encaustic tiles, geometrical patterns. Centre piece retains glaze. Larger tiles 13.5 cm square. Vicarage collection. (20.4.76) Now held by St Leonard's.

129. Four fragments of flooring tiles, lion passant and floral. L. Pimm collection. (14.2.83)

130. Flooring tile, fragment of wyvern or cockatrice. Drawing reconstruction. L. Pimm collection. (14.2.83)

131. Coat of arms from Mr Coates Barn on the east side of Back Lane, demolished 1963 which was later re-set in the east wall of the Bartholomew Room. The arms are reputed to be those of Aethelmaer. (13.2.75)

132. A very similar coat of arms, wrongly set on its side, built into the east wall of No. 6 Abbey Street, just under the eaves. It is suggested that both coat of arms were built into one of the abbey gatehouses. (27.5.75)

133 – 136 Corbels in Standlake church. One contains the same coat of arms as above but with the lion and the hunting horn reversed. The other has small fleur-de-lys and two pairs of interlaced rings, reputed arms of Abbot Miles Salley. (12.9.75)

137. Parliamentary Processional Roll of 1512 (*British Library Add.MS 5831*) showing a portrait and arms of Miles Salley, Bishop of Llandaff, Abbot of Eynsham *c.* 1496/7-1516. (25.5.83)

138. Detail of above.

139. Parliamentary Roll, 1512. Bishops in procession including Miles Salley, Bishop of Llandaff. 'Bod.196 m.4'. (8.10.80)

140. Arms of the See of Llandaff. (25.5.83)

141. Arms of Miles Salley when Bishop of Llandaff 1500-16, taken from Parliamentary Rolls 1512 and 1515 (*British Library Add. MS 40078*). (17.12.78)

142. Henry Taunt's photo of the Vicarage garden in 1890. From B.M. Pimm. (18.6.76)

143. Detail of the central arch of Taunt's photo. 'Earl's achievement'. i.e., arms of Chandos family. See 98. The arch was removed by 'Brydges 15/5/86'. (4.12.76)

144. Tiles on display in an Eynsham 'Abbey exhibition in the Market House. (L. Wright?) eagle St Leonard's.' (13.2.88)
145. St Mark's chapel Bristol. The tomb of Miles Salley. (24.10. 87)
146. Detail of above. (31.7.77)
147. Detail of above. (31.7.77)
148. Tomb slab of Abbot John de Cheltenham, Abbot of Eynsham 1317-30, in the vestry of Elsfield church, partly covered by safe. Re-used for Michael Pudsey d. 1645. (10.9.75) See *Eynsham Record* No.1, 1984.
149. Diagram of inscription on Abbot John of Cheltenham's tombstone, Elsfield, (27.6.77)
150. SW corner of tomb slab of Abbot John de Cheltenham in Elsfield church. (10.9.75)
151. NW corner of the same. (10.9.75)
152. North side of the same. (11.5.76)
153. Brass plate inserted in the centre of the tombstone of Abbot John of Cheltenham indicating that it was re-used by a certain Michael Pudsey 1561-1645. (10.9.75)
154. Sketch of brass indent in water-course of Hardwick Mill near Eynsham. Probably of Thomas de Wells, Abbot of Eynsham 1281-1307. (14.10.83) See *Eynsham Record* No.1 1984
155. One of the fragments of the above tombstone.
156. The wheel chamber at Hardwick Mill.
157. Pieces of Abbey stones set into the south wall of Lord's Cottages, Oxford Road, Eynsham. (28.9.74)
158. Abbey fragments. Newland House garden gatepost S. (20.8.74) Later demolished and some became part of the Brian Atkins collection.
159 Abbey fragments. Newland House garden gatepost N. (20.8.74)
160. Small E.E. capital and other fragments. Peter Hayes Collection. (11.5.81)
161-162. Miscellaneous Abbey fragments. Eynsham Vicarage. (20.10.84)
163. Masons mark on an Abbey block. 3 Bitterell. Mrs M. Streat. (15.10.82) Now re-set over garden gate.
164. 12th century foliated carving set into the south wall of 7 Newland Street, Eynsham. (5.11.76)
165. Column base or collar. Circular piece of shaft. 13th century. W.E. Beauchamp. (21.5.75)
166. Staddle stone?
167. Stump of fleur-de-lys. Gift of Lilian Buchanon. (23.5.78)
168. Carving, interlace pattern 13th century? Found in gable of Maltshovel House. 10 Newland St. W. Bainbridge. (19.9.76)
169. Eynsham Abbey fragment, 65 Newland St, Dr Hyde. (27.7.84) Finial from a shrine?
170. Fragment of carved foliage from Nursery site. Hunt, 107 Banbury Rd, Kidlington. (28.9.77)
171. 'Gravedigger's find'. St Peter's churchyard. (2.5.85)
172. Part of a buttress? Set into a wall in Thames Court, Eynsham.
173. Carved stone fragment or natural formation? Gift of M. Buchanon. (27.6.83)
174. Stone with Runic letters? Newland House. Dr E. Temple. (9.6.76)
175. 14th century plague graffiti from St Mary's church, Ashwell, Herts.
176. *Bodl.MS. 269, f.iii.* Frontispiece to Augustine Commentary on Psalms C-CL, *c.* 1125-50 with Abbey shelf mark. (11.9.86)

177. 15th century font in St Leonard's parish church, Eynsham. J.C. Buckler. *Bodl.MS Top Oxon a66 f. 249.* (19.2.79)
178. Sculpted head of cross 'fleuretty'. (6.11.86) Brian Atkins collection.

Appendix 4

A glossary of some architectural terms

Abacus: The top part of a capital. Generally square in Norman work, moulded and circular or octagonal in Gothic work.

Acanthus: A spiny plant with thick leaves with frilled edges used as a model for decorating mouldings, especially capitals. An imitation of Classical Corinthian forms.

Aisle: Extra space or wing alongside the nave and sometimes the chancel of a church and separated from it by an arcade.

Ambulatory: Literally a place to walk but used to denote the aisle enclosing a shrine or sanctuary behind the high altar in an abbey or cathedral. Often semi-circular or polygonal in plan.

Apse: A semi-circular or polygonal extension to the east end of a church or its aisles.

Arcade: A series of arches carried on piers or columns separating the nave from the aisle/s. See also **Blind Arcade.**

Arch: Saxon and Norman arches are usually semi-circular, Gothic arches variously pointed.

Ashlar masonry: Stones cut into regularly shaped squared blocks, smoothed and laid in horizontal courses often to face rougher work. A particular feature of post-Conquest architecture.

Ballflower: An ornament like a ball enclosed within three petals. A characteristic of Decorated Gothic architecture.

Baluster: A 'turned' Anglo-Saxon shaft.

Bar tracery: Moulded ribs or shafts which divide a window into patterns in the Gothic period. Introduced into England *c.* 1250.

Base: Moulded foot of a column. Norman bases are normally mounted on a square plinth. Water-holding bases are characteristic of Early English Gothic. Decorated and Perpendicular bases are frequently octagonal.

Bay: In a church, the compartments into which it is divided by the piers or columns of an arcade.

Beakhead: A form of Norman decoration taking the form of the head of a bird, beast or monster, the beak or jaw of which grips a roll moulding which is normally part of an arch of a doorway or window. Occasionally found on chancel arches or singly on a corbel.

Bell capitals: Capital in the shape of an inverted bell. A feature of Early English Gothic.

Billet: Norman ornamentation formed by cutting a round or rectangular moulding in notches, leaving regular gaps.

Blind arcade: An arcade with no openings attached to a wall as a form of decoration.

Boss: An ornamental block designed to hide the junction of the ribs of a vault. Not common before the Early English style. Very frequent in Decorated and Perpendicular periods.

Buttress: A section of a wall thickened to give greater support. Norman buttresses are generally flat and of small projection from the wall. Gothic buttresses are larger and more elaborate, being ornamented in the style of the period.

Cable/rope moulding: A Norman decoration resembling the twisted strands of rope.

Capital: The head of a column or pilaster. See cushion, scalloped, bell and waterleaf capitals.

Cavetto: Concave or hollow moulding.

Chamfer: The surface created by cutting off a square edge to create a bevel. When the resulting plane is concave it is known as a hollow chamfer.

Chancel: The eastern arm of a church beyond the nave where the altar is located. Sometimes referred to as the choir or presbytery.

Chantry: A chapel in which masses were sung for the soul of the founder.

Chevron: A late 11th to early 13th century ornament, usually applied to arches, in the form of V-shaped motifs or zigzag of a variety of types.

Chip carving: Geometric patterns (e.g. saltire) chiselled into a surface.

Classical: Ancient Greek and Roman architecture.

Clerestory: A row of windows in the upper part of a nave above the aisles, to let in more light.

Cloister: A covered and paved path round a quadrangle or garth attached to monastic churches. Used by monks for study, recreation and sometimes washing.

Column: The vertical support of an arch, made up of a base, shaft and capital.

Compound/Clustered piers: A pier with several shafts attached to or clustered round it.

Coping: The projecting top course of a wall, designed to throw off the rain and protect the wall below.

Corbel: A projecting block or bracket that supports a beam or parapet, frequently carved with heads or other motifs. A row of such corbels around a building is known as a corbel table.

Cornice: A moulded horizontal projection around the top of a building beneath the eaves of a roof or parapet.

Crenellation: A battlemented parapet. Rarely found in churches before the Decorated Gothic period.

Crossing: In a cruciform church the junction of the nave, transepts and chancel, often surmounted by a tower

Crockets: In Gothic architecture, leafy projections on the edges of any sloping feature, ornamenting gables, canopies, spires and pinnacles. A conspicuous feature of Decorated Gothic.

Curvilinear tracery: Tracery composed of sinuous curves. Associated with Decorated Gothic.

Cushion or block capital: Feature of Norman architecture. Basically cubic in shape but with the lower angles chamfered and rounded to fit the circular column. Each face thus becomes a semi-circle or 'shield'.

Cusp: A point formed by the meeting of two curves, small arches or foils in Gothic architecture.

Dado: A rail defining the lower part of an interior wall.

Decorated: See **Gothic.**

Dogtooth: A form of decoration of stylised star-shaped leaves forming small pyramids. Popular from the late 12th century and into the Early English Gothic. Used on hollow mouldings.

Dripstone: A projecting moulding over doors and windows to throw of the rain, also called a hood-mould. The corbels which terminate the dripstone are often heads, male and female or king and bishop.

Early English: See **Gothic.**

Fan vaulting: Characteristic of Perpendicular architecture.

Fillet: A narrow flat band running the length of a column. Characteristic of 13th century work.

Finial: The ornament, such as a bunch of foliage, terminating pinnacles or gables, especially in the Decorated period.

Flying Buttress: A buttress which transmits the natural outward thrust of a wall by means of an arch.

Foil: A small arc in the tracery of Gothic windows and separated from each other by cusps. The number of foils is indicated by a prefix such as trefoil, quatrefoil, cinquefoil, octofoil.

Foliated: Carved with leaf ornament.

Fret: A pattern created by mouldings meeting at right angles. Sometimes referred to as battlemented or Greek key.

Frieze: Sculpted horizontal panels.

Gable: The end wall of a building, the triangular top of which conforms to the slope of the roof which abuts it.

Gargoyle: A projecting spout designed to throw water from a gutter away from a wall. Sometimes carved with human or animal or grotesque figures. Popular in Gothic architecture.

Gothic: An architectural style which developed in the late 12th century and is notable for the use of the pointed arch and an emphasis on the vertical. Usually divided into Early English, Decorated and Perpendicular Gothic. Dates are approximations as one style gradually transitioned into another and there were significant regional differences. Not all of the following characteristics appear on any one building.
Early English *c.* 1175 – *c.* 1250: pointed arches, lancet windows, bell-shaped capitals, waterleaf and stiff leaf, round abaci, dogtooth, nailhead, plate tracery, compound piers, stone ribbed vaults, buttresses, slender towers with spires, use of Purbeck marble, deep-cut mouldings, restrained ornament.
Decorated *c.* 1250 – *c.* 1350: Sometimes subdivided into Geometric and Decorated. 'Geometric' *c.* 1250 – *c.* 1290: larger window openings, bar tracery of slender shafts, Y tracery, the decorative scheme at the head of windows sometimes based on cusped circles, trefoils, quatrefoils and even octofoils. 'Decorated' *c.* 1290 – *c.* 1350: Flamboyant sinuous tracery, rose windows, 'dagger' tracery, ballflower, ogee arches, richly carved crockets, lierne vaulting, flying buttresses, diamond shaped plan for piers, capitals with naturalistic foliage and flowers.
Perpendicular *c.* 1350 – *c.* 1550: Upright rectangular tracery panels, flatter four-centred arches with square hood moulds, spandrels with carved decoration, 'Tudor' flower decoration, slender piers, plainly moulded capitals or stylised carving in low relief, tall and slender bases and often bell-shaped with an octagonal plinth, finials and crockets finely carved with foliage, animal or human figures, fan vaulting, elaborate porches.

Grotesques: Carved ornament of fanciful, ludicrous figures.

Hood moulding: A projecting moulding above arches to throw off water. Also known as dripstone or label.

Impost: A horizontal stone block between a capital and the springing of an arch.

Interlace: Sculpted decoration imitating entwined stems or bands.

Intersecting blind arcade: Semi-circular arches in an arcade which interlace forming points. Usually Romanesque.

Jamb: The vertical side of a window or door.

Keystone: The central stone in an arch.

Label: See hood moulding.

Label stop: An ornamental 'boss' at the ends of a hood mould or label. Frequently carved with a human head.

Lancet: A window arch with a sharply pointed head. Common in Early English Gothic.

Lavatorium or Lavabo: In medieval monasteries, a cistern or tough used for washing hands. Usually situated near the refectory in the cloister or in a separate building in the cloister garth.

Lesene: See **Pilaster.**

Lierne vaulting: A vault with ribs that cross from one intersection of the ridge ribs to another. They are decorative and are not linked to any of the springing points of the vault.

Linenfold panelling: Wood carved decoration with the appearance of a fold of linen. Popular in high status buildings from the 15th and 16th centuries.

Long and Short Quoins: Characteristic of Saxon architecture where the corner stones of a building are alternately laid horizontally and perpendicularly.

Lozenge: Diamond shape decoration.

Megalithic: Literally, large stones. Sometimes used as quoins in medieval architecture.

Misericord: A shelf on the underside of a hinged seat which, when turned up, helped to support a monk or clergyman during long periods of standing. The underside of the shelf was frequently carved.

Mullion: The vertical bar dividing the lights of a window.

Nailhead: ornament consisting of small pyramids, regularly repeated. Present in late Norman architecture but particularly used in Early English Gothic.

Nave: The main body of a church, sometimes flanked by aisles and west of the tower crossing or chancel.

Necking: A moulding which separates a capital from its shaft.

Niche: A canopied recess in a wall for a statue.

Nook shaft: A shaft or column set in the angle of a wall or corner or the jamb of a doorway or window.

Norman architecture: See **Romanesque.**

Oculus/oculi: Round window/s.

Ogee arch: A pointed arch the sides of which are each formed of a double curve, one concave and the other convex. Characteristic of Decorated and Perpendicular Gothic.

Order of an arch: One of a series of recessed columns/jambs and arches which make up a splayed door opening or chancel arch.

Pellets: Rows of small or large balls on a moulding. Especially found in Norman architecture.

Perpendicular: See **Gothic**

Pier: Any isolated mass of building work, usually supporting an arch. Also used for column.

Pilaster: A shallow rectangular 'column' attached to a wall without base or capital. Characteristic of Saxon church architecture. Sometimes known as a lesene.

Pinnacle: A tapering vertical abutment terminating in a finial, sometimes ornamented with croquets. Mostly associated with the later Gothic style.

Plinth: the block on which the base of a pillar rests.

Pulpitum: A stone screen between the nave and the choir.

Quatrefoil: See **foil.**

Quoins: The dressed stones at the corners of buildings.

Rebates: A channel or recess cut along the inside edge of a window to secure glass or sometimes a wooden shutter.

Respond: A half pier or column attached to a wall to support an arch.

Retable: A frame enclosing painted panels set above the back of an altar.

Rib: A projecting band on a ceiling supporting a vault. Ribs are frequently moulded and enriched.

Roll moulding: A round or half-round moulding. In Gothic work with pronounced fillets.

Romanesque: A European style of architecture from the 10th until the end of the 12th century when it was superseded by the Gothic. In England used for Saxon and Norman work. Characterised by the use of the semi-circular arch, massive walls, columns and capitals, some of which might be roughly based on Classical models. Characteristic mouldings of the later Norman period are enriched with chevron, billets, lozenges, nailhead, pellets and beakhead amongst others.

Rood: The crucified Christ on a cross, often flanked by the figures of St John and Mary the mother of Jesus. The rood was often wooden and placed on a beam across the chancel arch and over a screen separating the nave from the chancel. Access to the rood was often by a staircase built into the wall adjoining it.

Rosette: An ornament like a rose commonly used to decorate medieval churches. Roses are a particular symbol of the Virgin Mary.

Rubble masonry: A wall built of uncut, irregularly shaped stones.

Saltire: A form of decoration in the form of X-shaped crosses set within squares. Particular characteristic of Norman ornament.

Scalloped capital: Common in Norman work. Similar to a cushion capital but with the curved portion carved with part-cones or deep grooves.

Sedilia: Recessed stone seats for officiating clergy in the south wall of a chancel near the altar.

Shaft: The body of a column or pillar between the base and the capital.

Soffit: The lower surface or underside of any part of a building including arches and voussoirs.

Spandrel: The roughly triangular space between an arched doorway and its squared head.

Splay: The sloping sides and sills of windows to allow as much light as possible.

Springer: The stone above an impost from which an arch springs.

Stiff-leaf foliage: Typical sculpture of capitals of the Early English Gothic, the name deriving from the stiff stalks rising from the necking.

String Course: A horizontal band or line of mouldings projecting from a wall.

Template: A pattern for guiding a stone carver.

Tracery: The intersection of the mullions and transoms forming a stone openwork pattern in the head of Gothic windows. Also seen on screens, panels or vaults. See also **bar tracery** and **curvilinear tracery.**

Transept: The rectangular projections north and south of the crossing in a cruciform church.

Transom: A horizontal bar to divide a window. Particularly found in Perpendicular architecture.

Triforium: A gallery or wall passage above the main arcade and below the clerestory in an abbey or cathedral. Sometimes known as a Blind-storey.

'Tudor' flower decoration: late Gothic ornament of a flower with square flat petals.

Tympanum: The stone between the lintel of a door and its arch. Often carved with figures and/or symbols.

Undercroft: Basement or cellar.

Vault: An arched roof usually supported or divided by ribs.

Volute capital: A capital decorated with spiral scrolls in imitation of Ionic Classical forms.

Voussoir: A wedge shaped stone forming part of an arch, the topmost being the key-stone and those next to the imposts, the springers.

Water-holding bases: An early gothic feature at the bottom of a column in which the gap between mouldings are deep enough to hold water.

Waterleaf: A carved wide leaf found on Gothic capitals. Somewhat reminiscent of Classical Corinthian capitals.

Zigzag: See chevron.

Bibliography

N.B. The abbreviation *ER* stands for the *Eynsham Record*, the journal published annually since 1984 by the Eynsham History Group.

Abbot Parry and Esther de Waal, *The Rule of Saint Benedict*, Gracewing, 2003.

Arber E. (ed.), *The Revelation to The Monk of Evesham (sic)*, English Reprints, 1869, London. Reprint of an edition in English printed by William de Machlinia *c.* 1482.

Atkins B., Buried Treasure, *ER* 2, 1985.

Atkins B., Editorial, *ER* 3, 1986.

Atkins B. Eynsham Parish Population since 1650, *ER* 4, 1987.

Atkins B., John Whiting's Survey of Eynsham, 1650, *ER* 6, 1989.

Atkins B., 'Tar's Grave', *ER* 13, 1996.

Atkins B., 'A View of Ensham ca. 1780', *ER* 16, 1999.

Atkins B., Eynsham's Muster Roll of 1542, *ER* 17, 2000.

Atkins B., Rescuing Eynsham Abbey Stones, *ER* 20, 2003.

Atkins B., History of the Wharf and Wharf Stream, *ER* 30, 2013.

Aubrey J., *Brief Lives*, Folio Society, London, 1975.

Bainbridge W., *Visible Remains of Eynsham Abbey*, Information Printing Ltd, Eynsham, 1980.

Bainbridge W., Looking for Abbots, *ER* 1, 1984.

Bainbridge W., Eynsham's Market House, *ER* 2, 1985.

Bapasola J., *The Finest View in England. The Landscape and Gardens at Blenheim Palace*, Blenheim Palace, Jarrold Publishing, 2009.

Barber T. and Boldrick S. (eds), *Art Under Attack – Histories of British Iconoclasm*, Tate Publishing, 2013.

Barclay A. and Boyle A. and Keevil G.D., A Prehistoric Enclosure at Eynsham Abbey, Oxfordshire, *Oxoniensia*, Vol. LXVI: pp. 105-162, 2001.

Baxter R., *The Royal Abbey of Reading*, The Boydell Press, 2016.

Blair J., Saint Frideswide Reconsidered, *Oxoniensia*, Vol. LII: pp. 71-127, 1987.

Blair J., Eynsham as a Central Place in Anglo-Saxon Oxfordshire, *ER* 5, 1988.

Blair J., *Anglo Saxon Oxfordshire*, Alan Sutton Publishing Limited, 1994.

Blair J. (ed.), *Waterways and Canal-Building in Medieval England*, Oxford University Press, 2014.

Blair J., *Building Anglo-Saxon England*, Princeton University Press, 2018.

Bond J., The Fishponds of Eynsham Abbey, *ER* 9, 1992.

Breay C. and Story J. (eds), *Anglo-Saxon Kingdoms, Art, Word,War*. The British Library, 2018.

Byng J., *Rides Round Britain*, D. Adamson (ed.), Folio Society, London, 1996.

Campbell J. and John E. and Wormald P., *The Anglo-Saxons*, Phaidon Press Ltd, 1982. Folio Society, 2018.

Carpenter D.X., *The Charters of William II and Henry I – Eynsham Abbey*, https://actswilliam2henry1.wordpress.com, 2016.

Cave C.J.P., *Roof Bosses in Medieval Churches*, Cambridge University Press, 1948.

Chambers E., *Eynsham Under the Monks*, Oxfordshire Record Society, Oxford 1936.

Chambers R.A., Eynsham Abbey Excavations, *ER* 7, 1990.

Cheetham F., *English Medieval Alabasters*, Phaidon Press, 1984.

Clark A., *The Life and Times of Anthony Wood, antiquary, of Oxford, 1632-1695, described by Himself*, Vol 1: 1632-1663. Oxford Historical Society at the Clarendon Press, 1891

Clarke D.T. and D., *St Laurence, Combe Longa*, Parochial Church Council of Combe Longa, 1994.

Cooper H.C.D., The Old Manor House, Eynsham, Oxon, *Oxoniensia*, Vol. XIX, 1954.

Cooper H.C.D., Eynsham Armorial, *Oxoniensia*, Vol. XXXVII, 1972.

Crossley A., Eynsham – A Suitable Case for Treatment, ER 1, 1984.

Crossley A., *Victoria History of the County of Oxford* Vol. XII: pp. 98-157, Oxford University Press, 1990. University of London Institute of Historical Research.

Curl J.S., *A Dictionary of Architecture and Landscape Architecture*, Oxford University Press, 2000.

Curthoys J., Christ Church, Eynsham Abbey and its Cartulary, ER 30, 2013.

Davies E.T., *A History of the Parish of Mathern*, Mathern Parochial Church Council, 1990.

Davis R.H.C., The Chronology of Perpendicular Architecture in Oxford, *Oxoniensia* Vol. XI/XII: pp. 75-89, 1947.

Davis R.H.C., A Catalogue of Mason's Marks as an Aid to Architectural History, *Journal of the British Archaeological Association*, 3rd Series XVII: pp. 43-76, 1954.

Deans H., Abbot James, ER 18, 2001.

Dodwell C.R., *Anglo-Saxon Art: A New Perspective*, Manchester University Press, 1982.

Douie D.L. and Farmer H. (eds), *Magna Vita Sancti Hugonis*, Vols 1 & 2, Nelson's Medieval Texts, Thomas Nelson and Sons Ltd, 1961.

Duffy E., *The Stripping of the Altars, Traditional Religion in England 1400-1580*, Yale University Press, 1992.

Dugdale W., *Monasticon Anglicanum*, Vol. 3: pp. 1-32, 1693. Additional authors: Dodsworth, Roger, John Stevens, John Caley, Sir Henry Ellis, Bulkeley Bondinel and Richard C. Taylor. Published by: Longman, Hurst, Rees, Orme and Brown, 1817-30.

Easting R. (ed.), *The Revelation of the Monk of Eynsham*, Oxford University Press, 2002.

Elton G.R., *England Under the Tudors*, The Folio Society, 1997.

Emden A.B., Medieval Floor-tiles in the Church of St. Peter in the East, Oxford, *Oxoniensia* Vol. XXXIV: pp. 29-45, 1970.

Eynsham Conservation Area Advisory Committee, *Eynsham, A Mediaeval Town by the Thames*, CAAC, 1984.

Farmer D.H., *The Oxford Dictionary of Saints*, Clarendon Press, Oxford, 1980.

Farmer D.H., *Saint Hugh of Lincoln*, Darnton Longman and Todd, 1985.

Ferguson G., *Signs and Symbols in Christian Art*, Oxford University Press, 1980.

Finberg H.P.R. (ed.), *The Deserted Villages of Oxfordshire*, Leicester University Press 1965. Occasional Paper.

Fish S., *A Supplication for the Beggars*, E. Arber (ed.), The English Scholar's Library, Unwin Brothers 1878. Reprinted by Amazon.co.uk Ltd, Filiquarian Publishing, 2015.

Fisher E.A., *Anglo-Saxon Towers – An Architectural and Historical Study*, David & Charles, 1969.

Foster C., Medieval floor tiles, with reference to Eynsham Abbey, ER 34, 2017.

Galbraith K., *The Iconography of the Biblical Scenes at Malmesbury Abbey*, Journal of the British Archaeological Association, Third Series, Vol. 28, 1965.

Garmonsway G.N. (ed.), *Aelfric's Colloquy*, Methuen's Old English Library, 1965.

Garmonsway G.N. (Trans.), *The Anglo-Saxon Chronicle*, J.M. Dent and Sons Ltd, Everyman's Library, 1967.

Gee E.A., Oxford Masons 1370-1530, *Archaeological Journal*, Vol. CIX: pp. 54-131, 1953.

Gies F. and J., *Life in a Medieval Village*, Folio Society, London, 2002.

Gomme G.L. (ed.), *The Gentleman's Magazine Library 1731-1868*, Elliot Stock, 1897.

Gordon E., Adventure at Hardwick Mill, *ER* 1, 1984.

Gordon E., Eynsham Charters, *ER* 2, 1985.

Gordon E., Eynsham Charters, *ER* 4, 1987.

Gordon E., Eynsham Charters, *ER* 5, 1988.

Gordon E., Eynsham Charters, *ER* 6, 1989.

Gordon E., Adam of Hanborough: Much Ado about a Ditch, *ER* 7, 1990.

Gordon E., *Eynsham Abbey 1005-1228 A Small Window into a Large Room*, Phillimore & Co. 1990.

Gransden A., The Customary of the Benedictine Abbey of Eynsham in Oxfordshire, *Corpus Consuetudinum Monasticarum*, Franciscum Schmitt – Sieburg, 1963.

Gray M. and Clayton N., Excavations on the site of Eynsham Abbey, 1971, *Oxoniensia*, Vol. XLIII, 1978.

Hamilton Thompson A., Historical Revisions – Cathedral Builders, *History*, Vol. 10, No. 38, July 1925, Historical Association.

Hardy A. and Dodd A. and Keevill G.D. *et al.*, *Aelfric's Abbey – Excavations at Eynsham Abbey, Oxfordshire, 1989-92*, English Heritage. Oxford University School of Archaeology, 2003.

Hardy A. and Smith R., *Eynsham: A village and its Abbey*, English Heritage, The Holywell Press, 2003.

Harris M., *From Acre End, Portrait of a Village*, Chatto & Windus Ltd, 1986.

Harris M.J., Medical Care in Eynsham, *ER* 14, 1997.

Harris M.J., *The Changing Faces of Eynsham*, Robert Boyd Publications, Witney. Book 1, 1997, Book 2, 1998, Book 3, 2002.

Harvey J., *English Medieval Architects*, Batsford, 1954.

Harvey J., *The Perpendicular Style 1330-1485*, Batsford, 1978.

Hearne T., *Joannis Lelandi Antiquarii De Rebus Britannicis Collectanea*, Forgotten Books, 2018.

Hearne T., *Remarks and Collections* printed for the Oxford Historical Society at the Clarendon Press. Vol VII (1719-22), reprinted by BiblioLife.

Heaney M., *Percy Manning, the man who collected Oxfordshire*, Archaeopress, 2017.

Heath-Whyte R.W., *An Illustrated Guide to the Medieval Wall Paintings in the Church of Saint Mary the Virgin at Chalgrove in the County of Oxfordshire*, Parochial Church Council of St Mary's Church, 2003.

Hendrix J.S., *Architecture as Cosmology. Lincoln Cathedral and English Gothic Architecture*, Peter Lang, 2011.

Hockedy D., The Mystery of Eynsham Cross, *ER* 23, 2006.

Holy Bible, Authorised Version, Oxford University Press, 1844.

Hurst J.D., *Savouring the Past, The Droitwich Salt Industry*, Hereford & Worcester County Council, Northwick Print, 1992.

Jones C.A., *Aelfric's Letter to the Monks of Eynsham*, Cambridge University Press, 2006.

Kahn D., *Canterbury Cathedral and its Romanesque Sculpture*, University of Texas Press, 1991.

Kauffmann C.M., *Romanesque Manuscripts 1066-1190*, Harvey Miller, London, 1975.

Keats-Rohan K.S.B., The Making of Henry of Oxford: Englishmen in a Norman World, *Oxoniensia*, Vol. LIV, 1989.

Kebell G., A Very Late Afterthought on an Eynsham Fire, *ER* 4, 1987.

Keevill G.D., *In Harvey's house and in God's house: excavations at Eynsham Abbey 1991-3*, Thames Valley Landscapes Monograph No. 6, Oxford Archaeological Unit, 1995.

Kemp B.R. (ed.), *Reading Abbey Cartularies*, Vols. I and II, Royal Historical Society, 1986/7.

Keynes S., King Aethelred's charter for Eynsham Abbey (1005) in *Early Medieval Studies in Memory of Patrick Wormald*, N. Brooks (ed.), Ashgate Publishing Ltd, 2008.

Kingsley Porter A., *Romanesque Sculpture of the Pilgrimage Roads*, Hacker Art Books, 1966. Reprint in 3 Volumes.

Knowles D., *The Monastic Order in England 940-1216*, Cambridge University Press, 1963.

Leland J., *Itinerary*, Lucy Toulmin Smith (ed.), Centaur Press Ltd, 1964.

Long E.T., Mural Paintings in Eynsham Church, *Oxoniensia* Vol. II, 1937.

Long E.T., Medieval Wall Paintings in Oxfordshire Churches, *Oxoniensia*, Vol. XXXVII, 1972.

Macaulay J., *The Gothic Revival 1745-1845*, Blackie, 1975.

MacGregor J., Finds at Hythe Croft, ER 10 1993.

Mason E., The D'Oyly Family and Eynsham Abbey, ER 22, 2005.

McCreadie M., A History of the River Thames at Eynsham, ER 21, 2004.

Moore J. Heritage Services, *An Archaeological Watching Brief at Abbey Farm Barns, Station Road, Eynsham, Oxfordshire*, February 2013.

Morris J., *Domesday Book, Oxfordshire*, Phillimore, 1978.

Moss R., *Romanesque Chevron Ornament*, British Archaeological Reports International Series 1908, Archaeopress, 2009.

Nairn I. and Pevsner N. and Cherry B., *The Buildings of England - Surrey*, Penguin Books, 1971.

Nash Ford D., *Royal County of Berkshire History*, Nash Ford Publishing, 2001.

Newman J., *The Buildings of Wales, Gwent/Monmouthshire*, Penguin Books, 2000. Founding Editor: Sir Nicholas Pevsner.

Page W. (ed.), Houses of Benedictine Monks: The abbey of Eynsham, *The Victoria County History of Oxford*, Vol. 2, London, 1907.

Parker J.H., *A Concise Glossary of Architectural Terms*, Ninth edition. First published 1846. Studio Editions Ltd, 1994.

Parrinder S., Romanesque Sculpture from Reading Abbey, Unpublished MA dissertation, Birkbeck College, University of London, 1982.

Parrinder S., Eynsham Abbey Stones – The Brian Atkins Collection, ER 31, 2014.

Parrinder S., The Co-op Wall, ER 31, 2014.

Parrinder S., Eynsham Abbey – The Final Accounts, ER 32, 2015.

Parrinder S., Graffiti in St Leonard's Church, ER 32, 2015.

Parrinder S., The Vision or Revelation of the Monk of Eynsham, *ER 33*, 2016.

Parrinder S., Thomas Hearne's Eynsham, *ER 33*, 2016.

Parrinder S., The Medieval Wall Paintings of Eynsham Abbey, ER 34, 2017.

Parrinder S., The Wrath of God - Eynsham and the Black Death, ER 35, 2018.

Parrinder S., Eynsham – Worth its Salt, ER 36, 2019

Parrinder S., Thomas Symonds – Antiquary Vicar of Eynsham, ER 36, 2019

Pevsner N. (ed.) and Verey D., *The Buildings of England - Gloucestershire: The Vale and the Forest of Dean*, Penguin Books, 1970.

Pevsner N. (ed.) and Verey D., *The Buildings of England - Gloucestershire: The Cotswolds*, Penguin Books, 1970.

Pevsner N. and Sherwood J., *The Buildings of England - Oxfordshire*, Penguin Books, 1974.

Pevsner N. and Cherry B., *The Buildings of England - Wiltshire*, Penguin Books, 1975.

Pevsner N. and Cherry B., *The Buildings of England - Hertfordshire*, Penguin Books, 1977.

Poulton-Smith A., *The Salt Routes*, Amberley, 2010.

Pounds N.J.G., *A History of the English Parish*, Cambridge University Press, 2000.

Richards D., An Eynsham Fire in 1696, *ER* 3, 1986.

Richards P., Do You Remember an Inn? An historical survey of Eynsham Public Houses. A *Good History* Special Issue No 1., 1997.

Richards P., An Eynsham Farmer, *ER* 17, 2000.

Richards P., *Eynsham: A Chronicle*, Eynsham History Group, Robert Boyd Publications, 2005.

Richards P., *Eynsham – A Place of 'sure foundation'*, Eynsham History Group, 2012.

Rogers J.K., "Enisham...was my birthplace" The Life and Career of a Sixteenth Century London Printer, *ER* 12, 1995.

Rosewell R., *Medieval Wall Paintings*, Boydell Press, 2008.

Salter H.E., *Eynsham Cartulary*, Vol. 1, Oxford Historical Society, Clarendon Press, 1907.

Salter H.E., *Eynsham Cartulary*, Vol. 2, Oxford Historical Society, Clarendon Press, 1908.

Salter H.E., *Medieval Oxford*, Clarendon Press for the Oxford Historical Society, 1936.

Saul N., *St George's Chapel Windsor in the 14th Century*, Boydell Press, 2005.

Scarisbrick J.J., *The Reformation and the English People*, Blackwell, 1984.

Seward D., *The Last White Rose*, Constable and Robinson Ltd, 2010

Smith A., *Roof Bosses of Winchester Cathedral*, Friends of Winchester Cathedral, 1996.

Stone L., *Sculpture in Britain – The Middle Ages*, Penguin Books, 1972.

Strong R., *Lost Treasures of Britain*, Guild Publishing, 1990.

Taylor H.M. and J., *Anglo-Saxon Architecture*, Vols 1 & 2, Cambridge University Press, 1965.

Taylor H.M., *Anglo-Saxon Architecture*, Vol. 3, Cambridge University Press, 1978.

Thompson A.H. (ed.), Visitations of Religious Houses in the Diocese of Lincoln, Vol. 1 1420-1436, *Lincoln Record Society*, Vol. 7, 1913.

Thompson A.H. (ed.), Visitations of Religious Houses in the Diocese of Lincoln, Vol. 2 1436-1449, *Lincoln Record Society*, Vol. 8, 1919.

Thurlby M., *The Herefordshire School of Romanesque Sculpture*, Logaston Press, 1999.

Townley S., 'Riottes, Extorcions and Inuries' A 16th century affray in Eynsham, *ER* 6, 1989.

Tristram E.W., *English Medieval Painting*, Hacker Art Books, 1976.

Turner H.L., *No Mean Prospect: Ralph Sheldon's Tapestry Maps*, Plotwood Press, 2010.

Van Lemmen H., *Medieval* Tiles, Shire Publications, 2016.

Walker J. (ed.), *Oxoniana, or Anecdotes Relative to the University and City of Oxford*, Vol. 1: p. 93, Slatter and Munday, 1806.

Ward A.W. and Walker A.R. (eds), *Cambridge History of English and American Literature*, in 18 volumes. Cambridge University Press, 1907-21.

Weaver J.R.H. and Beardwood A. (eds), Some Oxfordshire Wills proved in the Prerogative Court of Canterbury, *Oxfordshire Record Society* Vol. 39, 1958.

Weedon J., Hamstall's Trace, *ER* 6, 1989.

Weedon J., Church Medieval Wall Paintings, *ER* 23, 2006.

Willis R., *The Architectural History of Canterbury Cathedral*, 1845. Republished by Tiger of the Stripe, 2006.

Wood A., *The Life and Times of Anthony Wood, antiquary, of Oxford, 1632-1695, described by himself Vol. 1, 1632-63.* Extract quoted in *ER* 6, 1989.

Wood A. and Rawlinson R., *Parochial Collections* (Second Part), Transcribed and prepared for the Press by the Rev. F.N. Davis, Oxfordshire Record Society, 1922.

Wood M., *The English Mediaeval House*, Ferndale Editions, 1981.

Wright L., The Stanleys in Eynsham, *ER* 2, 1985.

Wright L., Eynsham Monks at the Dissolution, *ER* 9, 1992.

Wright L., *St Leonard's Eynsham. The story of an English Parish Church*, Parchments of Oxford, 3rd edition, 2009.

Wright L., Venetia Anastasia Stanley, *ER 27*, 2010.

Zarnecki G., *English Romanesque Sculpture 1066-1140*, London, 1951.

Zarnecki G., *Later English Romanesque Sculpture 1140-1210*, London 1953.

Zarnecki G., Romanesque Arches decorated with Human and Animal Heads, *Studies in Romanesque Sculpture*, The Dorian Press, London 1979.

Zarnecki G. and Holt J. and Holland T. (eds), *English Romanesque Art 1066-1200*, Arts Council of Great Britain, 1984.

Zarnecki G., Carved Stones from Newark Castle – Additional Notes, *Further Studies in Romanesque Sculpture*, Pindar Press, London 1992.

Zarnecki G., Germanic Animal Motifs in Romanesque Sculpture, *Artibus et Historiae*, No. 22, Wien, 1990. Reprinted in *Further Studies in Romanesque Sculpture*, Pindar Press, London, 1992.

Ziegler P., *The Black Death*, Folio Society, London, 1997.

Sources

Bainbridge collection of slides relating to Eynsham Abbey.

William Bainbridge's original slides are in the possession of Eynsham History Group, digitised by Martin Harris and indexed by the author – see Appendix 3. The following Figures were taken from the Bainbridge Archive: 56, 57, 95, 118, 131, 152, 161, 163, 171, 176, 177, 182, 220, 221, 232, 244, 245, 260, 274, 278, 284.

Bodleian Library, Oxford University

Auct. 1Q.5.28. Revelation of the monk of Eynsham.

MS Hearne's Diaries Vol. 50, 1714.

MS Top Oxon b 275. Rev Thomas Symonds Collection.

MS Top Oxon d 514. A. Cobb Drawings of Oxfordshire Buildings.

G.A. Oxon c 317 ([20]). Letter from M. Shurlock to Professor J.O. Westwood, April 15 1851.

MS Laud Lat 31. Eynsham's only certain surviving library book, 12th century

MS 269. St Augustine, Commentary on Psalms (Ps 101-50). 12th century manuscript thought to have been at Eynsham although not necessarily written there. Full page Virgin and Child (f.iii) and inhabited foliage initial (f.iiiv)

MS Wood B15. Notes of Oxfordshire churches visited.

MS Wood E1. Another version of *MS Wood B15* but with drawing of the abbey (*f 45*)

MS Rawl. D 97. 'The Diarie of the Life of Anthony á Wood Historiographer of the most famous Universitie of Oxford.' Includes an account of his visit to Eynsham (p. 30).

MS Selden Supra 66. '*Visio monachi de Eynsham*'. Also part of a Tudor inventory in English ff. iii-iv and a page of accounts in Latin stuck into the back.

MS Top Oxon a 66. J.C. Buckler drawings of Oxfordshire.

MS DD Queen's 288. April 6 1255, Eynsham quitclaims Drowda Hall to the Priory of Monk Sherborne. Two Abbey seals and reverse seals attached.

Corpus Christi College, Oxford.

CCC Oxford MS 533/1 f.9. Map of its Eynsham property drawn by Henry Wilcocke, April 1615

English Heritage Archive, Swindon.

Henry Taunt photo of the Vicarage garden, Eynsham, 1890. CC56/00796

Museum Resources Centre, Standlake.

Catalogue of Accessions.

Box 24 1995.342 EEA 90-92 OAU Photos of worked stone from the archaeological excavation.

Photos of worked stone taken by the author.

Oxfordshire History Centre, Oxford.

Palm 1/i ff 1-3. Manorial Accounts.

Palm IV. Whiting's Survey of Eynsham 1650.

PAR 100/3/F1/2. Churchwarden's accounts 1775-1864

MS d.d. Par Eynsham c 11.

MSS Oxf. Dioc. c 362, c365, c368.

? Cruikshank Mrs, *Notes on the History of Eynsham* or *Some Account of the History of Eynsham* Unpublished, undated typescripts *c.* 1930, possibly by the wife of the local doctor.

A Plan of the Estate belonging to William Holloway at Ensham, in the County of Oxford; Taken 1769 by Thomas Pride; Surveyor.

Goadby F.R.L. *Transcripts of Eynsham Parish Registers*, 1975.

Index of Proper Names in the main text

For Eynsham's Abbots see also Appendix 1. For Eynsham Abbey's properties and patrons see also Appendix 2. For authors see the Bibliography.